The Scotch-Irish
of Colonial Pennsylvania

The
SCOTCH-IRISH
of
Colonial Pennsylvania

By Wayland F. Dunaway

Baltimore
GENEALOGICAL PUBLISHING CO., INC.
1985

Reprinted, by arrangement, Genealogical Publishing Co., Inc.
Baltimore, 1979, 1981, 1985
Library of Congress Catalogue Card Number 79-52943
International Standard Book Number 0-8063-0850-8
Made in the United States of America

Preface

IT HAS OFTEN BEEN SAID of the Scotch-Irish that although they make history they leave to others the task of writing it, and this is largely true. The unfortunate part of it, however, is that the others who write history have often done so from a point of view unfriendly to this racial group; at least, this is the attitude of certain authors who have written the history of Pennsylvania, beginning with Proud. The notable contribution made by the Scotch-Irish to the development of Pennsylvania has not received from historians the attention it merits. It is our purpose, in some measure at least, to supply this lack.

The scope of our study is restricted in time to the colonial era, and in place to the province of Pennsylvania. In reality, however, it is somewhat more comprehensive than its title indicates, inasmuch as the activities of the Scotch-Irish in the later period are often passed in review, and much of the narrative, especially the first three chapters and the sixth chapter, applies to this group throughout the whole country no less than in Pennsylvania. On the other hand, their story as a distinct racial group is confined largely to the colonial period, being less clearly traceable in later times when they had merged with the general body of the people. Their later history is well worth narrating, to be sure, but this is not the story that we have set out to tell.

It is our purpose to tell this story objectively, nothing extenuating and setting down naught in malice. Though conscious that they have played a great part in history, the Scotch-Irish are well aware of the fact that there is no halo of sanctity around their heads. All they ask is that they be painted as they are, and this is all that we aim to do. Nothing more is required than that the evidence be assembled and that they be given their day in court; their deeds speak for themselves.

Grateful acknowledgement is made of the courtesies extended the author by the library staffs of The Pennsylvania State College, the Historical Society of Pennsylvania, the Library of Congress, the Presbyterian Historical Society, the Ridgway Branch of the Library Company of Philadelphia, the Historical Society of Western Pennsylvania, the Carnegie Library of Pittsburgh, the University of Pittsburgh, and the State Library of Pennsylvania.

The publication of this study has been made possible by grants extended from the Lamberton Fund by The Historical Society of Pennsylvania to the Pennsylvania Scotch-Irish Society. Although the Pennsylvania Scotch-Irish Society is not responsible for the inception or contents of the study, it was kind enough to endorse it when completed and to use its good offices in securing the grant to aid in its publication. This work is presented to the public as an authorized publication of the Pennsylvania Scotch-Irish Society, for whose aid and encouragement the author gratefully acknowledges his indebtedness. For the imperfections of the monograph the author alone is responsible.

W. F. DUNAWAY

State College, Pa.

CONTENTS

The Scotch-Irish
of Colonial Pennsylvania

1

Introduction

They regarded themselves as Scottish people who had been living in Ireland. HENRY CABOT LODGE

PENNSYLVANIA has been characterized by great racial diversity from the beginning. In this colony the major racial groups were the English, the Germans, and the Scotch-Irish, each of which occupied in predominant numbers a distinct geographical area— the English in the east, the Scotch-Irish in the west, and the Germans between the two. Inasmuch as each of these groups long preserved its own customs and traditions, there were three distinct civilizations in the Pennsylvania of colonial times.

The story of the Scotch-Irish as a peculiar people occupying a given area on the Pennsylvania frontier is confined largely to the provincial era, and it is not proposed to bring it down much beyond that period. The right is reserved, however, to trace them farther afield whenever it seems expedient. In later times they have spread all over the state and all over the country, and have lost to a considerable degree their distinctive characteristics as they became merged with the general body of the people. While still retaining the basic qualities that made them great, it was not their desire nor their destiny to remain localized in some particular spot or to continue to maintain their racial peculiarities and customs. Americans of the Americans, they think of themselves primarily as such, and only incidentally as a special racial group. They have never been greatly concerned about traditions of fatherland, nor encumbered by these, as is the manner of some. Entering heartily and unreservedly into the new life of the western

3

world, they promptly became Americanized and are of the very warp and woof of that American civilization which they did so much to promote. Once an isolated group, they are no longer so, being characteristic Americans in thought, word, and deed.

We are confronted at the outset with the word "Scotch-Irish," a designation which is objected to in some quarters though it has been in general use for two hundred years. The objection seems unreasonable in view of the fact that this term has been the customary usage in the nomenclature of American history and literature for so long a time, and is so commonly understood by the people, that it appears to be straining a point to challenge it at this late day, as some are inclined to do. There was a time, no doubt, when the Scotch-Irish themselves did not particularly care for the name because they thought it might cause them to be confused with the Irish, whereas they thought of themselves as Scotchmen; but that objection is not now raised by the Scotch-Irish, who are satisfied with the name and consider it a title of honor.[1] Those who object most seriously to the name are the Catholic Irish of the United States, chiefly it seems, because they want to claim the achievements of the Scotch-Irish for their very own.[2] Michael J. O'Brien, for instance, calls the distinction between the Scotch-Irish and the Irish "a bogus distinction that has been manufactured by the Irish immigrants, especially those from the province of Ulster;"[3] and Joseph Smith informs us that certain writers have "invented that ethnical absurdity, the Scotch-Irishman, and Scotch-Irish race." Smith further declares it to be "the duty of the American-Irish Historical Society to rebuke these things wherever found."[4] These writers, and those who hold with them, represent a point of view which flies into the face of fact by maintaining that the Scotch-Irish, who are of Scottish blood, are identical in race with those who are of Irish blood, merely because they sojourned for a time in Ireland. Such reasoning is far from convincing, and would be like claiming that a man born of American parents in China is of the same race as the Chinese;

1. C. A. Hanna, *The Scotch-Irish*, I, 26n.
2. John Fiske, *The Dutch and Quaker Colonies in America*, II, 352.
3. Michael J. O'Brien, *A Hidden Phase of American Nationality*, 343.
4. Joseph Smith, *The "Scotch-Irish" Shibboleth Analysed and Rejected*, 4, 19.

and we feel quite sure no man born of Irish parents residing at the time in China would consider himself a Chinaman, or, as an old Ulster Scot put it, "If a man is born in a stable, does that make him a horse?" Really now, it is as simple as that, and it requires no great discernment to distinguish between things so obviously different. The mere fact of a temporary residence of Scots in Ireland before emigrating to America does not transform them into people of a different race. The term "Scotch-Irish" means nothing more than a convenient name for Americans whose ancestors were Scots living in Ireland before they came to this country. It is a race-name primarily, with the term "Irish" tacked on as a place designation reminiscent of a sojourn in the Emerald Isle.

If a large number of Scots emigrated to Ireland and maintained themselves there as a distinct racial group, as is the case, and a name is used to designate this particular group after they emigrated to America, as is also the case, one is at a loss to understand why the Irish-Americans, a different race with a different background, should insist so strenuously that they are the same people unless, indeed, it be due to the desire of the Irish to claim the deeds of the Scotch-Irish for themselves. However that may be, it is plain enough to the discerning onlooker that Pat and Sandy are not one and the same, the great trouble being that while Sandy is well aware of this, Pat isn't. The gallant Irish people have laurels enough of their own without going out of their way to claim others that they do not need. Let it be distinctly understood that the term Scotch-Irish is used by the writer in no invidious sense, but merely because it happens to be the name of the people he is describing.

Others besides the Irish-Americans have objected to the name Scotch-Irish on the ground that it is an awkward compound, or that it is a hyphenated expression confusing (to some) in its meaning, or else that it is unknown in Ireland,[5] all of which is beside the point since the question is not as to whether the term is awkward, or what not, but as to whether it is the name of the

5. Fiske, *op. cit.*, II, 352; Albert Cook Myers, "The Scotch-Irish Quakers in Pennsylvania," in *The Pennsylvania Scotch-Irish Society Proceedings,* XIII, 47; Hanna, *op. cit.*, I, 162; Edward F. Roberts, *Ireland in America,* 6-7.

people concerned. Admitting that it is awkward, that is no reason for discarding it; all of us are known by our names, whatever they may happen to be. There is no end to names once given in ridicule that have remained to become titles of honor, as for example that of the Quakers, Baptists, and others. Once a name has been generally accepted, especially by those to whom it is given, and has entered into customary usage, it is absurd to find fault with it or to claim that it does not fit the case. One could wish that it were not a hyphenated name, though the hyphen has nothing to do with the traditions of fatherland which some racial groups cling to so tenaciously. The Scotch-Irish of America came to this country untrammeled by fatherland traditions, and for this reason became overnight thoroughly Americanized—themselves patriotic Americans. They are not hyphenated Americans, however, the hyphen having to do merely with their racial and place origin across the seas without any reference to an attempted perpetuation of the traditions of the Old World. In other words, the hyphen, as applied to them, has a very different meaning from that found in such terms as German-Americans, or other hyphenated Americans, the word American not entering into it in their case. They are Scotch-Irish and they are Americans, but they are not Scotch-Irish-Americans. They have never been under the delusion that they can maintain a dual citizenship and a divided allegiance. They have but one flag, and that is the Star Spangled Banner; the United States is a good enough fatherland for them. As for the objection that the term "Scotch-Irish" is not known in Ireland, this is freely admitted.[6] The objection is not valid, however, inasmuch as we are not concerned with a body of people living in Ireland, but with a group living in America, and therefore call them by their American name. Their history in Ireland is another story, in which they might well be called Ulster Scots; but in this country, where they have been called Scotch-Irish for two hundred years, it would be absurd to give them a name by which they are not known here. Far be it from us to call them the Ulster Scots of America or to designate them

6. J. S. MacIntosh, "The Making of the Ulsterman," in Scotch-Irish Society of America *Proceedings*, II, 92.

by any other name by which they may be called abroad.[7] Here their name is Scotch-Irish; let us call them by it.

That the term Scotch-Irish is of ancient origin is seen in the fact that students resorting to Scottish universities from Ulster were registered as "Scotus-Hibernus," the Latinized version of the name. This appears, however, to be the only manner in which this designation was used abroad, and the word Scotch-Irish is of American origin to all intents and purposes. Henry Cabot Lodge classifies the Irish and the Scotch-Irish as two distinct stocks, maintaining that the distinction is sound historically and scientifically, and that the name Scotch-Irish is "not only justifiable but is required by accuracy of statement."[8] In the interest of historical accuracy and scientific application ethnically, some distinctive name was necessary for the Scots who came to America by way of Ireland, and the name Scotch-Irish came to be universally used in America to designate this race-stock; it is too late to change it now, even if we would. It is fixed in the thought of the people and embalmed in literature for all time, and as such we use it without any qualms or apologies.

Though the Ulster Scots who emigrated to America thought of themselves as Scots and scorned to be called Irish,[9] it appears that they were quite commonly referred to by others as Irish until well into the eighteenth century. In fact, there is reason to believe that at first they objected to being called Scotch-Irish. John Elder, in writing to Edward Shippen in 1764 relative to the Conestoga Massacre, says: "The Presbyterians, who are the most numerous I imagine of any Denomination in the Province, are enraged at being charged in bulk with these facts, under the name of Scotch-Irish, and other ill-natured titles."[10] From this it appears that the Scotch-Irish were not as yet reconciled to being so called, preferring to regard themselves as Scots and resenting the tacking on of the word "Irish." Nevertheless, the name had long been current in Pennsylvania, as we shall proceed to show.

7. Terms in use abroad are Ulster Scots, Orangemen, Ulstermen, "sturdy Northern," etc.
8. Cited by H. J. Ford, *The Scotch-Irish in America,* 522.
9. E. L. Parker, *History of Londonderry, New Hampshire,* 68.
10. Cited by Hanna, *op. cit.,* 26.

The earliest use of the word Scotch-Irish that we have found occurs in a letter written by Reverend William Becket, an Episcopal clergyman stationed at Lewes, Delaware, to a Mr. Harris of Boston, October 11, 1728, in which he says: "The first settlers of this county were for the far greatest part originally English, but of late years great numbers of Irish (who usually call themselves Scotch-Irish) have transplanted themselves and their families from the north of Ireland into the Province of Pennsylvania."[11] Another early reference to this name is found in a letter of James Logan to Thomas Penn, December 19, 1730, touching on the occupation of Conestoga Manor, as follows: "This is the most audacious attack that has ever yet been offered. They are of the Scotch-Irish (so called here) of whom J. Steel tells me you seem'd to have a pretty good opinion but it is more than I can have tho' their countryman."[12] From these references it is evident that the Scotch-Irish were being very generally so called soon after they had begun to arrive in Pennsylvania in large numbers, and it is probable that the name was first applied to them by the Episcopalians and Quakers, who by no means intended it to be complimentary. Edmund Burke, in describing the migration of large numbers of settlers from Pennsylvania to the Southern colonies around the year 1757, says: "They are chiefly Presbyterians from the northern part of Ireland, who in America are generally called Scotch-Irish."[13] Thus it appears that, though often called Irish by others than themselves, the name Scotch-Irish was far more generally applied to them in the provincial era than our Irish friends would have us believe. If, then, the question be asked, "Who are the Scotch-Irish?," the answer is that they are a people who were originally Lowland Scots; that they emigrated on a large scale to Ulster about three centuries ago;[14] and that their descendants, being oppressed there, emigrated in large numbers to America, particularly to Pennsylvania, where they have long been known

11. *The Rev. William Becket's Notices and Letters concerning incidents at Lewes Town, 1727-1742*, MS Historical Society of Pennsylvania, 21.

12. *Penn MSS, Official Correspondence, 1683-1727*, II, 145.

13. Edmund Burke, *European Settlements in America*, II, 216.

14. For a description of the Ulster background of the Scotch-Irish, see the following chapter.

as Scotch-Irish to distinguish them from the Celtic, Catholic Irish, who were a different race-stock. This is the sense in which the term Scotch-Irish is used by the writer, who, in describing the Scotch-Irish of Pennsylvania, does not include the Scots coming to Pennsylvania directly from Scotland. Though the latter are, of course, of the same race as the Ulster Scots, they cannot properly be termed Scotch-Irish.[15]

Some additional points need to be cleared up before proceeding further with our story. Though the Scotch-Irish themselves are well aware that they are of pure Scottish descent and that the Irish part of the hyphenated name refers only to place origin in relation to their sojourn in Ireland, it appears that there are some people who suppose that the term Scotch-Irish signifies a blending of the Scots and Irish by intermarriage; and some writers have been so confused in their thinking as to make this assertion.[16] Hence it seems desirable to explode this fallacy. According to Hanna, an excellent authority, "the application 'Scotch-Irish' is not, as many people suppose, an indication of mixed Hiberno-Scottish descent."[17] Dr. John Hall, an eminent Presbyterian minister of New York, who was a native of Ulster, gives a convincing explanation of the matter, as follows:

"I have sometimes noticed a little confusion of mind in relation to the phrase 'Scotch-Irish,' as if it meant that the Scotch people had come over and intermarried with the Irish, and that thus a combination of two races, two places, two nationalities had taken place. This is by no means the state of the case. On the contrary, with kindly good feeling in various directions, the Scotch people kept to the Scotch people, and they are called Scotch-Irish from purely local, geographical reasons, and not from any union of the kind that I have alluded to. . . . They are Scotch through and through, they are Scottish out and out."[18]

This testimony from a learned divine, who was a native of Ulster and to the manner born, should be conclusive. Inasmuch,

15. Some writers use the term Scotch-Irish loosely to include the English and Huguenot elements of Ulster, but to the writer this seems to be unwarranted. Others include in the term the Anglo-Irish, wherever found in Ireland, which is also unwarranted.
16. This is the viewpoint of various Irish-American writers.
17. Hanna, *op. cit.*, I, 162-163.
18. Cited by Hanna, *ibid.*, 163-164.

however, as the fallacy that the Scotch-Irish are a cross between the Scots and the Irish is rather persistent in some quarters, other evidence is adduced to refute it. Reverend Dr. John MacIntosh of Philadelphia, who lived for a time in Ulster and was a close student of conditions there, gives the following statement of the case:

> "From Derry to Down I have lived with them. Every town, village, and hamlet from the Causeway to Carlingford is familiar to me. . . . It has been said that the Ulster settlers mingled and married with the Irish Celt. The Ulsterman did not mingle with the Celt. . . . The Ulster settlers mingled freely with the English Puritans and with the refugee Huguenots; but so far as my search of state papers, old manuscripts, examination of old parish registers, and years of personal talk with and study of Ulster folk disclose—The Scots did not mingle to any appreciable extent with the natives. . . . To this very hour, in the remoter and more unchanged parts of Antrim and Down, the country folks will tell you: 'We're no Eerish bot Scoatch.' All their folk-lore, all their tales, their traditions, their songs, their poetry, their heroes and heroines, and their home-speech, is of the oldest Lowland types and times."[19]

This does not mean to say, of course, nor does Dr. MacIntosh claim, that there was never an instance of marriage between the Ulster Scots and the Irish, for such unions undoubtedly occurred; but all the evidence points to the conclusion that these were rare, especially after the plantation of Ulster under James I. In fact, the King expressly directed that the settlers should be taken from "the inward parts of Scotland" and so located that they "may not marry with the mere Irish." The intermarriage of the Irish with the Scots occurred more frequently before the "Plantation" and was with the Scotch Highlanders and "wild islanders"—a group of Scots who were Catholics and were largely Celts, and would therefore be more inclined to intermarry with the Irish than would the Lowland Scots, who were Protestants and of a different racial strain. The number of the early Highlanders who emigrated to Ireland was, however, relatively few and did not belong to

19. J. S. MacIntosh, "The Making of the Ulsterman," in Scotch-Irish Society of America *Proceedings*, II, 96-97.

the Ulster Scots of the Plantation, as will be more fully explained in the following chapter. There is, it is true, abundant evidence to show that many of Cromwell's soldiers, who settled in the southern parts of Ireland after 1650, intermarried freely with the Irish and that their descendants, overcome "by the invincible Catholicism of the Irish women," lost their English characteristics and became "more Irish than the Irish themselves," but this was far from being the case with the Scotch Presbyterians settling in Ulster, where "intermarriages between the Scotch settlers of the seventeenth century, and their descendants in Ulster, have been so rare and uncommon as to be practically anomalous."[20]

This whole question is admirably disposed of by the *Edinburgh Review,* as follows:

"Another effect of the Plantation was that it effectually separated the two races, and kept them apart. It planted a new race in the country which never coalesced with the native population. There they have been in continual contact for more than two centuries; and they are still as distinct as if an ocean rolled between them. We have seen that all former schemes of plantation failed, because the new settlers became rapidly assimilated to the character, manners, and faith of the native inhabitants; even the descendants of Oliver's Puritan troopers being so effectually absorbed in the space of forty years as to be undistinguishable from the Celtic mass. The Ulster settlement put an end to the amalgamation of the races; difference of creed, difference of habits, difference of tradition, the sundering effects of Penal Laws, kept them apart. The Presbyterian settlers preserved their religious distinctness by coming in families, and the intense hatred of Popery that has always marked the Scottish mind was an effective hindrance to intermarriage. It is a curious fact, that the traditions of the Ulster Presbyterians still look back to Scotland as their home, and disclaim all alliance with the Celtic part of Ireland. Indeed, the past history of Ulster is but a portion of Scottish history inserted into that of Ireland; a stone in the Irish mosaic of an entirely different quality and color from the pieces that surround it."[21]

Certain other erroneous beliefs not infrequently encountered in this country may here be indicated for the sake of completeness,

---

20. Hanna, *op. cit.,* 160-161.
21. *The Edinburgh Review,* April, 1869 (American Edition), CXXIX, 223.

though this phase of the subject will be discussed more fully in the succeeding chapter. There appears to be a rather general impression that, at the time of the plantation of Ulster under James I, all the inhabitants of the old Irish stock were expelled from this region in order to make room for the newcomers, whereas this was by no means the case. In fact, many of them remained, either as small landholders or as hewers of wood and drawers of water; and today they are quite numerous, predominating in several of the counties of Ulster.[22] Again, the occupation of Ulster by the Scottish immigrants was not as overwhelming as is ordinarily supposed; many Englishmen settled there, together with a respectable number of Huguenots. It is doubtful, indeed, if the Scots at any time constituted a majority of the population of the province of Ulster. Furthermore, contrary to popular belief, the Presbyterians, while very numerous and influential, were not so all-pervading as we have been accustomed to believe, if indeed they were a majority at all, in Ulster as a whole. The English were mostly Episcopalians, the Irish were almost universally Catholics, and not all the Ulster Scots were Presbyterians; nor, for that matter, were all the Presbyterians Ulster Scots. There were undoubtedly quite a few Presbyterians in Ulster who were of English and French blood, and it is said that there were not wanting instances of Presbyterians among the native Irish, though these must have been rare. Some of the Ulster Scots were Episcopalians, Quakers, Baptists, and Methodists, though there can be no doubt that the overwhelming majority of them were Presbyterians, who brought their kirk with them to Ireland, just as they later brought it to America. It must be said also that while intermarriage of the Scots with the Irish was exceedingly rare, it seems reasonable to believe that there was some slight admixture of the two races.[23] It may be stated further that it would be a mistake for us to believe that all the Lowland Scots coming to Ireland settled in Ulster, since a respectable minority of them settled in other Irish provinces.

22. Lord Ernest Hamilton, *The Irish Rebellion of 1641*, 37-38. As we shall see later, the "Great Plantation" of Ulster was confined to only six of the nine counties of that province, commonly referred to as "the six escheated counties."

23. Hanna, *op. cit.*, 166; for the American-Irish viewpoint, see John C. Linehan, *The Irish Scots and the "Scotch-Irish,"* 63-64, 84, 93-96, 125.

2

The Ulster Background of the Scotch-Irish

We know that the term Ulster Scot is generic and simply means Scoto-Irish. I love the Highlander and I love the Lowlander, but when I come to the branch of our race which has been grafted on the Ulster stem, I take off my hat with veneration and awe. They are, I believe, the toughest, the most dominant, the most irresistible race that exists in the universe at this moment. LORD ROSEBERY

IN TRACING THE HISTORY of the Scotch-Irish of Pennsylvania, it seems desirable to describe their Ulster background in order to bring into clear relief the conditions under which they lived and the circumstances which motivated their emigration to the New World. Indeed, the complete picture of this remarkable group, which has played such an important rôle in history, cannot be given without tracing them even farther to their original home in Scotland. Limitations of space, however, preclude a detailed account of this phase of the subject, lest we be carried too far afield.

Scotland is divided into two geographical units, known as the Highlands and the Lowlands, marked by differences of race, religion, and customs, once clearly defined and still observable. It is with the Lowland Scots that we are chiefly concerned, since it was from this group that came the bulk of the immigrants to Ulster.[1] The Highlanders of Western Scotland and the adjacent islands are largely of Celtic origin, and it appears that the Gaels of the Highland clans were originally of the same Celtic stock as that of the native Irish before the latter were conquered by Eng-

1. John Harrison, *The Scot in Ulster*, 41; Thomas Croskery, *Irish Presbyterianism: Its History, Character, Influence, and Present Position*, 6-7.

land. But in the Lowlands of Scotland conditions were different, this region being once a part of Roman Britain and having a different racial composition. Unlike the Highlander, the Lowland Scot is an amalgamation of Celts, Romans, Frisians, Angles, Saxons, Danes, Norwegians, Normans, and Flemings, and is essentially of the same stock as the Englishman immediately to the south of him. These Scots have been called "as English in blood as they are in speech," though they doubtless retain a greater proportion of the Celtic strain than do the English, who are themselves composed of a variety of racial strains similar to those of the Lowland Scots. Professor James Heron of Belfast, Ireland, identifies the Ulster Scot with the Lowland Scot and says of the former that "the Angle and the Saxon, the Dane and the Norwegian, the Norman and the Fleming, all of which have gone to his formation, make a combination by which, I imagine, the Celt is overpowered and dominated."[2] From this race are sprung the Scotch-Irish of America.

The Lowland Scots not only furnished the bulk of the emigrants to Ulster, but from them have come an overwhelming proportion of the great figures who have made Scotland illustrious in history. According to Lecky, "The intellect, the industrial energy, the progressive instincts of Scotland were essentially Lowland. . . . The Highlands of Scotland were inhabited by a population speaking a language different from that of England, scarcely ever intermarrying with the Lowlanders, living habitually with arms in their hands."[3] The Highlanders, who furnished but a small part of the emigration to Ulster and that chiefly before the Great Plantation, had a much greater resemblance to the native Irish in race, language, and religion than had the Lowlanders. While a picturesque and valiant people, their contribution to the progress of civilization has been comparatively small; in fact, they were but "slowly and reluctantly subdued to civilization."[4]

Let us now pass over the Channel separating Scotland from Ireland and view the Ulster background of the Scotch-Irish. Ireland

2. Cited in H. J. Ford, *The Scotch-Irish in America*, 573.
3. W. E. H. Lecky, *A History of England in the Eighteenth Century*, II, 22, 36.
4. B. J. Witherow, *The Insurrection of the Paxton Boys*, 629.

is divided into four provinces and thirty-two counties. Of the provinces—Ulster, Leinster, Munster, and Connaught—Ulster, which is the northernmost, embraces the nine counties of Antrim, Armagh, Cavan, Donegal, Down, Fermanagh, Londonderry, Monaghan, and Tyrone. Comprising approximately one-fourth of the area and population of Ireland, it has long been regarded as the most prosperous and progressive section of the country. By reason of the confiscation of its soil by the English government and of its plantation by settlers from Scotland and England, it has for three hundred years been set apart from the remainder of Ireland, and, throughout this long period, has had a distinctive history. The differences existing between Ulster and the three remaining provinces have, in recent times, found expression in the establishment of two separate governments in the island— Northern Ireland, embracing most of Ulster, and the Irish Free State, comprising the three provinces to the southward.

The native population, largely Celtic in race and Catholic in religion, has undergone a considerable modification racially by reason of an admixture of Danish, Norwegian, English, and other racial strains with the original Celtic stock. A gallant and gifted people, they have produced a number of eminent men, but they have had a troubled history and have suffered many woes. Macaulay says of them, "The Irish . . . were distinguished by qualities which tend to make men interesting rather than prosperous. They were an ardent and impetuous race, easily moved to tears or laughter, to fury or to love."[5] In the great gamble of the nations for a place of dominance and security in the world, they lost at almost every turn in the wheel of fortune, and have never been able to realize to the full their national hopes and aspirations. Beginning with their partial conquest by Henry II in the twelfth century, they were for centuries subjected increasingly to the rule of England, by whom they were governed harshly as "a dependency won by the sword." By the time of Henry VIII, English authority had become fairly well established over the whole country, though full subjection did not come till

5. T. B. Macaulay, *The History of England,* I, 42.

the reign of Elizabeth, whose armies effectually crushed the native chieftains fighting to expel the invader.[6]

Throughout the long period of recurring wars and rebellions which devastated Ireland for centuries there had been several confiscations of the soil, accompanied by the plantation thereon of English settlers. This system did not develop on a large scale, however, until the reign of Mary, when extensive areas in the province of Leinster were seized by the Crown and planted by English settlers in Queen's County and King's County. In Elizabeth's reign, after Desmond's rebellion, other large districts in Munster were confiscated and disposed of to English tenants. In each case, however, some of the native inhabitants retained possession of their lands.[7] Up to the time of the death of Elizabeth, the actual confiscation and colonization of Irish soil was relatively slight and had hardly extended as far north as Ulster, except in County Monaghan.[8] The history of confiscation on a large scale begins with the accession of James I and the "great Plantation" of Ulster in his reign. Unlike the Marian and Elizabethan plantations, which were little more than the transference of forfeited lands from Irish to English landlords, the Ulster plantation under James I took root and resulted in a permanent settlement of Scots and English, profoundly affecting the subsequent history of that whole region.[9]

Before the "great Plantation" of Ulster began, however, there had been going on for some years a large settlement of Scots in Antrim and Down, the two counties nearest to Scotland. This settlement, which was not the result of wholesale confiscations of the soil, may be described briefly. Con O'Neill, an Irish chieftain who ruled the northern half of County Down, upon getting into trouble with the English government, was forced to cede to two Scots, Hugh Montgomery and James Hamilton, about two-thirds of his estate in order to secure their aid in extricating him from his difficulties. Through their intercession at court a pardon was

6. Lecky, *op. cit.*, 94.

7. *Ibid.*, 106; James Anthony Froude, *The English in Ireland in the Eighteenth Century*, I, 56.

8. W. F. T. Butler, *Confiscation in Irish History*, 35-37.

9. Cyril Falls, *The Birth of Ulster*. 7.

secured for O'Neill, and by letters-patent issued in 1605 by the Irish Council the major portion of his lands came into the possession of Montgomery and Hamilton. These Scottish gentlemen now proceeded to plant their newly acquired lands with settlers from Scotland, being the better enabled to do this because the region had been swept almost entirely bare of inhabitants during the late rebellion in Ulster led by Tyrone. This district became thoroughly Scottish in character. O'Neill, having by extravagant living and bad management become insolvent, was forced to sell the remaining third of his land, which also was settled largely by Scottish immigrants.[10]

Meanwhile Sir Arthur Chichester, Lord-Deputy of Ireland, had in 1603 acquired vast estates in the adjoining county of Antrim, across the river Lagan, in the region around Belfast. These lands he leased mostly to Englishmen, though this region later became prevailingly Scottish.[11] The northeastern part of County Antrim had long been occupied by the MacDonnells, a Scottish clan whose chieftain, Randal MacDonnell, had been rewarded, after Tyrone's rebellion, for his loyalty to the English government with a grant of the northern half of County Antrim; this district became "nearly as Scottish as the portion of County Down north of the Mourne Mountains." The MacDonnells, who were Scotch Highlanders and Catholics, were few in number, and Sir Randal, in order to develop his vast estate, found it necessary to introduce large numbers of Lowland Scots of the Protestant religion, as required by the terms of his grant. Hence this region became predominantly Scotch Presbyterian. Thus it happened that Counties Down and Antrim, by a series of large grants and purchases, had been settled by considerable numbers of Scots and English in the period beginning immediately after the accession of James I. Hence these counties were not included in the Great Plantation soon to be inaugurated by that monarch.[12]

A far-reaching colonization of Ulster took place under James I. While confiscations and settlements had been made by the Scots

10. Harrison, *op. cit.*, 7-23; J. B. Woodburn, *The Ulster Scot*, 56.
11. Harrison, *op. cit.*, 24-25.
12. Harrison, *op. cit.*, 26-27; Falls, *op. cit.*, 151-152; Froude, *op. cit.*, 69.

and English in Ireland under Elizabeth and her predecessors, these had been insignificant in comparison with the large-scale plantation now undertaken in Ulster. The Earls of Tyrconnell and Tyrone, powerful chieftains who owned and ruled a large part of Ulster, having conspired against the government and being fearful of vengeance, fled the country in 1607 and their estates were escheated to the Crown. In the following year Sir Cahir O'Dogerty, another great chieftain, started a rebellion resulting in his death and the confiscation of his estates. Other important chieftains having accompanied Tyrconnell and Tyrone into exile, the greater part of Ulster, embracing the counties of Armagh, Fermanagh, Tyrone, Londonderry, Cavan, and Donegal, passed into the hands of the Crown, and the way was now open for their colonization by English and Scottish settlers.[13] We have seen that Counties Down and Antrim had already been occupied to a great extent by the English and the Lowland Scots. Monaghan, the remaining county of Ulster, was not included in the great confiscation and plantation under James I. Sir Arthur Chichester had received a grant of a portion of this county and had effected a partial plantation there in 1607. Hence this county, like Down and Antrim, was not included in the Great Plantation.[14] There was no legal justification for confiscating the lands of the freeholders, in this case, such as existed in that of the others, and their inhabitants, being mostly Irish, were confirmed in their titles and left undisturbed. Thus it came about that, with the exclusion of County Monaghan and the previous plantation of Counties Down and Antrim, the Great Plantation of Ulster was confined to only six of the nine counties of that province, ordinarily referred to as "the six escheated counties."[15]

The conditions existing in the six escheated counties of Armagh, Cavan, Donegal, Fermanagh, Londonderry, and Tyrone, were such as to render their plantation by Scottish and English settlers comparatively easy. The long series of wars, particularly in

---

13. Miriam G. McClain, *The Rebellion of Sir Cahir O'Dogerty*, 78-87; Harrison, *op. cit.*, 34-35.

14. Woodburn, *op. cit.*, 61.

15. Lord Ernest Hamilton, *The Irish Rebellion of 1641*, 37-38.

the last years of Elizabeth's reign, had, to a great extent, depopulated that region, and the native inhabitants who remained were
not only without leaders, but were impoverished, ignorant, and
cowed by their misfortunes. The proprietary rights of such Irish
clans and chieftains as were left were disregarded, and many of the
old proprietors were expelled from their lands. Both the English
and the Scots of the time looked upon them as an inferior race
and regularly referred to them as the "mere Irish." Since most
of the Irish chieftains of Ulster had at one time or another rebelled against the Crown, it was not difficult to prefer charges
against them and to deprive them of their lands. Thus practically
the whole of the six escheated counties, amounting to about four
million acres, was thrown open for settlement.[16]

The plan adopted by King James for the plantation of this im-
mense tract of country was to divide it into estates of 1000, 1500,
and 2000 acres respectively, and to grant these to English and
Scottish Protestants. The grantees, known as "undertakers," were
required not only to live on the land themselves, but to erect places
for defence and enclosures for stock. By forbidding the undertakers to have Irish tenants, it was expected that the territory
would eventually become a British settlement.[17] The plan was
carried out ably and successfully under the direction of Sir Arthur
Chichester, Lord-Deputy of Ireland. Its fundamental purpose was
to displace the Irish Catholics and to make Ulster a Protestant
community occupied by immigrants from England and Scotland,
the Saxon supplanting the Celt. Large tracts of land were reserved for the Church, for schools, and for the sites of boroughs;
the remainder was divided among the English and Scotch undertakers, the public servitors of the Crown in Ireland, and some of
the old Irish proprietors who were accounted loyal. The allotments
to the English and Scottish grantees, however, were kept close
together to prevent, as far as possible, mixing with the Irish. In
fact, as has been noted, a law was passed forbidding the marriage of British settlers with the Irish, experience having proved
that such marriages invariably resulted in the adoption by the

16. Lecky, *op. cit.,* 108; Harrison, *op. cit.,* 34-36.
17. Harrison, *op. cit.,* 37; Butler, *op. cit.,* 40-41.

British of the Irish customs and religion. The native Irish were assigned to the less desirable and more remote districts. In 1609 the escheated lands were surveyed by commissioners, and all the details of the plantation were worked out with care. In 1610 the settlers, of whom many were English but more were Scots, began pouring into Ulster, and the plantation proceeded apace. The immigration to Ireland, now assuming large proportions, continued throughout the whole of the seventeenth century, by the end of which Ulster had become essentially British and prevailingly Scottish.[18] The plan was not carried out entirely as it was projected, however, since it was found that the native Irish were more or less indispensable as tenants, graziers, or laborers, and perhaps one-tenth of the escheated lands were allotted to them. No serious opposition to the plantation was encountered, and the result was an era of material progress such as Ulster had not known hitherto. The plantation was carried out most effectively in the counties of Armagh, Tyrone, Londonderry, and Fermanagh; only the eastern part of Donegal was colonized, and in Cavan the plan was largely a failure. The Scottish settlers outnumbered the English from the first, partly because their previous colonization of Down and Antrim had made them better acquainted with the country, partly because their geographical position favored them, partly because they endured the climate better than the English, and partly because their necessities were greater in inducing emigration.[19]

Other plantations of Ireland, affecting Ulster less directly than that of the six escheated counties and the settlement of Down and Antrim, followed later in the seventeenth century. The Cromwellian settlement after the Rebellion of 1641 resulted in another large confiscation of Irish lands in 1654. When the rebellion began, Ulster was still sparsely settled, it being estimated that, besides the native Irish, it contained some 100,000 Scots and 20,000 English. This rebellion, which began among the old Irish in

18. C. A. Hanna, *The Scotch-Irish*, I, 501; Hamilton, *op. cit.*, 67; Harrison, *op. cit.*, 35-37.
19. S. G. Wood, *Ulster Scots and Blandford Scots*, 15; S. A. Cox, "The Plantation of Ulster," in R. Barry O'Brien (ed.), *Studies in Irish History*, 36; Woodburn, *op. cit.*, 72-73.

Ulster, spread rapidly throughout the whole island, and for eleven years the land was deluged with blood. Upon its conclusion in 1652, the most far-reaching confiscation of land in Irish history ensued. More than six million acres were distributed among Cromwell's soldiers and among the numerous adventurers who had advanced money to Parliament, with the result that the greater part of Ireland passed into the hands of Protestant landowners, and the mass of the native Irish became, at least for a time, hewers of wood and drawers of water. Only about one-fourth of the island now remained in the hands of native proprietors. Nevertheless it transpired that many of Cromwell's soldiers intermarried with the Irish, became Catholics, and were eventually absorbed by the Irish. Hence the Cromwellian settlement was largely a failure in its attempt to make Ireland a Protestant country. It served, however, to introduce a number of Scots into Ireland and was followed by a large Scottish immigration into Ulster, in particular. Forty thousand Irishmen are said to have enlisted in foreign armies after the terrific vengeance of Cromwell for the Rebellion of 1641.[20]

The Revolution of 1688, resulting in the expulsion of James II and the accession of William and Mary to the throne, while accomplished almost wholly without bloodshed in England, was the occasion of a long and bloody civil war in Ireland, the greater part of which remained loyal to James. Ulster stood for William of Orange, but the remainder of Ireland was largely for James. Though the country was overrun by the forces of James and his Catholic adherents, the Protestants of Ulster made a heroic stand in the defense of Enniskillen and Londonderry, which held out against great odds. In 1690 William of Orange, now firmly seated on the throne of England, arrived in Ireland and administered a crushing defeat to James at the Battle of the Boyne. This was followed by a further confiscation of Irish lands and by the Williamite Settlement, as a result of which the Catholics lost an

20. Woodburn, *op. cit.*, 127-129; Butler, *op. cit.*, 160; Harrison, *op. cit.*, 67-79; Hamilton, *op. cit.*, 95, 110, 384; W. E. H. Lecky, *History of England in the Eighteenth Century*, II, 136-172; see also Lecky's *A History of Ireland in the Eighteenth Century*, I, 105-106, 244.

additional million and a half acres of land, though remaining as tillers of the soil. The estates thus confiscated were sold under an Act of Parliament, thereby bringing to an end the series of confiscations which within a century had amounted to about two-thirds of the whole landed property of Ireland. The movement of Scots to Ireland reached its climax at this time, it being estimated that no less than fifty thousand, most of whom settled in Ulster, arrived between the years 1690 and 1697. Thereafter the emigration of Scots to Ulster was negligible, being turned rather in the direction of America.[21]

Except in the case of the colonization of Ulster, there was no considerable removal of the Irish peasantry from the soil, where they remained as laborers. At the time of the Great Plantation there was no national spirit in Ireland, the country being in the hands of a few powerful chieftains and their retainers. Economic conditions were particularly bad. Agriculture was backward and manufactures were almost non-existent, while the recurring civil wars had depopulated the land and laid waste vast areas.[22] Prior to the plantation of Ulster, that whole province was exceedingly backward. Like the Highlands of Scotland, it was inhabited by clansmen obeying hereditary chieftains, accustomed to tribal laws and usages, neglecting agriculture, and living chiefly on their flocks and herds. The moral and religious state of the country was no less deplorable. The whole aspect of the region presented a picture of extreme poverty and wretchedness. According to Reid, the natives were even too poor to be plundered and "many betook themselves to the woods, where they lived almost in a state of nature, supported by plunder, and secure amidst the general poverty and desolation by which they were surrounded."[23]

With the coming of the Scottish and English settlers, however, the face of the country underwent a marked change and soon showed signs of improvement on every hand. In describing the

21. Anthony Marmion, *The Ancient and Modern History of the Maritime Ports of Ireland*, 51; Lawrence H. Gipson, *The British Empire before the American Revolution*, I, 255; Harrison, *op. cit.*, 86-87.

22. Maude Glasgow, *The Scotch-Irish in Northern Ireland and in the American Colonies*, 43-44; Butler, *op. cit.*, 239.

23. J. S. Reid, *History of the Presbyterian Church in Ireland*, I, 75-77.

colonization of the six escheated counties of Ulster, Froude says: "Unlike the Norman conquerors, who were merely military leaders, the new colonists were farmers, merchants, weavers, mechanics, and laborers. . . . They built towns and villages; they established trade and manufactures; they inclosed fields and raised farm-houses and homesteads where till then had been but robbers' castles, wattled huts, and mud cabins."[24] The vacant areas were largely occupied, the marshes were drained, and agriculture and manufactures flourished. Churches and schools multiplied, and Ulster became, as it has since remained, the most prosperous and progressive part of Ireland. This did not happen all at once, to be sure, nor were all the newcomers of a desirable type. It appears that, despite the claims of some Scotch-Irish orators, the first contingent of immigrants from Scotland left much to be desired. Reverend Andrew Stewart, minister of Donegore from 1727 to 1734, says that many coming from both Scotland and England were "the scum of both nations, who for debt, or breaking or fleeing from justice, or seeking shelter, came hither, hoping to be without fear of man's justice in a land where there was nothing, or but little as yet, of the fear of God. . . . Yet God followed them when they fled from Him—albeit it must be remembered that at first they cared little for any church."[25] He goes on to say, however, that a revival of religion followed, resulting in a great improvement in the moral and religious condition of the settlers. There seems to be no doubt that Stewart's censures applied only to a relatively small number of the first comers, and that the situation he describes was soon corrected. All evidence points to the conclusion that the great majority of the colonists were an industrious, self-respecting, moral people, and that the character of the later immigrants was superior to that of the first comers. In fact, it is well known that the stern discipline of the Presbyterian Church and the zealous efforts of other denominations moulded the Protestants of Ulster into a particularly high type

24. Froude, op. cit., I, 69.
25. Andrew Stewart, The History of the Church in Ireland since the Scots Were Naturalized (Supplement to Rev. Patrick Adair's A True Narrative of the Rise and Progress of the Presbyterian Church in Ireland), 315-321.

of citizenry, renowned no less for their moral and religious character than for their progress in education, trade, and industry.[26] In the earlier stages of the Great Plantation difficulties arose in the attempt to induce immigration from England and Scotland, but, when once the first comers had become settled in seeming security and prosperity, all doubts vanished and immigrants came in freely, especially Presbyterians from Scotland.[27]

Though there were numerous Englishmen and some French Huguenots and representatives of other racial elements sharing in the settlement of Ulster in the eighteenth century when the plantation was taking place, the predominant group was that of the Lowland Scots, who gave the prevailing tone and direction to the settlement. It was natural that the Scots should come more freely than the English because of their greater proximity to Ulster and the consequent quicker transit for themselves and their household goods. Furthermore, their poverty was greater, a circumstance which made the opportunities in Ireland appear more attractive to them than to the English. Hence they came in greater numbers from the beginning, and their preponderance increased as time went by.[28] There was a steady stream of emigrants from Scotland to Ireland, mainly to Ulster, throughout the whole of the seventeenth century. It is estimated that between thirty and forty thousand Lowland Scots arrived in Ulster between 1608 and 1618, and ten thousand are known to have arrived between 1633 and 1635; and the Cromwellian conquest was, as noted above, followed by a particularly large immigration of Scots to Ulster.[29] Froude estimates the number of Scots in Ireland following the Cromwellian Settlement at 100,000, nearly all of whom were Presbyterians. Only about half the Cromwellian settlers coming from England were Episcopalians, the remainder consisting of Presbyterians, Baptists, Independents, and Quakers.[30] Sir William Petty estimated the population of Ireland in 1672 at

26. Ford, *op. cit.*, 103; Hanna, *op. cit.*, I, 501.

27. Hanna, *op. cit.*, I, 498.

28. Ford, *op. cit.*, 92-93, 119-121.

29. Woodburn, *op. cit.*, 129.

30. Froude, *op. cit.*, 154-155; J. W. Kernigan, *The County of Londonderry in Three Centuries*, 41-43.

1,110,000, of whom there were 800,000 Irish, 200,000 English, and 100,000 Scots; the English were scattered all over the country, whereas the Scots were concentrated mostly in Ulster.[31] Prendergast informs us that after the Revolution of 1688, Ulster "was nearly colonized anew by the Scotch settlers and camp followers of King William's forces. Eighty thousand small Scotch adventurers, between 1690 and 1698, came into different parts of Ireland, but chiefly into Ulster."[32] In 1715 it was estimated by Archbishop Synge that 50,000 Scotch families had settled in Ulster since the Revolution.[33]

The Scots settled mainly in the northern and eastern parts of Ulster, where they greatly outnumbered the other immigrants. Of all the counties of Ulster, Down and Antrim have been the most completely transformed by the plantation, being thoroughly British and essentially Scottish. Scots predominated also in the counties of Londonderry, Tyrone, and eastern Donegal, but were outnumbered by the English in the counties of Armagh and Fermanagh, and were not especially numerous in the counties of Cavan and Monaghan. Belfast, though English in its foundation, became predominantly Scottish, and so remains today. The Scots spread all over Ulster, however, both in town and country; but Ulster as a whole is not today, nor has it ever been, so overwhelmingly Scottish and Presbyterian as some would have us believe.[34] It should be remembered, also, that not all of the Scottish immigrants settled in Ulster, though they were not found numerously in other parts of Ireland.

The Irish Presbyterians were mostly of Scottish birth or descent, though not all the Scots in Ireland, or even in Ulster, were Presbyterians, some being Baptists, Independents, Quakers, and Episcopalians. The majority of the population of Ulster has probably never been either Scottish or Presbyterian, since the Scots have never been the majority racial element, nor Presby-

---

31. Sir William Petty, *Political Survey of Ireland in 1652*, cited in Harrison's *The Scot in Ulster*, 83-84.

32. Cited in O'Brien, *op. cit.*, 36.

33. Harrison, *op. cit.*, 87.

34. *Ibid.*, 47-54, 103-105, 107-109; Wood, *op. cit.*, 26; Croskery, *op. cit.*, 44; Butler, *op. cit.*, 249.

terianism the predominant religion, except in the counties of Antrim, Down, Londonderry, and Tyrone. The Presbyterians represent an overwhelming proportion of the Scottish population of Ulster, just as they have always done since the time of the Great Plantation, but they are now outnumbered, as they have probably always been, by both the Catholics and the Episcopalians in Ulster as a whole. In the nine counties of Ulster the Catholics now represent a majority of the population, and there is good reason to believe that they have always done so. It appears, however, that Ulster has consistently had, since the Great Plantation, at least 90 per cent of both the Scottish and Presbyterian population of Ireland. In this province they established their full system of churches and church government and discipline. Here the Ulster Scots introduced a new type of thought, religion, and industry, and laid broad and deep the foundations of a new society that was to have a far-reaching effect not only in Northern Ireland, but in America as well.[35]

The Lowland Scots, the Ulster Scots, and the Scotch-Irish of America are, as has been noted, one and the same race, but the two latter branches of the race have had experiences in Ulster and America which have strengthened their character and toughened their native fibre by the very difficulties they have been compelled to overcome. This is the race that found Ulster a morass and transformed it into a garden, maintaining their position stoutly the while against their English overlords on the one hand and the combative Irish on the other. Firmly established in Ireland through the plantations of the seventeenth century, the Ulster Scot in his new environment ceased to be a Lowlander, though the seedbed of his race was the Lowlands of Scotland. While retaining his essential characteristics, new forces were brought to bear upon him which exercised a modifying influence upon his habits of thought and conduct. He was now in the midst of a hostile people whom he despised, and who in turn hated him as an alien and a usurper. This situation gave rise to a feud between the two races, resulting in the bloody massacre of 1641 when the Irishman sought to exterminate the Scot and to repossess the land

35. Croskery, *op. cit.*, 5-8; Froude, *op. cit.*, I, 154; Harrison, *op. cit.*, 106-109.

from which he had been ousted. The Ulsterman was hardened and toughened by this experience. Furthermore, living now under conditions such as he had not known in Scotland, he found it necessary to adjust himself to his new surroundings, and in the process he developed viewpoints and habits which still further differentiated him from the Lowlander. Again, he was not only surrounded by the unfriendly Irish, but was also brought into close contact with other races with which he became allied, often by marriage. Alongside him in Ulster lived the English Puritan, the French Huguenot, and the Hollander, whose influence upon him was felt in giving a new spur and direction to his activity. He was led to engage more energetically in trade, manufactures, and commerce than he would probably have done had he remained in Scotland. He was now as apt to be a business man or a manufacturer as to be a farmer; he developed rapidly into a man of affairs with a somewhat broader viewpoint. Thus the Ulster Scot became a modified Lowlander, more versatile than his brother across the Channel, more adaptable, and less traditional, provincial, and clannish. His local attachments have been weakened by his growing sense of the injustices heaped upon him in the land of his adoption, and he is now almost a man without a country. He is ready to seek new adventures beyond the seas. Exasperated by his wrongs, he will make one more migration— this time to the New World, where freedom abounds and opportunity beckons. Here, amid new surroundings, he will undergo a further change, and here he will go his farthest lengths and attain his greatest heights. No longer a Lowland Scot or an Ulster Scot, he becomes the Scotch-Irishman of America—still of the same race as the Lowlander and the Ulster Scot, to be sure, but different from either by reason of his adjustment to a changed environment; more fertile in resource, less insular and angular, less stern in his outlook upon life, and with a keener sense of humor.[36] Practical, as always, he is now ready for anything, doing with his might what his hand finds to do. A greater destiny awaits him than he has ever dreamed of.

36. For a discerning elaboration of this point of view, see J. S. MacIntosh, "The Making of the Ulsterman," in Scotch-Irish Society of America *Proceedings*, II, 92-104.

3

Emigration of the Ulster Scots to Pennsylvania

In the two years which followed the Antrim evictions, 30,000 Protestants left Ulster for a land where there was no legal robbery, and where those who sowed the seed reaped the harvest. FROUDE

THE EMIGRATION of the Ulster Scots to the New World is one of the significant movements of history, not only on account of its volume but because of its far-reaching effects upon American life.[1] Beginning in the last decade of the seventeenth century, it continued uninterruptedly throughout the whole of the eighteenth century and well into the nineteenth, nor has it ever ceased. Its greatest relative importance, however, was in the eighteenth century from about 1717 until 1775.

CAUSES OF EMIGRATION

The causes leading to the emigration of the Ulster Scots, while partly political and partly religious, were chiefly economic, although there was a growing sense of oppression due to a combination of these causes. Having by their energy and skill redeemed Northern Ireland from its physical and moral degradation and transformed it into a prosperous community, their reward at the hands of the English Government was a series of political, economic, social, and religious persecutions, resulting in a wholesale emigration to America, particularly to Pennsylvania. Never a submissive people, they decided to seek a new home in the

1. The Ulster Scots comprised about 90 per cent of the Scots in Ireland in the eighteenth century. The remaining 10 per cent, scattered elsewhere over the Island, are, for our purposes, included in the term "Ulster Scots," commonly employed to designate them.

wilderness rather than to endure the accumulated wrongs inflicted upon them, being urged the more thereto by their restless disposition and their love of adventure. Hence they gathered unto themselves their household goods and departed with no good feelings toward their oppressors, whom they were later to confront on the battlefields of the Revolution, where they evened up the score. Furthermore, being merely sojourners in Ireland and, in some sense, men without a country, they found it easier to emigrate than would have been the case if the ties binding them to a fatherland had existed. Not all of them emigrated to America, however; some returned to Scotland, while others went to England, France, Germany, Spain, and the West Indies.[2]

The most potent, as well as the most constant, cause of emigration was economic. This assumed the forms of repressive trade laws, rack-renting, famine, the decline of the linen industry, and a general feeling of economic insecurity. Impoverished by reason of these conditions, their present livelihood precarious and the outlook gloomy, they felt constrained to emigrate. Restrictions on Irish trade began in 1699, when the woolen manufacture, then the staple industry of Ireland, was restricted by the passage of an act forbidding the exportation of Irish woolen manufactures to any part of the world except to England and Wales. This act, inspired by the jealousy of English manufacturers, deprived the people of Ulster, where the industry was centered, of their colonial and foreign markets, and was the principal cause of the emigration from Ulster early in the eighteenth century.[3]

Another inducing cause of emigration was that of rack-renting landlordism, which drove many thousands of Ulstermen beyond the seas. An enormous quantity of land had been leased to tenants on leases extending over a long period of years. In 1717 these leases began to expire, and when a renewal was sought the rents were doubled or trebled, reaching a point where farming ceased to be profitable. Having improved the lands by their industry and

2. W. E. H. Lecky, *A History of England in the Eighteenth Century*, II, 260.
3. James Anthony Froude, *The English in Ireland in the Eighteenth Century*, I, 392; George O'Brien, *The Economic History of Ireland in the Eighteenth Century*, 5, 179, 181-183; Carl Wittke, *We Who Built America*, 45.

turned a wilderness into a smiling countryside, the tenant farmers not only received no compensation for the improvements effected, but merely furnished the landlords an excuse for raising the rent beyond all reason. The situation appearing hopeless, a heavy emigration at once began. The native Catholic Irish, long habituated to a life of abject poverty, took up the leases and continued to live in squalid misery, but the Ulster Scots, refusing to be held up in this manner, left the country in large numbers. In some instances, districts of considerable area were almost depopulated.[4]

The recurring bad harvests and resulting famines which afflicted Ireland in the eighteenth century were the occasion of another large exodus of Ulstermen. Especially severe were the famines of 1727 and 1740, which led to two of the largest waves of emigration from Ulster in this century. The year 1770 was also one of scarcity, which was one of the causes of the exceptionally heavy emigration in the several years following. Famine years were invariably marked by a large increase in the volume of emigration.[5]

A major cause of the great exodus of 1771-1773 was the decline of the linen manufacture. This industry centered in Ulster, which was far and away the leading industrial district of Ireland, and especially in the city of Belfast. The decline of this industry was rapid after 1770, and many thousands were thrown out of employment. In their extremity, they joined the swelling host of emigrants to America. Arthur Young stresses this point, while Froude informs us that "the linen trade . . . had entered upon a period of stagnation, and the consequent distress gave an impetus to the emigration to the land of promise."[6]

Of great significance also as a cause of emigration was the religious persecution suffered by the Ulster Scots at the hands of the Established Church of Ireland, where the Church of England, though represented by but a small part of the population, had been established by law. The religious oppression of the

---

4. J. S. Reid, *History of the Presbyterian Church in Ireland,* III, 224; J. B. Woodburn, *The Ulster Scot,* 214, 221; Maude Glasgow, *The Scotch-Irish in Northern Ireland and in the American Colonies,* 155.

5. O'Brien, *op. cit.,* 17, 103-105; Woodburn, *op. cit.,* 216, 229; H. J. Ford, *The Scotch-Irish in America,* 198.

6. Arthur Young, *Tour in Ireland, 1776-1779,* I, 123, 144; Froude, *op. cit.,* 124-125.

Protestant Dissenters, mostly Presbyterians in Ulster, weighed heavily upon the inhabitants. The Presbyterians, comprising the bulk of the Ulster Scots, had transferred their system of churches and church government to Ireland, and were strongly organized. Their growth and prosperity aroused the animosity of the Church of England, and they became the victims of unjust laws and petty persecutions directed against them by the ruling powers in Church and State. All of the Episcopal bishops and some of the Episcopal landlords inserted in their leases clauses prohibiting the erection of Presbyterian churches on their estates. Marriages performed by Presbyterian clergymen were declared illegal, and those performing them were subjected to fines in the ecclesiastical courts. Even their right to conduct services for the burial of the dead was questioned, sometimes at the grave itself. The Test Act of 1704, enacted as a blow against Protestant Dissenters in general and against the Ulster Presbyterians in particular, excluded them from all civil and military offices under the Crown by requiring all who served in these capacities to take communion of the Established Church. Not only were they thus deprived of the rights of citizenship, but were required to pay tithes to support the clergy of the Episcopal Church, whose bishops were the chief instigators of their civil and religious disabilities. A statement put forth by the Presbytery of Tyrone in December 1729 specifically mentioned "the discouragements under which they lay by the Sacramental Test, excluding them from all places of public trust and honor, as among the chief causes driving them to other parts of the empire where no such discouragements existed."[7]

It may here be noted that the political cause of the emigration of the Ulster Scots stemmed from the religious cause as set forth above, as embodied in the Test Act of 1704. Disqualified thereby from holding political office or commissions in the army, they naturally felt themselves to be discriminated against politically no less than religiously and economically. According to Harrison, the Test Act "at once emptied the town councils of the Ulster

---

7. W. F. Latimer, *A History of Irish Presbyterains*, 155; E. A. D'Alton, *History of Ireland*, I, 481; W. E. H. Lecky, *A History of Ireland in the Eighteenth Century*, I, 427-429; Reid, *op. cit.*, 225-226; Woodburn, *op. cit.*, 214, 228-229; Wittke, *op. cit.*, 44-45.

towns; it deprived of their commissions many who were serving as magistrates in the counties. It drove out of the Corporation of Londonderry several of the very men who had fought through the siege of 1689."[8] The oppressive measures directed against the Dissenters were instigated by the Bench of Bishops of the Irish House of Lords and were aimed chiefly at the Ulster Scots to bring pressure to bear on them to make them conform to the Established Church rather than endure the galling disabilities to which they would otherwise be subjected. But the bishops reckoned without their host, for the Ulster Scots were made of sterner stuff than to compromise their principles. They refused to conform, and, though many remained to endure the persecutions that fell to their lot, thousands of others, perhaps a majority, sought civil and religious liberty in America.[9]

A further stimulus to emigration was the activity of ship-agents in promoting it. The assisted immigration of the indentured servant system played a large part in inducing emigration by making it possible for thousands to go who would otherwise have been forced to remain at home. In colonial times Ireland, and Ulster in particular, furnished the largest supply of indentured servants from English-speaking countries. Agents of ship companies went through the country, advertising the advantages of the New World and offering to transport necessitous emigrants who would sign agreements to sell their services for a term of years upon their arrival at American ports, and thereby defray the expense of passage. Many ships were engaged in this trade, and undoubtedly many passengers were conveyed from Ireland to America on these terms. This trade continued brisk down to as late as 1807, when it was interrupted by the Embargo of that year, but declined rapidly thereafter and ceased altogether in 1831.[10]

Froude summed up the causes of the emigration of the Ulster Scots in the following eloquent language:

8. John Harrison, *The Scot in Ulster*, 89.

9. Woodburn, *op. cit.*, 229; Reid, *op. cit.*, III, 226; Latimer, *op. cit.*, 155.

10. C. A. Herrick, *White Servitude in Pennsylvania*, 143, 159, 167, 260; G. F. Keiser, *Redemptioners and Indentured Servants in the Colony and Commonwealth of Pennsylvania*, 36, 81.

"Men of spirit and energy refused to remain in a country where they were held unfit to receive the rights of citizens . . . Flights of Protestant settlers had been driven out earlier in the century by the idiocy of the bishops . . . Religious bigotry, commercial jealousy, and modern landlordism had combined to do their worst against the Ulster settlement . . . Vexed with suits in ecclesiastical courts, forbidden to educate their children in their own faith, treated as dangerous in a state which but for them would have had no existence, and associated with Papists in an Act of Parliament which deprived them of their civil rights, the most earnest of them at length abandoned the unthankful service. They saw at last that the liberties for which their fathers had fought were not to be theirs in Ireland . . . During the first half of the eighteenth century, Down, Antrim, Armagh, and Derry were emptied of their Protestant families, who were of more value to Ireland than California gold mines."[11]

VOLUME OF EMIGRATION

The emigration of Ulster Scots to America on a large scale dates from the beginning of the eighteenth century. There was, however, a slight emigration of this group to the New World in the last decade of the seventeenth century, though it appears that only a small percentage of it was at this time directed to Pennsylvania. The first Scotch-Irish settlers in America located on the eastern shore of Maryland about 1649, and in South Carolina in 1682.[12] It is probable that there were a few Scotch-Irish in southeastern Pennsylvania in 1685.[13] A Presbyterian church was organized in Philadelphia in 1695, and it is likely that there were some Scotch-Irish in the membership. James Logan, who arrived at Philadelphia in 1699, was a Scotch-Irish Quaker, secretary of the province and confidential agent of William Penn. Nevertheless, the emigration of Ulster Scots prior to 1700 was slight, consisting of a few individuals or of small groups who, not yet oppressed at home, felt the impulse to seek a better environment abroad.[14] The mass emigration of the Ulster Scots, due to

11. Froude, *op. cit.*, I, 392; II, 125, 131.
12. Ford, *op. cit.*, 170-171, 212.
13. G. S. Klett, *Presbyterians in Colonial Pennsylvania*, 38.
14. Maude Glasgow, *op. cit.*, 155.

the several causes enumerated above, began early in the eighteenth century and increased in volume as the century advanced.

While there was a steady stream of emigration of Ulster Scots throughout the whole of the eighteenth century, there were certain periods when the tide was unusually strong; these were the years 1717-1718, 1727-1728, 1740-1741, and 1771-1773. The causes of emigration which we have described did not operate equally during these heavy waves of emigration, and it is possible to determine those which were especially influential at a given time. The emigration in 1717-1718, when the first mass emigration of the Ulster Scots began, was caused by the destruction of the woolen industry, by the disabilities arising from the Test Act, and by the rack-renting of the landlords, the last of which was the most immediate and potent cause.[15] In a letter dated October 23, 1717, Jonathan Dickinson says that "from ye north of Ireland many hundreds" arrived at Philadelphia "in aboute four months";[16] and on October 17, 1719, he writes, "This summer we have had 12 or 13 sayle of ships from the North of Ireland wth a swarm of people."[17] He further states, in a letter under date of November 12, 1719, that twelve ships, laden with passengers from Ireland, had recently arrived at Philadelphia.[18]

Following this first wave of emigration, the tide ebbed somewhat until 1727-1728, when it reached an even greater height than before and was still going strong in the seventeen-thirties. The causes which had produced the earlier exodus were still potent now, but to these was added the immediate cause of a series of poor harvests, culminating in the famine of 1727-1728 with its attendant want and misery. A contemporary account of conditions in Ireland in this period is given in the following excerpt from the *Pennsylvania Gazette:*

"The English papers have of late been frequent in their Accounts of the unhappy Circumstances of the Common People of Ireland;

15. Lecky, *A History of England in the Eighteenth Century*, II, 260; Reid, *op. cit.*, III, 225; C. K. Bolton, *Scotch-Irish Pioneers in Ulster and America*, 270; Ford, *op. cit.*, 187; Harrison, *op. cit.*, 90.

16. Jonathan Dickinson, *Copy Book of Letters*, 163.

17. Jonathan Dickinson, *Letter Book*, 294.

18. Jonathan Dickinson, *Copy Book of Letters*, 288.

That Poverty, Wretchedness, Misery and Want are become almost universal among them; That . . . there is not Corn enough rais'd for their Subsistence one Year with another; and at the same Time the Trade and Manufactures of the Nation being cramp'd and discourag'd, the labouring People have little to do, and consequently are not able to purchase Bread at its present dear Rate: That the Taxes are nevertheless exceeding heavy, and Money very scarce; and add to all this, that their griping, avaricious Landlords exercise over them the most merciless Racking Tyranny and Oppression. Hence it is that such Swarms of them are driven over into America."[19]

The *Gazette* follows up this account with an extract from a London newspaper written by Robert Gambie of Londonderry to a mercantile firm in London, in July 1729, in which he says: "There is gone and to go this Summer from this port Twenty-five Sail of Ships, who carry each, from One Hundred and twenty to One hundred and forty Passengers to America; there are many more going from Belfast, and the Ports near Colrain, besides great numbers from Dublin, Newry, and round the Coast. Where this will end God only knows."[20] So great was the exodus at this time that the landlords became alarmed and drew up a memorial to the government in which it was stated that "about 4000 useful Protestants have left this Kingdom since the Beginning of last Spring; and your memorialists are well assured, that the infatuation is now so general, that not fewer than 20,000 have already declared, and seem determined to transport themselves in the ensuing Spring."[21] The only result accomplished by this memorial appears to have been that the Presbyterian Synod, which met at Dublin about this time, was requested "to use their Influence with the People, in persuading them not to desert the kingdom."[22]

This emigration assumed such proportions as to attract the attention of the authorities in both Ireland and Pennsylvania. In Ireland it was feared that the country would be depopulated of its highly useful Protestant inhabitants, chiefly the Ulster Scots,

19. *Pennsylvania Gazette,* November 20, 1729.
20. *Ibid.*
21. *Ibid.*
22. *Ibid.*

whereas in Pennsylvania the large immigration of Scotch-Irish at this time was viewed with alarm by James Logan, Secretary of the Province. Archbishop Boulter, Lord Primate of All Ireland, in a letter dated March 13, 1728, says: "The humour of going to America still continues, and the scarcity of provisions certainly makes many quit us. There are now seven ships at Belfast, that are carrying about 1000 passengers thither."[23] Writing to the Duke of Newcastle November 23, 1728, Boulter says:

"We have had for several years some agents of the colonies in America, and several masters of ships, that have gone about the country and deluded the people with stories of great plenty and estates to be had for the going for, in those parts of the world; and they have been the better able to seduce people by reason of the necessities of the poor of late. The people that go from hence make great complaints of the oppressions they suffer here, and, not from government, but from their fellow-subjects of one kind and another; as well as the dearness of provisions; and they say these oppressions are one cause of their going . . . One man in ten may be a man of substance, and may do well enough abroad, but the case of the rest is deplorable. They either hire themselves to those of substance for their passage, or contract with the masters of ships for four years' servitude when they come hither . . . The whole north is in a ferment at present, and people every day engaging one another to go next year to the West Indies. The humour has spread like a contagious distemper, and the people will hardly hear of anybody that tries to cure them of their madness. The worst is, that it affects only Protestants, and reigns chiefly in the north, which is the seat of our linen manufacture."[24]

So great was this exodus that one of the Lords-Justices, alarmed at its extent and desirous of ascertaining its causes, asked Francis Iredel and Robert Craighead, two Presbyterian clergymen, to enquire into the matter and submit a report of their findings to the government. The answer of the Presbytery of Tyrone to this query was returned in December, 1729, and mentioned as causes of the exodus that "the bad seasons for three years past, together

23. Hugh Boulter, *Letters Written by his Excellency Hugh Boulter, D.D., Lord Primate of all Ireland to several Ministers of State in England, and some others,* I, 230-231.
24. *Ibid.,* 225-226.

with the high price of lands and tithes, have all contributed to the general run to America, and to the ruin of many families, who are daily leaving their houses and lands desolate."[25] The report also specified as serious causes of discontent, even where no other causes were involved, the disabilities arising from the Sacramental Test, which excluded them from all places of public trust and honor under the government.[26]

That the heavy immigration into Pennsylvania, which far exceeded that into any of the other colonies, was viewed with misgivings by the provincial authorities is revealed in the letters of James Logan. Writing to J. Chalmers of Belfast, September 26, 1727, he says, "We are very much surprised here at the vast crowds of people pouring in upon us from Ireland."[27] Two months later he writes to John Penn that, "We have from the North of Ireland great numbers yearly, 8 or 9 ships this last fall discharged at New Castle."[28] His alarm is not yet excited, however, but two years later, he says in a letter to John Penn: "It now looks as if Irel^d or the Inhabitants of it were to be transplanted hither. Last week I think no less than 6 ships arrived at New Castle and this place [Philadelphia], and they are every 2 or 3 days when the wind serves dropping in loaded with Passengers, and therefore we may easily believe there are some grounds for the common apprehensions of the people that if some speedy Method be not taken, they will soon make themselves Proprietors of the Province."[29]

That this wave of immigration continued strong for some years later may be seen in a letter of James Steel, Receiver-General of the province, in November 1737, in which he refers to the "vast numbers of people still flocking into your Province," and specifically mentions Ireland as one of the principal sources of this immigration.[30] A letter written from Londonderry June 3, 1735, speaks of the "great number of *Protestant Inhabitants* that have gone this season from this Province to America (not fewer than 1800

25. Cited by Reid, *op. cit.*, III, 227.
26. *Ibid.*, 226.
27. *Logan Papers*, IV. Letter Books of James Logan, 148.
28. *Logan Papers*, IV, 153-154.
29. *Logan Papers*, III. Letters from James Logan, 303.
30. *Penn MSS.*, Official Correspondence, III, 63.

from this port, and in the same proportion I am inform'd from all the other ports of the North);"[31] while a letter of the same date from Dublin declares, "Great numbers are gone and more are going this year to America (as they say) to avoid the oppressions of the Landlords and Tythemen."[32] A further proof of the continuance of a strong stream of emigration from Ireland in the seventeen-thirties is found in the letter of an Irish ship captain to Thomas Penn, under date of May 3, 1736, complaining bitterly of the obstructions placed on Irish emigration to Pennsylvania at this time. He represents that many poor people were fleeing from Ireland to escape "the oppressions of the Landlords and tyeths," and that the authorities were placing obstacles in the way of their departure. He further states that ten ships, of which eight were bound for the ports on the Delaware River, had already been detained at Belfast for more than two weeks, with about 1800 emigrants "in most deplorable circumstances."[33]

Another great wave of emigration from Ulster began in 1740-1741. While the grievances previously described were still operating to produce discontent and to induce emigration, the immediate occasion of this particular exodus was the famine of 1740-1741, which was quite as severe as that of 1727-1728, and probably even more devastating in its effects.[34] It is estimated that within two years at least 400,000 people in Ireland perished from starvation. A large movement of population to America at once began, and continued for some years above the ordinary volume; in fact, for a decade or more.[35] Proud informs us that in 1749 and for several preceding years it amounted to nearly 12,000 annually in Pennsylvania alone.[36] The emigration around the year 1749 was further stimulated by a trade depression caused by overproduction in silk weaving, throwing many weavers out of employment and impelling them to emigrate.[37] In fact, it might be

31. *Pennsylvania Gazette*, September 18, 1735.
32. *Ibid.*
33. *Pennsylvania Magazine of History and Biography*, XXI, 485-486.
34. Obrien, *op. cit.*, 17, 105; Woodburn, *op. cit.*, 217; Glasgow, *op. cit.*, 156.
35. Woodburn, *ibid.*
36. Robert Proud, *History of Pennsylvania*, II, 274.
37. O'Brien, *op. cit.*, 17.

said that the exodus at this time constituted of itself another wave of emigration resulting from industrial depression and continuing briskly for several years.

The immigrant tide slackened in the period of the French and Indian War and was not noticeably strong thereafter until 1771, when a new wave of emigration from Ulster, stronger than any that had preceded it, began to gather headway and reached its climax in 1772-1773. It constituted by far the largest immigration to America of any single racial group in the years immediately preceding the Revolution. This exodus, besides the usual causes of emigration, was motivated particularly by the decline of the linen trade centering in Ulster and by a new outburst of rack-renting. It is computed that during 1771-1773 twenty-five or thirty thousand emigrants sailed from Ulster alone to ports in the New World, especially to those on the Delaware. Arthur Young states that for many years Belfast "had a regular emigration of about 2000 annually; but in 1772 the decline of linen manufacture increased the number, and the same cause continuing, in 1773 they were at the highest, when 4,000 went" from that port.[38] Newenham estimates the emigration of 1771-1773 at 28,600 from the ports of Ulster, especially Belfast, Newry, and Derr, in ninety-one ships.[39] Froude computes the number of Protestants emigrating from Ulster in 1772-1773 at 30,000, and says "ships could not be found to carry the crowds that were eager to go."[40] Grattan Flood states that during 1771-1773, 101 ships sailed from Ulster ports to America with full complements of passengers, carrying about 32,000 emigrants in these three years alone, while 20,000 more sailed from Dublin and 10,000 each from Cork and Waterford, "not taking into consideration the occasional sailings from Galway, Killala, Limerick, Sligo, Youghal, and other ports." He is of the opinion that "it would not be rash to assume that 150,000 Irish emigrants went to America within a few years before the

38. Anthony Marmion, *The Ancient and Modern History of the Maritime Ports of Ireland*, 84; Arthur Young, *op. cit.*, 144.
39. Thomas Newenham, *A Statistical and Historical Inquiry into the Progress and Magnitude of the Population of Ireland*, 59.
40. Froude, *op. cit.*, II, 125.

outbreak of the war in the colonies."[41] This estimate would appear to be an exaggeration, but there can be no question that the emigration in these years was the heaviest at any given time in the eighteenth century. Inasmuch as a goodly number of the emigrants from Ireland sailed from ports in Scotland and England also, the evidence points to the conclusion that from 1770 to 1775 at least 50,000 left Ireland for America, the majority of whom settled in Pennsylvania.

Two facts stand out clearly with reference to the emigration from Ireland to America in the colonial era: it was large and it was Protestant. It is computed that from 1728 to 1750 Ulster lost one-fourth of her manufacturing population, and that the counties of Down, Antrim, Armagh, and Londonderry "were almost emptied of their Protestant inhabitants." In the great exodus beginning in 1771, Ulster is said to have lost one-fourth of its population and one-fourth of its trading cash within five years.[42] Newenham estimates that between 1750 and 1800 about 200,000 emigrated from Ireland, though not all of these came to America; and Woodburn is of the opinion that at least 200,000 emigrated from Ulster alone between 1700 and 1776.[43]

All the authorities are agreed upon the statement, and the evidence warrants it, that Irish emigration to America in the eighteenth century was overwhelmingly Protestant and mainly Presbyterian; and that the bulk of the emigrants were Ulster Scots, although there was a respectable number of Protestants emigrating from other parts of Ireland. The emigration of the Catholic Irish was very slight in this period, nor did it become noteworthy until well into the nineteenth century. Archbishop Boulter, as noted above, complained that the heavy emigration of 1728 "affects only Protestants, and reigns chiefly in the North," and the same statement would have been equally true of the later waves of emigration.[44] Lecky speaks of the Catholics as occupying the cottages vacated by the departing Protestants, and declares

41. W. H. Grattan Flood, *Irish Emigration to the American Colonies, 1723-1773,* 206.
42. Maude Glasgow, *op. cit.,* 157; Froude, *op. cit.,* 131; Reid, *op. cit.,* 339.
43. Newenham, *op. cit.,* 65; Woodburn, *op. cit.,* 213.
44. Boulter, *op. cit.,* I, 226.

that "for nearly seventy-five years the drain of the energetic Protestant population continued, and their places, when occupied at all, were occupied by a Catholic cotter population sunk in the lowest depths of ignorance and poverty."[45] The Test Act, with its religious and civil disabilities, was aimed primarily at Dissenters and there is no reference to it as a cause of Catholic emigration, whereas we have seen that it was one of the main causes of the Protestant exodus. The Woolen Act affected scarcely any other element of the population except the Ulster Scots; and the decline of the linen manufacture, a Protestant industry, did not affect the population as a whole. The rack-renting of the landlords sent large numbers of Protestants overseas, but affected only a negligible number of Catholics, who remained rooted to the soil. Arthur Young informs us that the emigrants "were generally Dissenters, very few Churchmen or Catholics," and in a later volume says, "The Catholics never went," though in the latter statement he was mistaken since a few of them did emigrate to America at intervals throughout the colonial era.[46] According to Sweet, a very good authority, there were only 24,000 Catholics in the entire United States in 1783,[47] and this number included many, perhaps a majority, from countries other than Ireland. It appears probable that Ireland furnished not more than 10,000 Catholics in America during the colonial period, and that the major part of the Catholic population came from England, Germany, and France.

It is impossible to determine with certainty the number of Scotch-Irish immigrants into America in the colonial era, but taking into account the estimates of the authorities cited above and the known facts about the continuous and heavy emigration from Ireland to these shores extending over a period of three quarters of a century and more, we venture to compute this immigration at about 250,000 in the eighteenth century. Upon the basis of a careful study of the evidence bearing upon the question, we believe this estimate to be approximately correct, and that it is in all probability more likely to be an underestimate rather than other-

45. Lecky, *A History of England in the Eighteenth Century*, II, 260-261.
46. Young, *op. cit.*, I, 123-124; II, 260-261.
47. W. W. Sweet, *The Story of Religions in America*, 293.

wise.[48] Next to the English, this racial group was by far the most numerous of any entering America in the colonial era.

LATER EMIGRATION OF THE ULSTER SCOTS

While the colonial era is the most significant for the study of Scotch-Irish immigration into America, it would be a mistake to suppose that it ceased to be important when that era ended. In the post-colonial period there continued to be a large emigration from Ulster, and well down into the nineteenth century the emigration from this region exceeded that from the remainder of Ireland, and was still composed mostly of Protestants. William Priest, an English traveler in America, in a letter written in 1796 says: "The emigration from Ireland has this year been very great; I left a large vessel full of passengers from thence at Baltimore. I found three at Newcastle; there is one in this city [Philadelphia]. The number of passengers cannot be averaged at less than 250 each vessel, all of whom have arrived in the last six weeks."[49] As late as 1820 Ulster was still supplying two-thirds of the emigrants from Ireland and in 1835 was furnishing "the bulk of the emigrants." Though it is true that the first phase of Irish emigration to America closed with the outbreak of the American Revolution, and that it was interrupted by that struggle and by the Napoleonic wars, the flow never ceased, continuing mainly from Ulster for a generation or more. But the tide of the Ulster Scots had reached its flood in the seventeen-seventies, and thereafter began to ebb. It was not until after 1835 or 1840, however, that the Ulster emigrants declined to the minority position which they have since occupied in Irish emigration.[50] According to Professor Hansen of the University of Illinois: "My own impression is that in colonial times about five-sixths and in the nineteenth century, up to about 1840 or a couple of years later, about two-thirds [of the "Irishmen"] were from the North of Ireland and Protestant. This impression is based upon three months of doing

48. Fiske estimates the Scotch-Irish in America at one-sixth the population in 1776. See his *Dutch and Quaker Colonies in America*, II, 354. This, however, is an overestimate.
49. William Priest, *Travels in the United States of America, 1793-1797*, 146.
50. W. F. Adams, *Ireland and Irish Emigration to the New World, from 1815 to the Famine*, 120, 158, 191; Edward F. Roberts, *Ireland in America*, 70-72.

nothing but reading Irish newspapers covering the period 1830-1850."[51]

There is no reason to believe that there was any mass emigration of the Catholics before about 1840; prior to this time it was much smaller than that of the Protestants from Ulster. Though the heavy Catholic Irish immigration into America set in about 1840, it did not become pronounced until the famine of 1845, following which it continued for many years to be the largest stream of any racial group coming to our shores. That the Ulster emigration remained reasonably strong, however, is unquestionable. Furthermore, it is noteworthy that the emigration from Ulster to America has continued down to the present time to be larger than is ordinarily supposed. Burr estimates that "Ulster furnished, from 1850 to 1910, over one-fourth the total emigration from Ireland, so that it may reasonably be supposed that the Orangemen migrating to the United States numbered at least one-tenth the Irish total."[52] The Ulster Scots have by no means ceased to emigrate to America, and their number is still considerable.[53] They have in all probability constituted at least 10 per cent of Irish immigration since 1850. It would be a mistake, however, to think that everybody coming from Ulster was of Scottish descent. The evidence seems to warrant the conclusion that the Ulster Scots furnished not more than half the emigrants from that province since about 1850, the remaining half being composed mainly of Irish Catholics and of Ulstermen of English descent.

PORTS OF EMBARKATION AND DEBARKATION

Belfast, the most prosperous and progressive city of Ireland, was the chief port of embarkation for the Ulster Scots bound for America, but other Ulster ports frequently referred to in this connection were Newry, Londonderry, Larne, and Port Rush. Other Irish ports from which emigrants often sailed were Dublin, Cork, and Waterford, especially at the time of the great exodus

51. Cited in John N. Finley, *The Coming of the Scot*, 176.
52. C. S. Burr, *America's Race Heritage*, 95.
53. *Census of the United States*, 1930.

of 1771-1773. Occasional ports of embarkation were Galway, Killala, Limerick, Sligo, and Youghal. It appears that after 1790 Dublin ranked next to Belfast as the principal port for emigration. As the colonial period advanced, the passenger trade, consisting chiefly of emigrants, became a regular branch of commerce increasing continually in importance. A considerable proportion of the passengers consisted of indentured servants.[54] Many Ulster Scots embarked for America from English ports also, and some from Scottish ports, especially in the late colonial era. The English ports from which the largest number sailed were London, Liverpool, and Bristol. While the emigration of the Irish Protestants from English and Scotch ports was much smaller than from those of Ireland, nevertheless it was, in the aggregate, by no means inconsiderable.[55]

The principal American ports at which the Scotch-Irish emigrants debarked were Philadelphia, Newcastle, and Lewes, on the Delaware, and Charleston, South Carolina. But few landed at Boston or at any other New England port after 1720 because of the inhospitable reception accorded them in that section. A respectable number landed at New York, Baltimore, and Norfolk, and any southern port was likely to receive a few. The largest number, however, entered the country through the ports along the Delaware, especially Philadelphia.[56] Late in the colonial era some landed preferably at Baltimore as being the most convenient way to reach western Pennsylvania. The route overland to Pittsburgh by way of Braddock's Road from Baltimore was shorter than that by way of Forbes's Road from Philadelphia, besides presenting less difficulty in crossing the mountains.[57]

Emigrant ships commonly carried from 120 to 140 passengers, though some carried fewer and others more, depending on the size of the ships and the volume of traffic at different times.[58]

54. Newenham, op. cit., 59; Adams, op. cit., 118-120; Arthur Young, op. cit., II, 57.
55. Pennsylvania Gazette, November 20, 1729; Michael J. Obrien, Irish Immigrants from English Ports in the Eighteenth Century, 208.
56. H. L. Osgood, The American Colonies in the Eighteenth Century, II, 520; Hanna, op. cit., II, 60.
57. Priest, op. cit., 92n.
58. Pennsylvania Gazette, November 20, 1729.

That the voyage was long and hazardous and the conditions aboard ship were often distressing, is shown by the following excerpt from the *Pennsylvania Gazette:*

> "It is to be observed that to complete their Misfortunes, they have commonly long and miserable Passages, occasioned probably by the unskilfulness of the Mariners; the People, earnest to be gone, being oblig'd to take any Vessel that will go; and 'tis frequently with such as have before been only Coasters, because they cannot always get those that have been us'd to long Voyages to these Parts of the World; and being besides but meanly provided, many starve for Want, and many die of Sickness by being crowded in such Numbers on board one Vessel."[59]

Most emigrants had to carry with them their provisions for the voyage, together with such of their household goods as could be transported conveniently. Craftsmen brought along also the tools of their trade. All took with them such ready money as they possessed, but the average emigrant had little, while the indentured servants had practically none and were compelled to sell their services to pay their passage over.[60] The voyage ordinarily took from eight to ten weeks, but was longer if conditions were unfavorable, and there was the ever present danger of encountering pirates. Instances are on record of ships taking five months to complete the voyage, and heartrending accounts of starvation are all too numerous.

The Ulster Scots emigrating to America included among their number both those who were well-to-do and those who were needy, though the evidence points clearly to the conclusion that the great majority of them were needy. This state of affairs, however, was not peculiar to the Scotch-Irish immigrants, since the great bulk of the immigrants to America, of whatever race or nationality, have always been poverty-stricken. While there were doubtless some idle and worthless people among them, as among all other racial groups, there is every reason to believe that the Ulster emigrants were composed principally of a sturdy,

59. *Ibid.*
60. Glasgow, *op. cit.,* 156; Froude, *op. cit.,* I, 125.

enterprising, self-respecting, and liberty-loving group second to none other, the best proof of which is their actual achievements here. As in the case of other large immigrant groups of that day, they were composed of farmers, tradesmen, laborers, craftsmen, and a small number of professional men. But whatever their occupation or condition in life, it appears that all of them came with a feeling of hatred in their hearts for the English Government as the source of the injustices they had endured. Upon this all authorities are agreed.

Pennsylvania the Favorite Colony

The emigration of the Ulster Scots to America has been discussed in the large rather than from the strictly Pennsylvania standpoint, which is our more immediate concern, for reasons that seem justifiable to the writer. Had the subject been treated simply with reference to Pennsylvania, the facts adduced would have been essentially the same, while the broader implications of the subject, which are pertinent and important, would have either been touched upon casually or else given in a wrong perspective. The causes prompting the emigrants to leave Ireland were the same for those who entered the ports of Boston or Charleston as for those who landed at Philadelphia or Newcastle. The ports from which they embarked were the same regardless of that part of America for which they were bound. They were of the same occupations and social status and endured the same hardships of the voyage, whatever their American destination. Conditions in Ireland influenced emigrants bound for Pennsylvania in no way differently from those bound for New York or South Carolina. Conditions on this side of the water, however, were not the same in all the colonies, and for this reason attention is now directed to Pennsylvania in particular.

Pennsylvania was by far the favorite colony of the Scotch-Irish immigrants to America, and became their headquarters and distributing center in the New World.[61] As noted above, the ports at which a majority of these people landed were Philadelphia,

61. Osgood, *op. cit.*, II, 520; E. M. Proper, *Colonial Emigration Laws*, 80; Ford, *op. cit.*, 181, 199.

Lewes, and Newcastle, on the Delaware. While some few remained in Delaware and others crossed into New Jersey and Maryland, an overwhelming majority of those debarking at these ports settled in Pennsylvania. Edmund Burke, in describing European settlements in America, says: "In some years more people have transported themselves in Pennsylvania than into all the other settlements together; in 1729, 6208 persons came to settle here as passengers or servants, four-fifths at least of whom were from Ireland;"[62] and MacDougal informs us that "Pennsylvania was the chief centre of Scottish settlement, both from Scotland direct and from Ulster."[63] An indication of the destination of the majority of the emigrants from Ulster is seen in a contemporary account given by an Irish sea captain, who says, "Of the ten ships detained in the harbor, eight were bound for the Delaware River."[64] James Logan expresses wonder that "very few [Irish] come to any other Colony but this [Pennsylvania]."[65]

There need be no wonder, however, as to why Pennsylvania was the favorite colony of the Scotch-Irish immigrants. They found here to a greater degree than existed elsewhere the political, economic, social, and religious conditions that appealed to them. They desired civil and religious liberty and economic opportunity, and these were to be found in Pennsylvania as nowhere else in America. Only in Rhode Island was religious liberty equally secure, but that was a small colony, already well settled, and land was neither so abundant nor so fertile as in Pennsylvania. Furthermore, the inhospitable reception they met with in New England, especially in Massachusetts, convinced them that they were not wanted there, whereas Penn had "invited People to come & settle his Countrey."[66] Again, the excellent laws, low taxes, and general reputation of Pennsylvania throughout the world for its liberal institutions, together with the favorable reports of the first comers to the colony, served still further to persuade the Scotch-Irish that this was the haven they had long been seeking. Hence Pennsyl-

62. Edmund Burke, *An Account of European Settlements in America*, II, 205.
63. D. MacDougal, *Scots and Scots' Descendants in America*, 26.
64. *Pennsylvania Magazine of History and Biography*, XXI, 486.
65. *Logan Papers*, III, Letters to James Logan, 303.
66. *Logan Papers*, Letter Book, IV, 153-154; *Pa. Arch.*, 2 Ser., VII, 96-97.

vania became their headquarters and camping ground in the New World, and the center from which they were distributed to the westward and southward in succeeding generations.

Prior to about 1718, Scotch-Irish immigration was directed to New England rather than to Pennsylvania. Being mostly Presbyterians and stout Calvinists, they had much in common with the Puritan settlers of New England, who had themselves fled from persecution to seek a refuge in the wilderness. What more natural, therefore, than that the Presbyterians of Ireland, conscious of a somewhat similar background and a certain community of interest in relation to the New Englanders, should bend their course in that direction. Upon arrival, however, they soon found that they were not welcome among the Puritans and that obstacles were thrown in their way. They were at once confronted with a bigotry, intolerance, and exclusiveness of which they had never dreamed, and which was quite as great as that they had left behind in Ireland.[67] Hence, after a few settlements had been made in that bleak and inhospitable region, they turned their steps toward Pennsylvania and the South. Thus it happened that the majority of the emigrant ships carrying Ulster Scots to the New World landed their passengers on the shores of the Delaware.

As to the number of Scotch-Irish in Pennsylvania at the close of the colonial era, say 1790, it is impossible to speak with certainty, just as we can do no more than estimate the numerical strength of the other racial groups in the state at that time. We know that they came to this colony in a steady stream, sometimes reaching a heavy tide, throughout the whole of the eighteenth century, and that they were preceded by smaller numbers in the seventeenth century. Hanna estimates the Scottish element in Pennsylvania in 1790 at 100,000, but this includes both the Scots and the Scotch-Irish.[68] If this estimate is correct, as there is every reason to believe it is, and if the Scotch-Irish numbered 80 per cent of the total, which would seem to be a conservative estimate, then we are warranted in computing the Scotch-Irish population of Pennsylvania in 1790 at 80,000. The available evidence supports

67. Ford, *op. cit.*, 189-192.
68. Hanna, *op. cit.*, I, 83.

this conclusion as being approximately correct, and is so accepted by the writer. This number was substantially increased both by immigration and by natural increase in the last decade of the eighteenth century, and it is probable that in 1800 there were at least 120,000 inhabitants of Pennsylvania who were of Scottish lineage, of whom 100,000 were Scotch-Irish. These figures are believed, however, to be an underestimate rather than otherwise, a modest estimate being given to avoid even the appearance of extravagant claims.[69]

69. The writer is aware of the study made by Howard F. Barker entitled *National Stocks in the Population of the United States as Indicated by Surnames in the Census of 1790*, but is far from accepting the claims of this study insofar as it pertains to the Scotch-Irish of Pennsylvania. Apart from the rather fantastic notion of attempting to estimate the numerical strength of the various racial groups on the mere basis of name, it would seem to be still more fanciful to try to distinguish between the Scots and the Ulster Scots on this basis, inasmuch as they were the same stock, as were the Ulster Scots and the Scotch-Irish. To distinguish between a German or a French name and an English name may be fairly easy, but to distinguish between a Scottish name and a Scotch-Irish name is carrying the theory of determining racial origin on the basis of names to what would seem to be an extreme bordering on absurdity. Furthermore, the conclusions reached by this method are contradicted, in the case of the Scotch-Irish at least, by the plains facts of history, which show not what might have taken place ideally but what did take place actually. Contemporary records and the unanimous conclusion of historical scholars support the statement that the immigration of the Scotch-Irish into America in the colonial era was the largest immigration movement of non-English stock into the country in that period, whereas Barker's study, based on names only, makes the Scots coming directly from Scotland outnumber the Scotch-Irish in the ratio of 8 to 6. Again, with reference to Pennsylvania in particular, this study gives the Scotch-Irish but 11 per cent of the population as compared with 8.6 per cent from Scotland direct, whereas the record is clear that there was no such proportion of Scots, while there was a much larger proportion of Scotch-Irish. Hence the writer does not hesitate to discard the conclusions of Barker with reference to the Scotch-Irish of Pennsylvania as being at variance with the facts in the case as revealed by clear historical evidence. See Howard F. Barker, "National Stocks in the Population of the United States as Indicated by Surnames in the Census of 1790," in *Annual Report of the American Historical Association* (1931), I, 126-359, especially 270, 306-307.

4

Scotch-Irish Settlements in Pennsylvania: First Phase

Large Scotch-Irish settlements were made in Chester, Lancaster, and Dauphin Counties in the first third of the century. From Dauphin County the stream of settlement crossed to the west side of the Susquehanna. H. J. FORD

OF THE THREE MAJOR racial groups of Pennsylvania the English were the first to arrive, and the Scotch-Irish the last. When the Scotch-Irish began to enter the province in numbers sufficiently large to effect substantial settlements, they found the land in the original English counties already largely occupied, while the German counties immediately to the westward were in process of being occupied; hence the newcomers passed these by to settle farther out on the frontier. Before they began to come in any considerable numbers, however, the Scotch-Irish entered as individuals or in small groups toward the close of the seventeenth century and in the first decade of the eighteenth. The Scotch racial strain in Pennsylvania appears to have been represented at first chiefly by those coming directly from Scotland rather than from Ulster, but when the immigration assumed large proportions the Ulster Scots promptly became and thereafter remained by far the more numerous group.

SETTLEMENTS EAST OF THE SUSQUEHANNA RIVER

Immigration of the Scotch-Irish into Pennsylvania prior to 1717 was too slight to attract much attention, but in that year began the first important wave of immigration of this racial group into the province, to be followed immediately by important settlements. Jonathan Dickinson, in a letter dated October 23, 1717, speaks of the arrival of "many hundreds" from the North of Ireland in the preceding four months; and in a letter to John Herriot, November 12, 1719, again refers to a recent large influx of Scotch-Irish.[1] This considerable stream of Ulster immigrants continued steadily until 1727, when it was followed by a much heavier wave of immigration from Ulster.[2] Where did these immigrants effect their first group settlements? A few of them doubtless settled in Philadelphia and its environs and in Delaware, but the large majority sought the frontier. Moreover, it is well established that prior to the immigration of 1717-1718, the Scotch-Irish had already effected settlements as early as 1710 in present Chester County and were pressing forward to the Susquehanna.[3]

The first Scotch-Irish group settlements in Pennsylvania were made in the western part of Chester County, in Lancaster County, and in the southern part of Dauphin County, as we now know these districts, though they were all embraced in Chester County until 1729. The earliest of these settlements were effected at Fagg's Manor, New London, and Octorara, in the western part of present Chester County, beginning in 1710, and "the Scotch-Irish spread over the whole of the western part of the county from the Maryland line to the Welsh Mountains," composing a majority of the pioneer settlers in this region.[4] It seems likely that a number of these pioneers landed at Newcastle rather than at Philadelphia, and from there pushed their way westward to Chester County, where their first group settlements in Pennsylvania were made.[5] Others appear to have come from Maryland and the Chesapeake region up the Susquehanna River.[6]

As the stream of immigration increased, the Scotch-Irish advanced into Lancaster County, and here their settlements became

1. Jonathan Dickinson, *Copy Book of Letters*, 163, 288.
2. *Ibid.*, 288; See also Jonathan Dickinson's *Letter Book*, 294.
3. Franklin Ellis and Samuel Evans, *History of Lancaster County*, 19.
4. W. H. Egle, *History of the Commonwealth of Pennsylvania*, 526, 541; also W. H. Egle, "Landmarks of Early Scotch-Irish Settlement in Pennsylvania," in Scotch-Irish Society of America *Proceedings and Addresses*, VIII, 73.
5. W. B. Noble, *History of the Presbyterian Church of Fagg's Manor*, 4.
6. H. L. Osgood, *The American Colonies in the Eighteenth Century*, II, 520.

numerous and important at an early date. Their first settlement in this county was made in 1714 along Chickies Creek, where Donegal Presbyterian Church was soon organized in the vicinity of Donegal Spring; Donegal Township was settled principally by this group. This was the most notable of all the very early Scotch-Irish settlements in Pennsylvania, and was a minor nursery and headquarters of the group for some years. According to Colin McFarquhar, Donegal Presbyterian Church was organized in 1719 or 1720, though some writers claim 1714 as the date of organization.[7]

Another pioneer Scotch-Irish settlement in Lancaster County was made in the Pequea Valley, where they began to filter in from 1710 to 1714, contemporaneously with the Donegal settlement. According to Hensel, the Scotch-Irish trail in Lancaster County led from Pequea to Leacock, and from Leacock to Donegal, and this may have been the case. At any rate, the Pequea Valley settlement was among the first made in Lancaster County, though not as important as the Donegal settlement.[8] Pequea Presbyterian Church, a memorial of this early occupation, was organized in 1724.[9] About the time that Pequea was being settled, though probably a little later, the Scotch-Irish effected important settlements in the neighboring townships of Leacock and Coleraine, where they were the pioneers, and were well established prior to 1724. By this time western Lancaster County from Octorara Creek to Conewago Creek had been occupied by this racial group as the majority element of the population.[10] While the first important Scotch-Irish settlements in Lancaster County were in the northern part of the county, known as the "Upper End," it turned out finally that their most permanent settlements were in the "Lower End," the name given to the five townships of Southern Lancaster; here they still abide in strength and are more numerous

7. *Centennial Memorial of the Presbytery of Carlisle*, I, 50; Lancaster County Historical Society *Papers*, VIII, 221; IX, 160.

8. W. U. Hensel, *Presbyterianism in the Pequea Valley, and Other Historical Addresses*, 7, 20.

9. W. F. Worner, "The Old Pequea Presbyterian Graveyard," in Lancaster County Historical Society *Papers*, XXIV, 40.

10. W. H. Egle, "Landmarks of Early Scotch-Irish Settlements in Pennsylvania," in Scotch-Irish Society of America *Proceedings and Addresses*, VIII, 73-74.

than anywhere else in Pennsylvania east of the Susquehanna River.[11] The name of Donegal Township, which was originally called West Conestoga, was changed to Donegal in 1722 in response to the wishes of the Scotch-Irish inhabitants, who "then composed nearly the entire population of that township." They appear to have been mostly squatters in this district at first and for some years balked at paying quitrents, though willing to pay provincial and county taxes.[12] Thus it is seen that at an early period there were important settlements of Scotch-Irish in present Lancaster County in the region east of the Susquehanna and bordering on that river, especially in Donegal Township.

From Donegal, in northwestern Lancaster County, the Scotch-Irish spread northward into present Dauphin and Lebanon Counties to the lands on the Conewago, Swatara, Monada, and Paxtang Creeks, east of the Susquehanna River.[13] In the vicinity of the mouth of the Conoy River in northwestern Lancaster County there was a Scotch-Irish settlement as early as 1718. Within a few years settlements were extended further toward the northwest "mostly into the broad and well-watered valley of Conestoga Creek," which is the division line between the present Lancaster and Dauphin Counties, about half way between Elizabethtown and Middletown. Early tax lists show that the whole Donegal district in Lancaster County and the pioneer settlements in southern Dauphin County "contain only a few names that are not Scotch."[14] The Scotch-Irish were the pioneer settlers along the Swatara in western Lebanon County; they settled in Derry Township before 1720, this being a part of their extension movement along the east bank of the Susquehanna. Those who settled the county at this time were originally a part of the Donegal group, and "settled chiefly in the town of Lebanon and along the South-

11. E. Melvin Williams, "The Scotch-Irish in Pennsylvania," in *Americana*, XVII, 380-381.

12. Ellis and Evans, *op. cit.*, 20, 23; Lancaster County Historical Society *Papers*, XVII, 251.

13. *Centennial Memorial of the Presbyteries of Donegal and Carlisle*, I, 50-51.

14. J. S. Africa, *The Settlement of the Southern Border Counties by the Scotch-Irish*, 13; A. Boyd Hamilton, "The Conewago Congregation of Presbyterians, Londonderry Township, Dauphin County, 1730-1796," in Dauphin County Historical Society *Publications*, 45.

ern and western borders of the county, where they remained for several generations."[15] The Scotch-Irish settlements dating from about 1720, were the first to be made within the present limits of Lebanon County. They were also the pioneers in Hanover Township in this county, it being the part of Dauphin County that was cut off to form Lebanon County.[16]

From 1720 to 1730 the Scotch-Irish were moving northward from Donegal Township in Lancaster County to present Dauphin County, settling principally on the Swatara and its affluents, with "scattered settlements along the foot of the first range of mountains." The Presbyterian churches of Derry, Paxtang, and Hanover, the first two of which were organized in 1729 and the last in 1736, are historic memorials of the early Scotch-Irish settlements in this county. As the first permanent settlers in Dauphin County, the Scotch-Irish occupied the original townships of Derry, Paxton, and Hanover in considerable numbers as early as 1726.[17] By 1753 they had reached their maximum number in this county, their relative strength declining thereafter by reason of the emigration of themselves and their descendants to the South and West in large numbers.[18]

While the general movement of the Scotch-Irish in Pennsylvania was westward toward the Susquehanna and beyond, there was a notable exception to this in the early settlement effected by them in upper Bucks County (now Northampton County) in 1728. The pioneer settlers in present Northampton County comprised a group of Scotch-Irish, who, beginning in 1728, made a settlement at the Forks of the Delaware (Easton) in East Allen Township. Since William and Thomas Craig were prominent among these pioneers, the settlement was long known as the "Craig Settlement" or the "Irish Settlement," which by 1731 was sufficiently

15. George Mays, "The Palatine and Scotch-Irish Settlers of Lebanon County," in Lebanon County Historical Society *Papers*, I, 318; M. D. Learned, "The Pennsylvania German and His Scotch-Irish Neighbors," in Lebanon County Historical Society *Papers*, II, 320.

16. Egle, *History of Pennsylvania*, 865, 870 .

17. *Ibid.*, 640, 644, 647; G. E. Morgan, *The Settlement, Formation, and Progress of Dauphin County, Pennsylvania*, 12-13-15.

18. W. W. McAlarney (ed.), *History of the Sesquicentennial of Paxtang Church*, 45-46.

numerous to organize a Presbyterian church and to be known as the "Craig Settlement." The lands thus occupied were not legally open to settlers, and it was not until 1735, when Chief-Justice Allen acquired a large estate of five thousand acres in this district from Thomas Penn, that the Scotch-Irish settlers there received from him the titles to their lands. Judge Allen was friendly to the settlers, and his ownership of a large estate in the vicinity appears to have given to the settlement a stability which proved an additional incentive to the Scotch-Irish to continue to come to this region. As its numbers increased it came gradually to be known as the "Irish Settlement." By 1737 a church had been organized and the settlement, now well established, was flourishing. Ely is of the opinion that this colony was probably "an offshoot from the settlement at Neshaminy."[19]

Somewhat later than the founding of the Craig Settlement was the location of another group of Scotch-Irish in Lower and Upper Mount Bethel Townships in Northampton County, which was called "Hunter's Settlement" after Alexander Hunter, a leader among them. This settlement extended northward from Martin's Creek through Lower and Upper Mount Bethel Townships, beginning about 1730. In 1738 it was large enough to organize Mount Bethel Presbyterian Church, and was developing rapidly. In 1752 there were six hundred Scotch-Irish in Northampton County.[20]

A characteristic Scotch-Irish settlement was effected in present Bucks County, beginning about 1720 and still receiving additions in 1740. Between 1730 and 1740 the settlers purchased considerable land in the lower part of Warrington and Warwick Townships. Other Scotch-Irish settlements were made in Tinicum and Bedminster Townships and in Deep Run, Plumstead, and New Britain Townships, but by far the most important settlement made by the Scotch-Irish in Bucks County "was the one made at the

19. W. S. Ely, "Scotch-Irish Families," in Bucks County Historical Society *Papers*, II, 523; J. C. Clyde, *History of Allen Township Presbyterian Church and the Community Which Sustained It*, 9-13; Egle, *History of Pennsylvania*, 970-971.

20. H. M. Kieffer, *Some of the First Settlers of the Forks of the Delaware*, 10; Northampton County Historical and Genealogical Society *Publications*, I, 427, 430-431, 525, 528; Hanna, *op. cit.*, II, 104; Egle, *History of Pennsylvania*, 983.

forks of the Neshaminy, with Warwick as its centre." Prior to
1726 they had located in Warwick, Warrington, and Warwick
Townships, "with a scattering number in Buckingham, New-
town, the Makefields, and New Britain," and by 1730 were well
established throughout this area. Neshaminy Presbyterian Church,
in Warwick Township, was organized by the Reverend William
Tennent in 1726, near the site of the famous "Log College," of
which he was the founder and presiding genius. The Neshaminy
settlement, dating from about 1720, with its church and its school,
exerted a great and lasting influence and was a notable landmark
in the history of Pennsylvania.[21]

Such were the early Scotch-Irish settlements east of the Susquehanna River. There were, to be sure, individuals and a few small
scattering groups of these people in southeastern Pennsylvania of
whose history there is no record, as, for example, in the city and
county of Philadelphia and in Berks County; but it appears that
there were no large and characteristic Scotch-Irish settlements east
of the Susquehanna other than those we have described. They
were found in considerable numbers farther out on the frontier
in a bailiwick peculiarly their own in the Cumberland Valley
and beyond. Though their trek toward the Susquehanna resulted
in important settlements, their headquarters were to be beyond
that river in the Cumberland Valley, but between this valley and
the Susquehanna they made other settlements in present York
and Adams Counties, which will now be described before following their main line of march to the westward.

SETTLEMENTS IN YORK AND ADAMS COUNTIES

York, the fifth county of Pennsylvania to be erected, was taken
from Lancaster County in 1749, and in 1800 Adams County was
cut off from the western part of York. After 1749 and prior to
1800, the territory embraced in these two counties was commonly
referred to as the "York Country." Among the pioneer settlers in

---

21. W. S. Ely, "Some of the Early Settlers in Bucks County," in Scotch-Irish Society of
America Proceedings, IX, 93-94; also his Land o' the Leal, 1-2; Egle, "Landmarks of
Early Scotch-Irish Settlement in Pennsylvania," in Scotch-Irish Society of America Pro-
ceedings, VIII, 73.

this region were the Scotch-Irish, whose advance guard arrived there as early as 1726, coming from Chester and Lancaster Counties.[22] This territory not being included in the Land Purchase of 1718, no settlements could legally be made there until the Indian claims were satisfied. Owing to special arrangements, however, a portion of it was opened to settlement in 1726. The occasion of this was the intrusion of Marylanders into the southern portion of present York County. To head off this movement the provincial government, with the consent of the Indians, in 1722 surveyed a tract of about 75,000 acres to be called Springettsbury Manor, which was opened to settlement. Samuel Blunston, a magistrate living at Wright's Ferry on the Susquehanna, was authorized to issue licenses on special terms to settlers in this region; these permits were known as "Blunston's licenses." Among the settlers there were English, Germans, and Scotch-Irish. Thus it happened that, though the Indian claims to the region west of the Susquehanna were not extinguished until the Land Purchase of 1736, many settlers found their way thither either under Blunston's licenses or as squatters.[23]

The Scotch-Irish pioneers in York County settled mainly at Monaghan and in the "Barrens." The Monaghan Settlement, in the northwestern part of the county, was made by those coming by way of southern Dauphin County and crossing the Susquehanna at Harris's Ferry, proceeding in the general direction of the present road from Harrisburg to Carlisle.[24] This settlement, however, was neither so important nor so permanent as that of the "York Barrens," which was established in the southeastern part of the county. This region, embracing about 130,000 acres of "arenaceous, gravelly, and loamy soil and comprising the townships of Chanceford, Fawn, Peach Bottom, Hopewell, and Windsor," was occupied by the Scotch-Irish in force between 1731 and 1735.[25] According to Rupp, writing in 1844:

22. Grier Hersh, "The Scotch-Irish in York and Adams Counties," in Scotch-Irish Society of America *Proceedings*, VIII, 319-320.
23. Egle, *History of Pennsylvania*, 1169.
24. Hersh, *op. cit.*, 321; Africa, *op. cit.*, 13.
25. I. D. Rupp, *History of Lancaster and York Counties, Pennsylvania*, 567.

"The term *Barrens* has not been applied to this portion of the county from the sterility of the soil; but from the circumstance that the Indians for many years and until 1730 or 1731, to improve this portion of their *Great Park* for the purpose of hunting, fired the copse or bushes as oft as their convenience seemed to call for it; and thus when the whites commenced settling here, they found no timber, hence they applied the term *Barrens,* a common appellation at that time, to such portions of country, however fertile the soil."[26]

In present Adams County the Scotch-Irish, who were the pioneers in this region, effected the "Marsh Creek Settlement" and the "Great Conewago Settlement" in the general vicinity of the present town of Gettysburg, around the year 1740. These settlements were small, however, and the Scotch-Irish influence in Adams County has never been especially noteworthy.[27]

The Scotch-Irish settlers in Lancaster, Lebanon, Dauphin, York, and Adams Counties were located in a region predominantly German and rapidly becoming more so. Hedged in on all sides by increasing numbers of Germans in what was to become an integral part of Pennsylvania German-Land, they soon found themselves in an uncongenial environment. Between them and the Germans arose mutual antagonisms, resulting in frequent disturbances as time passed. The ill feeling between the two races sometimes took the form of riots at elections and was a cause of concern to the provincial authorities. As a consequence, the Penns instructed their agents in 1743 to sell no lands to the Scotch-Irish throughout this region, but to make them generous offers of removal to the Cumberland Valley, farther to the westward. Since these offers were liberal, many of the Scotch-Irish accepted them, and all the more readily as they were inclined to be clannish and were glad to remove to a district peculiarly their own, where their first great mass settlement was in process of being effected. Furthermore, many of them had been merely squatters on the land they occupied and, having no legal titles to it, found it no great hardship to remove to a beautiful and fertile section immediately

26. *Ibid.*
27. Hersh, *op. cit.,* 321; Africa, *op. cit.,* 13.

to the westward, under the sanction of the provincial government. This was the beginning of that movement of the Scotch-Irish from the lands which they first occupied to other lands farther west— a movement that was to continue to such an extent as to result in the depletion or the practical extinction of many of their original settlements in eastern Pennsylvania. As the Scotch-Irish moved out the Germans moved in, extending their original holdings throughout this area.[28] Due partly to the advantageous offers of removal and partly to the great wave of immigration from Ulster in 1727-1728, conditions were ripe for their rapid settlement of the Cumberland Valley in large numbers, a circumstance fraught with tremendous significance in the history of Pennsylvania and of the country at large.

Settlements in the Cumberland Valley

The first great settlement of the Scotch-Irish in Pennsylvania was in the Cumberland Valley, now comprising the counties of Cumberland and Franklin—one of the most beautiful and fertile sections of the commonwealth. This valley became the headquarters of the Scotch-Irish not only in Pennsylvania but in America as well. It was the seed-plot and nursery of their race, the original reservoir which, after having been filled to overflowing, sent forth a constant stream of emigrants to the northward and especially to the South and West. For a generation other racial groups were but scantily represented here. It was estimated that in 1751, when there were about five thousand people in the Valley, all except fifty families were either Scotch or Scotch-Irish, principally the latter.[29] It is probable that at that time and for many years thereafter there was no area of similar extent in Pennsylvania as homogeneous as the Cumberland Valley, the camping ground of the Scotch-Irish, where about 90 per cent of the population were of that race down to the Revolution.[30]

28. H. J. Ford, *The Scotch-Irish in America*, 267; John Watson, *Annals of Philadelphia and Pennsylvania*, II, 109.

29. P. A. Durant and J. F. Richard, *History of Cumberland County*, 25.

30. John Stewart, "Scotch-Irish Occupancy and Exodus," in Kittochtinny Historical Society *Papers*, II, 17.

The causes of the rapid settlement of the Cumberland Valley by the Scotch-Irish may here be noted. Attention has been called to the fact that, beginning in 1727 and continuing for a decade or more, there was a particularly heavy immigration of Scotch-Irish into Pennsylvania, and that the provincial authorities encouraged settlement west of the Susquehanna by this racial group. Provincial policy favored settlement in the Cumberland Valley by the Scotch-Irish not only because of the ill feeling existing between them and the Germans, but also as a "cordon of defense" on the frontier against the Indians, as well as a means of safeguarding the territory against the intrusion of Marylanders along the southern border of the province. For some years also, in recognition of the hardships suffered by these settlers on the extreme frontier, they were excused from taxes, even for county purposes, and forbearance was exercised in postponing collection of payments for the land.[31] Furthermore, the character of the region to be occupied was inviting, the best land in the province to the eastward had already been taken up, and the newcomers were generally too poor to buy lands in that section. Again, the Scotch-Irish, always a border people, had no aversion to the frontier, and, being somewhat clannish, "didn't care to settle among a people so alien in language as the Germans or so peculiar in religious beliefs as the Friends."[32] For these several reasons the settlement of the Valley proceeded apace.

The first settlers in the Cumberland Valley, entering by way of the northeast and probably crossing the Susquehanna at Harris's Ferry, were Richard Parker, James Macfarlane, Andrew Ralston, and Tobias Hendricks. Parker located two miles west of the present town of Carlisle in 1725; Macfarlane, about five miles farther west in 1726. Ralston settled at "the Big Spring" in 1726, and Hendricks "within three miles of the river" in 1727. These men, with their families, were the pioneer settlers of this region

31. C. P. Wing, *History of Cumberland County, Pennsylvania*, 23; *Centennial Memorial of the Presbytery of Carlisle*, 71.

32. J. B. Scouller, *History of the Big Spring Presbytery of the United Presbyterian Church*, 6-7; George Norcross, "The Scotch-Irish in the Cumberland Valley," in Scotch-Irish Society of America *Proceedings*, VIII, 190.

and were soon followed by others numerous enough to receive the ministrations of Presbyterian clergymen above Conewago Creek in 1727. It is estimated that in 1731 there were about four hundred families in the Cumberland Valley.[33] It was not until several years later, however, that the real movement of the Scotch-Irish into this region got well under way.

The significant movement of the Scotch-Irish into the Valley began in 1730 and, though slight at first, rapidly gained momentum until within a decade the whole district was dotted with their settlements; there were also a few English and Germans here and there. Some of the Scotch-Irish came from east of the Susquehanna River, but others came direct from Ireland. After 1736, when Hopewell and Pennsborough Townships were erected, the influx of settlers was large.[34] The first comers in this region settled either as squatters or under the authority given by Blunston's licenses, but in 1736 the Indian claims to the land were extinguished, and thereafter the settlements could be legalized through purchase at the land office at Philadelphia. It must be admitted, however, that there were some who overlooked the detail of visiting the land office and proceeded to locate where fancy dictated. Others, though willing to pay were unable to do so, at least not until they had made their improvements and had accumulated the wherewithal to pay. This situation, however, was by no means peculiar to the Scotch-Irish, but prevailed quite generally on the frontier, regardless of the racial group to which the settlers belonged.[35] As early as January 1, 1726, James Logan had complained to Hannah Penn that "there are at this time near a hundred thousand acres possessed by persons, who resolutely sit down and improve, without any manner of Right or Pretence to it."[36]

One of the earliest settlements in the Cumberland Valley was that made by Benjamin Chambers, who in 1730 located at Falling Spring in the vicinity of the present town of Chambersburg,

33. W. H. Egle (ed.), *Notes and Queries, Historical and Genealogical*, II, 157-158.
34. Scouller, *op. cit.*, 6, 53-54.
35. *Logan Papers*, III, 354; *Penn MSS.*, Official Correspondence, II, 179.
36. *Penn MSS.*, Official Correspondence, I, 185.

which was named after him. With three brothers he emigrated at the age of seventeen from County Antrim, Ireland, and settled on Fishing Creek in Lancaster County. Four years later, Benjamin, the youngest of the four brothers, crossed the Susquehanna and settled at Falling Spring, having secured four hundred acres under a Blunston license. Here he erected a sawmill and a grist mill and farmed a large plantation, becoming a very substantial citizen. In 1764 he laid out the town of Chambersburg, which was to become the county seat of Franklin County. Other Scotch-Irishmen located in the same vicinity, becoming numerous enough to organize Falling Spring Presbyterian Church in 1738.[37]

While the Chambersburg settlement was being founded, a group of Scotch-Irish located on Middle Spring Creek, where in 1730 they began to occupy the land roundabout. They later laid out the town of Shippensburg, next to York the oldest town west of the Susquehanna River. The progress of this community may be illustrated by the fact that here was organized within a decade the Middle Spring Presbyterian Church in Southampton Township, Cumberland County. The pioneer Scotch-Irish settlers in the Cumberland Valley, as elsewhere, commonly located on the borders of streams and in the vicinity of springs in order to be assured of a plentiful supply of water. Hence we find their first settlements along the water courses such as the Conodoguinet, Yellow Breeches, Big Spring, Middle Spring, Falling Spring, and Conococheague Creeks in this valley, just as we found them earlier along the Octorara, Pequea, Chickies, Conestoga, Conewago, Swatara, Monada, and Paxton Creeks in Lancaster, Lebanon, and Dauphin Counties; their pioneer settlements and churches were generally named after the streams on which they had located.[38] Inasmuch as they regularly organized Presbyterian churches as soon as they had gathered in sufficient numbers to render this practicable, the location of these churches furnishes the best evidence of their settlements in their westward movement across the province.

37. L. H. Gerrard, *Chambersburg in the Colony and the Revolution*, 1-2, 4, 6-7, 32; I. H. M'Cauley, *Historical Sketch of Franklin County, Pennsylvania*, 9, 35.

38. G. E. Swope, *History of Big Spring Presbyterian Church*, 9.

Other pioneer Scotch-Irish settlements in Cumberland County were those made at Meeting House Spring (Carlisle), Silvers' Spring, and Big Spring. One of the earliest of these settlements was that on Conodoguinet Creek, about halfway between Harrisburg and Carlisle, in the general vicinity of the present town of Mechanicsburg. This region was occupied by Scotch-Irish pioneers in 1730; by 1734 they had increased sufficiently to organize Silvers' Spring Presbyterian Church, which appears to have been the oldest church in the Cumberland Valley.[39] Meanwhile other pioneers had been settling somewhat farther to the westward in the vicinity of the present town of Carlisle, in the township of Middleton, where a Presbyterian church, known as Meeting House Spring, was organized in 1735. Others, moving still farther to the westward, effected a settlement about the same time in the vicinity of Big Spring, at the present town of Newville, where a congregation had gathered in 1735 and a Presbyterian church was organized not later than 1737.[40]

Besides the notable settlement made by the Scotch-Irish at Falling Spring (Chambersburg), other important early settlements were made by them in the lower part of the Cumberland Valley (Franklin County) in the seventeen-thirties, especially along the Conococheague and its tributaries down to the Maryland line. The rapid settlement throughout this area was doubtless due in part to the special inducements held out by the Penns to "come in and occupy the lands along the border to prevent the encroachments of the Marylanders."[41] The present town of Mercersburg, originally known as Black's Town, was settled by the Scotch-Irish about 1736 and, the country roundabout being occupied rapidly, in 1738 the Upper West Conococheague Presbyterian Church was organized. Meanwhile another Scotch-Irish settlement farther east, known as the "Conococheague Settlement," was made prior to 1738 in the vicinity of the present town of Greencastle toward the Maryland line. It appears that this settlement was begun in 1731 or 1732 and was composed almost

39. Alfred Nevin, *Churches of the Valley*, 63; C. A. Hanna, *The Scotch-Irish*, II, 103.
40. Swope, *op. cit.*, 10; Nevin, *op. cit.*, 48; Hanna, *op. cit.*, 103.
41. D. K. Richardson, *The Presbyterian Church of Greencastle*, 6.

entirely of Scotch-Irishmen coming from Lancaster and Dauphin Counties, and from Ulster. That the settling of this region was rather rapid is seen in the fact that a Presbyterian congregation was in existence here as early as 1738.[42] Another early Scotch-Irish settlement was effected at Rocky Spring, about four miles west of Chambersburg, prior to 1739.[43]

By 1750 the Cumberland Valley was dotted with Scotch-Irish settlements throughout its entire area, a district which had become almost exclusively the possession of this racial group, with whom were mingled small numbers of English and German settlers constituting perhaps 10 per cent of the population. It was well adapted to farming, and the Scotch-Irish, in this early period, were mostly farmers, but later they developed a marked aptitude for trade and the professions.[44] They were not, however, to remain the predominant racial group in the Cumberland Valley, for reasons that will be discussed in another connection.[45]

SETTLEMENTS IN THE JUNIATA VALLEY

Though there were many Germans and smaller numbers of other racial stocks occupying the Juniata Valley,[46] the pioneer settlers of this region were prevailingly Scotch-Irish. Beginning as early as 1741, settlement of the valley proceeded slowly, being retarded by the ruggedness of the country, the lack of transportation facilities, and the French and Indian War. According to Jones, the historian of the Juniata Valley, the pioneers in this district were "nearly all Scotch-Irish." It appears that the early settlements throughout this area were in large part the result of the movement of the Scotch-Irish from the Cumberland Valley and from their other centers farther east, together with the pressure for new lands caused by another heavy wave of immigration

---

42. Richardson, op. cit., 5-6; Nevin, op. cit., 162-163; Linn Harbaugh, "German Life and Thought in a Scotch-Irish Community," in Scotch-Irish Society of America Proceedings, X, 89, 91, 94.

43. Nevin, op. cit., 177, 188.

44. A. S. Bolles, Pennsylvania: Province and State, II, 134.

45. See Chapter VI, passim.

46. For the purposes of this study the Juniata Valley is taken in the wide acceptance of the term to include the counties of Juniata, Mifflin, Huntingdon, Perry, Blair, and Bedford.

from Ulster around 1749-50.[47] Since most of the best lands to the eastward had already been occupied, it was but natural that there should be a movement to the hitherto unoccupied lands of the Juniata Valley. Furthermore, since the Scotch-Irish had long been the predominant racial group on the frontier and had by this time become the typical frontiersmen of the province, they naturally moved westward when they began to feel crowded in their old quarters. Thus we find them braving the hardships and dangers of the wild, which but served as a challenge to their adventurous natures.

When settlement of the Juniata Valley began in 1741, the lower part of this area was the first to be occupied. It was not, however, until after the French and Indian War that large and permanent settlements were effected throughout this territory. Since the Indian claims to this region were not relinquished until the Albany Purchase of 1754, lands that were occupied there before this time were without legal warrant and the settlers ran the risk not only of Indian hostility but also of being ejected as squatters. These considerations did not deter them, however, though eventually some were forcibly ejected as squatters, while others were massacred in the Indian wars. From 1755 to 1764 the hazards of settlement throughout this region were great, and even when there were no Indian wars in progress the hardships and privations were ever present.

It appears that a few venturesome individuals among the Scotch-Irish of the Cumberland Valley crossed the Kittatinny Mountain and settled in the Great Cove in present Fulton County in 1740 or 1741. These were soon followed by others locating in the Great Cove and on Aughwick and Licking Creeks in sufficient numbers to cause the Indians in 1742 to lodge a complaint with the provincial authorities against this intrusion on their lands. Though the governor issued a proclamation warning the settlers away from this district, it was not heeded. In 1750 the pioneers here numbered sixty-two, mostly Scotch-Irish. While these settlements were being made, others were in progress in the valleys of Big Tonoloway and Little Tonoloway Creeks in the southern part of Fulton

47. U. J. Jones, *History of the Early Settlement of the Juniata Valley,* 39.

County; the settlers here also were principally Scotch-Irish.[48] The first settler at the mouth of Licking Creek was a Scotch-Irishman by the name of Hugh Hardy, who located here about 1750 and was soon followed by a small colony of Scotch-Irish families.[49] Great Cove Presbyterian Church, organized in 1766, is a memorial of this early occupation.[50] Further settlement was retarded by the French and Indian War and by Pontiac's War, but thereafter the county was occupied more rapidly; progress in this region was slow, however, the lands in the remainder of Fulton County being less fertile than those first settled.

Farther to the westward, the Scotch-Irish began to enter present Bedford County as early as 1750 or 1751, when Robert Ray (Rea) founded a trading post on the north bank of the Juniata; this was originally known as Raystown, but was later named Bedford. Garrett Pendergrass, another Scotch-Irishman, settled in the same neighborhood in 1752. In 1758 a goodly number of Scotch-Irish, along with a few Germans, following in the wake of Forbes's army, settled in and around Bedford and on Dunning's Creek. Bedford was laid out as a borough in 1766, but was not incorporated until 1795. The Scotch-Irish predominated in Bedford County, where they comprised the main body of the pioneers and took the initiative in securing the organization of the county in 1771. After 1760 there was a strong German minority group, some of whom here, as elsewhere in the Juniata Valley, were among the pioneer settlers.[51]

Meanwhile straggling settlements were being made in present Perry County. Though the majority of the pioneers in this county were Scotch-Irish, the first settler appears to have been Frederick Starr, a German, who located with some companions "probably east of Big Buffalo Creek."[52] After the opening of the land office in 1755 for the sale of lands in Sherman's Valley and on the

---

48. W. P. Schell, *The Annals of Bedford County*, 6, 17; Egle, *History of Pennsylvania*, 764-766.

49. Schell, *op. cit.*, 6-7; Jones, *op. cit.*, 164.

50. Hanna, *op. cit.*, II, 105.

51. Schell, *op. cit.*, 6-7, 23-25, 27, 30, 42; Jones, *op. cit.*, 164.

52. H. H. Hain, *History of Perry County, Pa.*, 149; T. H. Burrowes, *State-Book of Pennsylvania*, 194; Egle, *History of Pennsylvania*, 1007.

Juniata, additional settlers came; the French and Indian War, however, prevented further immigration into this region for some years. When the war was over, settlement proceeded more rapidly and by 1776 there was a considerable population in Perry County, especially in the vicinity of the mouth of the Juniata River and in Sherman's Valley. The pioneers were prevailingly Scotch-Irish, but there were many Germans and a few English.[53] Eventually the Germans became the predominant racial strain in this county, and so remain to this day.[54]

The first settlers of Juniata County were mainly Scotch-Irish coming from the Cumberland Valley and locating in the Tuscarora Valley in 1749. The pioneers were Robert Haag, Samuel Bingham, James Grey, and John Grey, who, after clearing some lands, erected Bingham's Fort. Two years later Captain James Patterson and his companions made a settlement on both sides of the Juniata River near the present village of Mexico. These were joined by George Woods, Robert Innis, and a few others prior to 1754. Some of the pioneers came from the vicinity of Carlisle, while others came from the Conococheague settlement in Franklin County.[55] The first settlers in present Mifflin County were Arthur Buchanan, his two sons, and several other Scotch-Irish families, who came from the Conococheague by way of Aughwick and located near the mouth of Kishacoquillas Creek in 1754. This being a particularly beautiful and fertile section, many others followed in 1754 and 1755; in the latter part of 1755, the French and Indian War being in progress, they built Fort Granville for their protection. Owing to the Indian wars, the Kishacoquillas Valley, despite its fertility, was not settled to any great extent until about 1769, when it began to fill up rapidly with settlers "nearly all Scotch-Irish," and was "pretty thickly settled" by 1772.[56] At a later period this valley became prevailingly German, being occupied principally by the Amish, as it is today.

In 1748-1749 some adventurous Scotch-Irish crossed the Tus-

53. Hain, *op. cit.*, 148-149; Jones, *op. cit.*, 67.
54. T. F. Gordon, *A Gazeteer of the State of Pennsylvania*, 343.
55. Jones, *op. cit.*, 84; Burrowes, *op. cit.*, 198-199.
56. J. W. Jordan (ed.), *A History of the Juniata Valley and Its People*, 343; Jones, *op. cit.*, 91, 111, 116; Burrowes, *op. cit.*, 198-199; Egle, *History of Pennsylvania*, 940-942.

carora Mountains and occupied lands in present Huntingdon County as squatters, but were driven out and their cabins were burned by the provincial authorities in order to keep peace with the Indians. Huntingdon County was within the Land Purchase of 1754, however, and settlements in this region were legal thereafter. Nevertheless, settlement was retarded by the French and Indian War and did not begin in earnest until its conclusion in 1763, when many warrants were issued by the land office to Scotch-Irish pioneers from the Cumberland Valley. Checked for a time by Pontiac's War, settlement again became brisk in 1766, and within a year most of the best lands in the valleys and river bottoms had been taken up. The town of Huntingdon, originally called by the Indian name of Standing Stone, was founded by Provost William Smith in 1767; in 1766 it consisted of only a few cabins. Aughwick (Fort Shirley), in the extreme southern part of Huntingdon County, was settled in 1749. Another early settlement was made in Woodcock Valley, north of Huntingdon. Much of the later progress of Huntingdon County, as of the entire Juniata Valley, was due to the development of the iron industry following the Revolution. Water Street, an old village, was founded by a small group of Scotch-Irish, among whom was Patrick Beatty, the father of seven sons. As a canoe landing for the interior country, it was long an important point, the region roundabout being originally known as Canoe Valley.[57]

In 1749 several Scotch-Irish families settled in Morrison's Cove in present Blair County; most of these were either driven out or massacred by the Indians, and but small progress was made in settling the county until after the Indian wars. About 1755 a small colony of German Baptist Brethren settled in the southern part of this cove, or valley. In 1769 Adam Holliday, a Scotch-Irishman, took out a warrant for a thousand acres of land surrounding the present town of Hollidaysburg, which was named after him. While some of the pioneers who had been ejected by the provincial authorities in 1750 returned later, the real settlement of Blair County did not get well under way until after the Land Purchase

57. M. S. Lytle, *History of Huntingdon County, Pa.*, 36-37, 71-72, 74; Jordan, *op. cit.*, 55; Jones, *op. cit.*, 134; Burrowes, *op. cit.*, 210-212.

of 1768. Thereafter, settlers gradually occupied Morrison's Cove, the best land in the county. The pioneers in this area were mainly Scotch-Irish and Germans, but Scotch Valley was settled by Samuel Moore and other Scotchmen in 1768. The latter appear to have come directly from Scotland, and their descendants in this section are numerous. The county was named after John Blair, an early settler who was either a Scot or a Scotch-Irishman. There can be no doubt, however, of the Scotch-Irish origin of such place-names as Tyrone and Newry in this county.[58]

As we have noted, the pioneer settlers in the Juniata Valley were mainly Scotch-Irish, though there were many Germans and a few English, Scots, and French among them. The first settlements throughout this territory were made before the Indian claims had been extinguished. This gave rise to Indian complaints, and the provincial authorities, anxious to preserve the peace with the savages as well as to discourage squatters from occupying the land, took strong measures to eject them, burning their cabins in some instances and threatening them with dire penalties should they return. Richard Peters, Secretary of the Province, in several letters written to the proprietaries in the spring and summer of 1750, describes the means employed to expel the squatters from the Juniata Valley. After wrathfully exclaiming that "the Range of Country said to be seized by these vile people extends from Juniata and its waters all along the Indian Path through both the Coves about half the way to the Allegheny," he goes on to say that if the squatters will not voluntarily withdraw he knows of no other means of meeting resistance than to burn their cabins.[59] Later he expresses the view that to burn the cabins is a milder method than imprisonment, which would deprive their families of support and protection; and that mere threats would accomplish nothing.[60] Hence, accompanied by several magistrates and some Indians, he set out in May 1750 upon his mission of ejecting the squatters, going by way of Harris's

58. Jones, *op. cit.*, 207-208, 311-312; Burrowes, *op. cit.*, 207, 209; Egle, *History of Pa.*, 399-400.
59. *Penn MSS.*, Official Correspondence, V, 3.
60. *Ibid.*, 39.

Ferry. He describes the accomplishment of his task as follows:

"We took our Rout into the center of the Trespassers on Little Juniata or what is called Shermans Creek having between us an almost impassable ridge of Hills called the Tuscarora Hills. . . . We took the shortest cut to Big Juniata. . . . By this short Cut we came on the Settlements at Juniata, by surprise, took them Prisoners, burnt their Houses and sent the chief Mutineer to Jayl. The very next day a party of the magistrates returned to Shermans creek, burnt some houses and put all under Recognizances and Bonds for their Appearance and removal in a month, a few in two months. . . . The principal work was still behind a numerous settlement in the Tuscarora Gap or Path Valley thro which the Indian Traders road passed to Allegheny, a more numerous Settlement in the Big Cove, and a small one in the Little Cove and Big and Little Conolloway. . . . The Company proceeded to the Path valley and effected the work there destroying and burning small houses and laying all under Recognizances and bonds and the same was done at a place called Aughwick a branch of the little Juniata and in the Big Cove. . . . The Settlements here were many and valuable but they saw no help and so submitted to the same fate as the rest."[61]

By such harsh methods the squatters in the Juniata Valley were ejected, but many of them returned to their homes after the magistrates had left. In a letter to Thomas Penn, under date of March 16, 1752, Peters says: "The Trespassers beyond the Hills still continue, nay are considerably encreased, and it is an exceeding Embarrassment to know what to do."[62] Further trouble with the Indians was avoided by the Land Purchase of 1754, which included the region embraced in the Juniata Valley. The Indian wars, however, not only rendered settlement in this area hazardous, but resulted in the temporary abandonment of it by many of the inhabitants. Hence it was not until about 1766 or 1767 that it was reoccupied in force by the settlers who had fled, and that settlement on a larger and more permanent basis got well under way.[63] By 1776 the more desirable portions of this mountainous district

61. *Ibid.*, 29-31.
62. *Ibid.*, 219.
63. Robert McMeen, "The Scotch-Irish of the Juniata Valley," in Scotch-Irish Society of America *Proceedings*, 119-120.

had received a considerable body of settlers, of whom the majority were Scotch-Irish, the Germans being the strongest minority group. In the post-colonial period much of the increase in population and wealth throughout the Juniata Valley was due to the development of the iron industry.[64]

Such was the first phase of Scotch-Irish settlement in Pennsylvania, extending from the Delaware to the Susquehanna and from the Susquehanna to the Alleghenies. In the area east of the Susquehanna they were outnumbered by both the English and the Germans, who had been the first to arrive, but from the Susquehanna to the Alleghenies they were the most numerous racial group. As pioneers, they were the advance guard blazing the trail through the wilderness far out on the frontier. They were the first line of defense against the savages, bearing the brunt of the Indian wars, and courageously enduring the hardships of pioneer life as the typical frontiersmen of provincial Pennsylvania. Step by step they had advanced along a perilous path, surmounting whatever difficulties arose, moving ever farther into the wilderness and reclaiming it to the new civilization. For a while they paused at the foothills of the Alleghenies, but not for long. In the next chapter we shall see them crossing the mountains in force into Southwestern Pennsylvania, and spreading into the central, north central, and northwestern sections of the commonwealth.

64. A. C. Bining, *Pennsylvania Iron Manufacture in the Eighteenth Century*, 60-61.

5

Scotch-Irish Settlements in Pennsylvania:
Second Phase

*A distinct section, occupied predominantly by Scotch-Irish, was
formed in Western Pennsylvania, which was to have an important
effect on the internal politics of that province.* HERBERT L. OSGOOD

AFTER REACHING the foothills of the Alleghenies, the westward
movement of the Scotch-Irish in Pennsylvania was checked for a
time by the mountain barrier, by the remoteness and inaccessibility
of the trans-Allegheny region, by the Indian wars, by the uncertainty of land titles caused by the boundary dispute between
Pennsylvania and Virginia, and by the failure of the Penns to
extinguish the Indian claims to this territory prior to 1768. Nevertheless, despite the hazards involved, there were not wanting a
few daring souls who located west of the mountains at an early
date. During the French and Indian War and Pontiac's War the
first comers were forced to flee for their lives to the more settled
parts of the province, if indeed they escaped massacre at the hands
of the savages. With the return of peace, however, and the Land
Purchase of 1768, the occupation of the trans-Allegheny region
began in earnest.

SETTLEMENTS IN SOUTHWESTERN PENNSYLVANIA

Southwestern Pennsylvania, in the restricted sense in which
the term was long understood, embraced the present counties of
Somerset, Westmoreland, Fayette, Allegheny, Washington, and

Greene, and it is in this sense that it is here more immediately employed.[1]

In Southwestern Pennsylvania, a section which has played a great part in American history, the Scotch-Irish were the predominant racial group for many years and here they still abide in strength.[2] To this region they gave tone and direction politically, economically, and socially. It was a characteristically Scotch-Irish community, forming a second and larger reservoir of their race than the earlier one in the Cumberland Valley. The Scotch-Irish influence is perhaps more pervading in Southwestern Pennsylvania than anywhere else in the commonwealth today, but here as elsewhere, though they cherish their traditions, they have no distinctive language or customs, their early peculiarities having long since disappeared as they merged into the general body of the English-speaking citizens of the state.

The majority of the first settlers in Southwestern Pennsylvania were not Pennsylvanians coming from east of the mountains, but Virginians and Marylanders entering the region by way of Braddock's Road and securing the land under Virginia titles. Virginia claimed this territory under her charter, and communications were easier with that province and with Maryland than they were with eastern Pennsylvania over the mountains. Furthermore, the Ohio Company, a Virginia enterprise which fostered settlement throughout this region, in 1750 sent out Christopher Gist to explore it and to report conditions. Hence the pioneer settlers throughout this area were mostly of English stock, though some of those coming from Virginia and Maryland were Scotch-Irish and a few were German. Not until after the Revolution did the Scotch-Irish, coming from eastern Pennsylvania and from North Ireland, prevail in this district.[3]

1. In a more modern and comprehensive signification the term "Southwestern Pennsylvania" might well include also the present counties of Cambria, Indiana, and Beaver, with portions of Armstrong and Butler Counties, and will be so used later.

2. Herbert L. Osgood, *The American Colonies in the Eighteenth Century*, II, 421.

3. E. W. Hassler, *Old Westmoreland: A History of Western Pennsylvania during the Revolution*, 6, 12; James Veech, *The Monongahela of Old*, 99; Joseph Smith, *Old Redstone, or Historical Sketches of Western Presbyterianism*, 31; W. F. Dunaway, "The English Settlers in Colonial Pennsylvania," in *Pennsylvania Magazine of History and Biography*, LII, 328-330.

Although Indian traders had visited the trans-Allegheny region as early as 1720, no white settlements were effected there prior to 1752, when Christopher Gist located at Mount Braddock in present Fayette County, where he was soon joined by eleven families. Prior to 1769 there were only a few scattered settlements west of the Alleghenies, and these were mostly in Fayette County. Their number at this time was estimated at 150 families, or about 800 persons, the large majority of whom were English. Inasmuch as the Indian claim to this territory had not yet been settled, those locating here under Pennsylvania jurisdiction were squatters. Furthermore, the Proclamation of 1763, promulgated by the British Government and reinforced by the proclamations of the governors of Pennsylvania and Virginia, forbade settlements west of the mountains. These proclamations were ignored, however, by those already settled there and also by those intending to join them; nor were prospective settlers deterred by the conflicting jurisdiction between Pennsylvania and Virginia.[4]

Although there was some immigration into Southwestern Pennsylvania from east of the mountains prior to that time, the significant movement of the Scotch-Irish into this district began in 1769 with the opening of the land office for the sale of lands in the "New Purchase" of 1768. Between 1760 and 1765 some settlements were effected by military permits in the vicinity of Fort Pitt, Fort Burd, Fort Ligonier, and at other points along Forbes's Road, but these were few and widely scattered, being regarded "as mere appendages to the forts and as accessories to the trade and intercourse with the Indians." It was customary to grant military permits to settlers "along the roads and at stations on the rivers, where they were of advantage to the military authorities."[5]

Despite the conflicting claims of Virginia and Pennsylvania to Southwestern Pennsylvania and the resulting uncertainty of land titles, the settlement of this region proceeded at an accelerated

4. George Chambers, *A Tribute to the Principles, Virtues, Habits and Public Usefulness of the Irish and Scotch Early Settlers of Pennsylvania*, 132-134; Franklin Ellis, *History of Fayette County, Pennsylvania*, 56; G. D. Albert, *History of Westmoreland County, Pennsylvania*, 41.

5. Veech, *op. cit.*, 82; Hassler, *op. cit.*, 6; Albert, *op. cit.*, 36.

pace from 1769 to the Revolution. Prior to 1779, when Virginia yielded to Pennsylvania her claims to this territory, the majority of the settlers there were Virginians holding their lands under Virginia title. When immigrants from eastern Pennsylvania began to cross the Alleghenies, many of the settlers found it convenient to purchase lands under Virginia warrants because the purchase price was only 2s 6d per hundred acres, whereas the Pennsylvania price was five pounds per hundred acres, besides one penny per acre quitrent. In 1774 Governor Dunmore of Virginia opened several offices for the sale of lands in present Fayette, Washington, Allegheny, and Greene Counties, and warrants were granted merely upon paying the trifling sum of 2s 6d for fees, "and even this was not demanded."[6]

Prior to the opening of the Pennsylvania land office April 3, 1769, for the sale of the lands of the New Purchase, there were probably not more than 1200 settlers in all Southwestern Pennsylvania. Of these about 800 were found in present Fayette County in the Redstone, Youghiogheny, and Turkey Foot settlements, and there were small settlements around Fort Pitt, Fort Burd (Brownsville), and Fort Ligonier. There were also a few settlers under military permit along Braddock's Road and Forbes's Road, and at Croghan's settlement on the Allegheny.[7] Most of these, coming by way of Braddock's Road, were of English stock, though there were some Scotch-Irish and a few Germans among them. A few Scotch-Irish had entered the region as settlers under military permits or as squatters coming from eastern Pennsylvania. With the extinguishing of the Indian claims to this district, however, the Scotch-Irish, coming mainly from the Cumberland Valley and the Juniata Valley, entered the region in large numbers and by 1784 had become the prevailing racial element.

Meanwhile, Virginia having yielded her claims to this territory, and Pennsylvania having passed a law in 1780 for the gradual abolition of slavery, many of the Virginians resident here, finding themselves in Pennsylvania whereas they had thought them-

6. I. D. Rupp, *Early History of Pennsylvania and the West, 1751-1833*, 46; Ellis, *op. cit.*, 65.

7. Albert, *op. cit.*, 40-41, 50.

selves in Virginia and being dissatisfied also with the law against slavery, began to emigrate to Kentucky in considerable numbers. Thus, with the Virginians going out and the Pennsylvanians coming in, it was not long before the latter began to preponderate in this area. Many of the Virginians sold their holdings to immigrants from east of the mountains at very reasonable rates, not infrequently disposing of them by barter. This was especially true of those residing in present Washington, Fayette, and Greene Counties, where they were the most numerous.[8] In fact, this particular district, as far north as Pittsburgh, might well be regarded as in some sense an extension of the Virginia frontier, when first settled. The movement to Kentucky, beginning in 1780, continued brisk for some ten or fifteen years.[9]

Thus it happened that, with the Land Purchase of 1768, the conclusion of the Indian wars, the settlement of the boundary dispute between Pennsylvania and Virginia, the greater security of land titles, and the great wave of immigration from Ulster to Pennsylvania on the eve of the Revolution, all within a decade, the time was ripe for the rapid settlement of Southwestern Pennsylvania, and thither the settlers flocked in ever increasing numbers. The natural urge for westward expansion surmounted the mountain barrier and caused an irresistible movement into the fertile valleys of the Monongahela, the Youghiogheny, the Kiskiminitas, and their tributaries. As in eastern Pennsylvania, the pioneers located first along the rivers and the creeks flowing into them, and when these lands had been occupied they followed the creeks farther inland. By 1776 the region between the Youghiogheny and the Monongahela had been fairly well settled, and there were many settlers in present Washington and Greene Counties, besides a few along Chartiers Creek and at Pittsburgh. The entire region comprising the present counties of Somerset, Fayette, Westmoreland, Allegheny, Washington, and Greene, had received a steady stream of immigrants from east of the mountains. During the Revolution its volume slackened, but thereafter increased rapidly, and by 1790 the population of the four trans-

8. Ellis, *op. cit.*, 127-128; Smith, *op. cit.*, 49; Veech, *op. cit.*, 99-100.
9. Ellis, *op. cit.*, 127.

Allegheny counties of that day—Westmoreland, Washington, Fayette, and Allegheny—was 63,628.[10]

As has been noted, the Scotch-Irish did not constitute a majority of the pioneers of Southwestern Pennsylvania until after the Revolution, but by 1790 and for many years thereafter they predominated throughout this region, which became in time the most characteristically Scotch-Irish section of the commonwealth. When this section emerged from the pioneer stage into a well-settled community with an ordered civilization, the Scotch-Irish were not only the most numerous racial group in this area but were the ones chiefly responsible for its political, economic, and social progress; it was largely a Scotch-Irish civilization. It may be said also that while they did not predominate throughout this region as a whole prior to 1784, there were instances of particular settlements where they were in the majority, probably as early as 1770 and certainly before 1780.[11]

The Scotch-Irish invasion of Southwestern Pennsylvania in mass numbers really began with the opening of the land office for sales in the New Purchase in April 1769, when there began a movement across the Alleghenies from the Scotch-Irish settlements in the eastern part of the province, especially from their headquarters in the Cumberland Valley. Somewhat small at first, this movement increased steadily until the Revolution, when it slackened perceptibly until the war was over and then became strong for several decades. Within a month after the opening of the land office in 1769, about 3200 applications for warrants were made, some of them by speculators but the large majority by bona fide settlers. Much the largest number of settlers under the New Purchase were Scotch-Irish, coming either from eastern Pennsylvania or directly from Ulster, though there were doubtless a few from Virginia and Maryland. It appears that of the Ulster immigrants to Pennsylvania in the large exodus of 1771-1773, the majority

10. J. W. Dinsmore, *The Scotch-Irish in America,* 35-36; A. W. Patterson, *History of the Backwoods, or the Region of the Ohio,* 198; J. I. Brownson, in *The Centennial Celebration of Washington County, Pennsylvania: Proceedings and Addresses,* 14; Boyd Crumrine, *History of Washington County, Pennsylvania,* 147; Hassler, *op. cit.,* 8; Smith, *op. cit.,* 30; Chambers, *op. cit.,* 134.

11. Veech, *op. cit.,* 99.

located in Southwestern Pennsylvania either immediately upon landing or after a brief sojourn in the Scotch-Irish centers east of the mountains. Thus the movement of the Scotch-Irish westward from existing settlements in the province was accompanied by a considerable immigration of those from abroad; this continued for a generation or more with the result that this racial group predominated throughout the trans-Allegheny region. Reverend David McClure, a Presbyterian minister who traveled through this district in 1772-1773, says in his diary under date of April 8, 1773: "The Inhabitants west of the Appalachian Mountains are Chiefly Scotch-Irish. They are either natives of the North of Ireland, or the descendants of such and removed here from the middle colonies. There are some Germans, English, and Scotch."[12] Had Mr. McClure traveled more extensively in what are now Fayette, Washington, and Greene Counties, he would have found more English there than he supposed, but elsewhere in Southwestern Pennsylvania, especially along the route he traveled, the Scotch-Irish were even then already in the majority and were destined soon to become so in Washington, Fayette, and Greene Counties also. There were probably more Germans in this region than came under the notice of Mr. McClure, but from the beginning they were largely outnumbered by the Scotch-Irish in the district as a whole, though there were some early settlements in which they predominated, especially in present Somerset County.[13] The early tax lists show that in Somerset County the Germans prevailed in Brothers Valley, Stony Creek, and Elklick townships, and comprised about half the population in the remaining townships of the county, but that they were overwhelmingly outnumbered by the Scotch-Irish in all the other counties of Southwestern Pennsylvania, especially in the closing decades of

---

12. *Diary of David McClure*, 112; Daniel Agnew, "The Scotch-Irish of Pennsylvania," in Scotch-Irish Society of America *Proceedings*, II, 252; S. T. Wiley, "The Scotch-Irish in Southwestern Pennsylvania," in *ibid.*, III, 233, 235; James Carnahan, *The Pennsylvania Insurrection of 1794, commonly called the "Whiskey Insurrection,"* 119; Alfred Creigh, *History of Washington County, Pennsylvania*, 47; Albert, *op. cit.*, 44-45; Smith, *op. cit.*, 30.

13. T. H. Burrowes, *State-Book of Pennsylvania*, 228; Albert, *op. cit.*, 47.

the eighteenth century.[14] According to Stella H. Sutherland, an excellent authority:

> "Germans were never a conspicuous element in the population of Bedford, Cumberland, Westmoreland, and Washington. Their nomenclature is almost entirely wanting from the tax lists of these counties, even in the late colonial period. The lure of frontier life in Pennsylvania meant little or nothing to them. They were not expert Indian traders, as were the Scotch-Irish; and many of them held views antithetical to war. So they appear in sheltered valleys, content to grow rich by crafts and by extraordinary agricultural economy."[15]

Nevertheless it appears that in the early nineteenth century the Germans became, next to the Scotch-Irish, the largest racial group in Southwestern Pennsylvania throughout a considerable portion of its area, and that in certain restricted districts they were in the majority. Throughout this territory as a whole, however, they predominated only in Somerset County.

Somerset County was crossed in its southwestern extremity by Braddock's Road and in its northern part from east to west by Forbes's Road, the former being constructed in 1755 and the latter in 1758. With the building of these roads, hastily constructed for military purposes to facilitate the advance of the armies of Braddock and Forbes against Fort Duquesne, the settlement of Somerset County began, though very gradually at first. The early settlements in this county are not well known, but the first appear to have been at Brothers Valley, Turkey Foot, and Somerset. The Brothers Valley settlement, located in the vicinity of the present town of Berlin, was made by a colony of Germans. The Turkey Foot settlement, established about the same time, was made by some twenty families from New Jersey, who were mostly Baptists and presumably were mainly of English stock. The Somerset settlement, near the center of the county in the region known as "the Glades," was effected by English and Scotch-Irish about 1765. Later augmented by a number of arrivals, mostly Scotch-

---

14. *Pennsylvania Archives*, 3 ser., XII-XXII.
15. Stella H. Sutherland, *Population Distribution in Colonial America*, 149.

Irishmen from the Cumberland Valley, it increased rapidly until the Revolution. The Scotch-Irish, however, appear to have been a minority group in this county from the beginning, being outnumbered by the Germans.[16]

In Westmoreland County, where the pioneer settlers were principally Scotch-Irish, the first settlement appears to have been made in 1759 on Brush Creek by Andrew Byerly, who had a military permit. Though no considerable settlements were made in Westmoreland County prior to the opening of the land office for the sale of lands in the New Purchase in 1769, some early settlements were made under "tomahawk title" along the Conemaugh and the Loyalhanna and in Ligonier Valley prior to 1768. Thereafter the population of the county increased rapidly and in 1790 numbered 16,018, of whom the majority were Scotch-Irish. The next most numerous were the Germans, though these were in the minority in all the townships of the county except Hempfield and Huntingdon.[17] Many of the pioneers came from the Scotch-Irish "nursery" in the Cumberland Valley, some of whom located north of the Conemaugh, while others established the Derry settlement between that river and the Loyalhanna. The Sewickley settlement was comprised mainly of Scotch-Irish, though there were some Germans in the neighborhood. Prior to 1773 a group of Scotch-Irish settled Hannastown, the original county seat, situated about three miles northeast of the present town of Greensburg, locating around the tavern of Robert Hanna on Forbes's Road. The settlers at Robb's Town were mostly Scotch-Irish, as were those in the same general vicinity.[18] By 1775 Ligonier Valley was well settled, the focus of settlement being Fort Ligonier on Forbes's Road; there were other small but fairly numerous settlements along this road and along the Loyalhanna and its tributaries as far as Hannastown. Nearly all the pioneers in this part of the county were Scotch-Irish, whereas the centers of German settlement were along Turtle Creek and Brush Creek.[19] The

16. W. H. Egle, *History of the Commonwealth of Pennsylvania*, 1078-1079; Burrowes, *op. cit.*, 228-230.

17. Albert, *op. cit.*, 32, 36, 40-41, 44-45, 47.

18. C. Hale Sipe, *Fort Ligonier and Its Times*, 247, 250; Hassler, *op. cit.*, 8.

19. Patterson, *op. cit.*, 186; Hassler, *ibid.*

predominance of the Scotch-Irish in Westmoreland County in the colonial era, as well as the sites of their principal settlements, may be seen in the fact that there were seven Presbyterian congregations established in this area prior to the Revolution and five others in the post-Revolutionary period prior to 1795.[20]

The first settlement to be effected in Fayette County was made by Christopher Gist in the vicinity of Mount Braddock in 1752 under the auspices of the Ohio Company. This settlement was scattered, however, by Indian ravages following Braddock's defeat in 1755 and it was not until 1759 that settlers again entered this region under the protection of Fort Burd, at the junction of Redstone Creek with the Monongahela.[21] Though driven out again during Pontiac's War, the settlers returned when peace was restored, and from 1765 to 1770 a considerable number of immigrants located in the valley of Redstone Creek, on the Youghiogheny, and in the valley of the Cheat. Most of these pioneers were English coming from Virginia and Maryland by way of Braddock's Road, but there were some Scotch-Irish and a few Germans among them. Prior to 1770 only a few settlers entered Fayette County from east of the mountains and, except in a few isolated settlements, this group did not begin to preponderate until after the Revolution. Some Scotch-Irish pioneers located on Dunlap's Creek and between the Redstone and the Youghiogheny.[22] Hanna lists six Presbyterian churches founded in Fayette County at an early date, three of which were established before the Revolution, two during the Revolution, and one in 1791. Of these, two were in Dunbar Township, an early Scotch-Irish center.[23] Though this was only half the number of Presbyterian churches found in Westmoreland County at this time, it should be remembered that in 1790 Fayette County was not so populous as Westmoreland and had a much smaller area. Nevertheless there can be no doubt that the Scotch-Irish, while a majority group in the county, were relatively less numerous than in Westmore-

20. Hanna, *op. cit.*, 106-107.
21. The name of Fort Burd was changed to Redstone Old Fort, and still later to Brownsville.
22. Ellis, *op. cit.*, 56-57, 64, 127; Veech, *op. cit.*, 83, 99-100.
23. Hanna, *op. cit.*, 106-107.

land, a circumstance due in part to the larger percentage of English in Fayette.

Settlements in present Washington County began about 1756, but it was not until 1769 that the region began to be occupied to any considerable extent; thereafter it proceeded rapidly.[24] The first settlers, who were principally English, came from Virginia and Maryland by way of Braddock's Road to Redstone Old Fort on the Monongahela and thence westward into the county. For many years there was no road west of the Monongahela, hence the pioneers located close to the banks of the river and its affluents; later, they advanced into the interior. The Scotch-Irish population of the county became more noticeable about 1773 and thereafter increased steadily; it came mainly from the Cumberland Valley and from other Scotch-Irish centers in Chester, Lancaster, York, and Dauphin Counties, but was augmented by a goodly number of immigrants coming directly from Ulster. There were nineteen Presbyterian churches established in Washington County between 1774 and 1798, thirteen of which were organized prior to 1790.[25] Inasmuch as this was the largest proportion of Presbyterian churches to be found in any county west of the Alleghenies and churches of other denominations were but few, the evidence is conclusive that the Scotch-Irish were overwhelmingly strong in Washington County in 1790 and that this was the most distinctively Scotch-Irish community in Western Pennsylvania. There were numerous English settlers here also, but the German element was scantily represented at this time.[26]

Greene County, originally a part of Washington County, from which it was separated in February, 1796, was settled in the first instance by pioneers from Virginia and Maryland, especially by a colony of Virginia Baptists located on Muddy, Ten Mile, and Whitely Creeks.[27] In the post-Revolutionary period, however, the

24. Crumrine, *op. cit.*, 140, 223, 398.

25. James Veech, in *Centenary Memorial of Presbyterianism in Western Pennsylvania and Parts Adjacent*, 301; J. I. Brownson, in *The Centennial Celebration of Washington County, Pennsylvania: Proceedings and Addresses*, 17; Creigh, *op. cit.*, 47; Burrowes, *op. cit.*, 249; Sherman Day, *Historical Collections of the State of Pennsylvania*, 659; Hanna, *op. cit.*, 106-107.

26. Sutherland, *op. cit.*, 149; Egle, *op. cit.*, 1141-1142.

27. Veech, in *Centenary Memorial . . .*, 327; Egle, *op. cit.*, 771.

Scotch-Irish became the predominant racial group in the county. The German element was particularly small in this county, whose early population consisted mostly of Scotch-Irish, Scots, English, and a handful of Germans, Irish, and French.[28] Owing to the lack of roads, Greene County was settled slowly and in 1800 had a population of only 8,605 as compared with 28,298 in Washington County, which was the most populous county in Western Pennsylvania down to 1820.

Due to its geographical location and especially to its possession of the strategic Forks of the Ohio, the gateway of the West, Allegheny County early became the scene of struggles between the French and the English and also between the Virginians and the Pennsylvanians, all contending for the mastery of what was recognized on all sides as being the key to empire. Here, however, we are concerned only with its settlement, which was attended by many hazards not easily surmounted. Upon finally emerging from a troublous beginning, it was found to be predominantly a Scotch-Irish community. While others contributed in no slight degree to the development of this region, nevertheless it was the Scotch-Irish who, in the main, gave tone and direction to its political, economic, and social life.

Allegheny County was settled chiefly by the Scotch-Irish, along with smaller numbers of Scots, English, Germans, and other racial groups. Though most of the Scotch-Irish came to this county, as to other parts of Southwestern Pennsylvania generally, from the Scotch-Irish centers east of the Alleghenies, a large number came directly from Ulster, especially in the post-Revolutionary period.[29] Following the capture of Fort Duquesne by General Forbes in 1758, a small settlement grew up around the fort, now renamed Fort Pitt. The settlers were dispersed, however, during Pontiac's War, but a new start was made in 1765; the town grew slowly, being remote and subject to Indian incursions. Arthur Lee, who visited the place in 1784, states that "Pittsburgh is inhabited almost entirely by Scots and Irish, who live in paltry log houses."[30]

28. Sutherland, *op. cit.*, 246; Burrowes, *op. cit.*, 149.
29. Chambers, *op. cit.*, 148; Rupp, *op. cit.*, 47; Burrowes, *op. cit.*, 257.
30. Cited in *The Olden Time*, II, 340.

Though settlements were made at various places along the Monon-gahela and its tributaries, the real settlement of the county did not get well under way until 1769. That the Scotch-Irish were strong in these parts may be gathered from the fact that ten Presbyterian churches were established in this county between 1771 and 1794, seven of which were in existence in 1790.[31] There was a fairly rapid settlement in parts of Allegheny County west of the Monongahela between 1770 and 1775, most of the lands being acquired under Virginia titles, especially along Chartiers Creek; and it appears that the majority of the settlers prior to the Revolution were from Virginia. A few settlements were estab-lished a short distance up the Allegheny, but most of them were located on the Monongahela and its branches. In general it may be said that the Scotch-Irish did not begin to preponderate in this county until after the Revolution.[32]

The Whiskey Insurrection served to advertise Southwestern Pennsylvania, the region in which it centered. Allegheny County, along with the other settled portions of the trans-Allegheny coun-try, being now better known to the outside world, attracted a substantial number of the militiamen as permanent residents. This expedition, like those of Braddock and Forbes, showed to the peo-ple east of the mountains how desirable Southwestern Pennsylvania was, and led to a considerable increase of the population of this section as a result.[33]

Summing up our description of the Scotch-Irish in Southwestern Pennsylvania, it may be observed that inasmuch as this region was long regarded as an extension of the Virginia frontier and that Virginia held jurisdiction over the greater part of it prior to yielding her claim to Pennsylvania, the majority of the first settlers throughout this area were of English stock entering the district by way of Braddock's Road, though some, even of those coming from Virginia and Maryland, were Scotch-Irish. Few settlers were found in this region prior to 1764 and not a large number before

31. Hanna, *op. cit.*, 106-107.
32. A. A. Lambing and J. W. F. White, *Centennial History of Allegheny County*, 38-41, 50.
33. I. D. Rupp, *op. cit.*, 47; Burrowes, *op. cit.*, 261.

1769, and the first settlements were mainly along the river courses. After 1769 population increased more rapidly, the larger number of immigrants coming now from eastern Pennsylvania, especially from the Scotch-Irish centers previously established. The English, however, prevailed in Southwestern Pennsylvania until the close of the Revolution, following which this district became increasingly a Scotch-Irish community, mingled with smaller numbers of English, Germans, and other racial elements. Prevailingly Scotch-Irish by 1790, this territory became increasingly so in the next generation and formed a second reservoir of this race, which overflowed northward and westward as time passed. Owing to the greater number of Scotch-Irish settling in this region and to the relatively fewer removals than from the Cumberland Valley and other Scotch-Irish centers east of the mountains, Southwestern Pennsylvania became in time the principal stronghold of this race in the commonwealth.

Such is the story of Scotch-Irish settlement in the old historic Southwestern Pennsylvania of colonial times. In the decades following, however, settlement expanded to the northward to Beaver, Butler, Armstrong, Indiana, and Cambria Counties, and we will include these as being in a more modern view a part of present-day Southwestern Pennsylvania.

SCOTCH-IRISH SETTLEMENTS IN UPPER SOUTHWESTERN PENNSYLVANIA

The settlements effected by the Scotch-Irish in the counties bordering on old Southwestern Pennsylvania to the northward belong not to the colonial era, strictly construed, but to a later period when the proprietary government had been abolished, the Revolutionary War had receded into the past, and the commonwealth had supplanted the Penns in disposing of the vast, unlocated, and unsold lands of Pennsylvania. Hence there was a definite break in the continuity of the story, along with sharp contrasts between conditions in the two periods of settlement. Here it may be noted that the Scotch-Irish, though leading the advance into this new territory and still forming an important element of the population, did not establish themselves so firmly nor predominate so largely as they had done in the Cumberland Valley and in the old Southwestern Pennsylvania. No such reservoirs of their race were formed here as in the earlier centers, nor was their influence so prevailing. Furthermore, the records of their settlements, never too abundant, become even less satisfactory as they grow more meagre. In the new counties comprising what we have designated as Upper Southwestern Pennsylvania, the pioneers were mainly Scotch-Irish and Germans, coming principally from Westmoreland, Washington, Fayette, and Allegheny Counties, with smaller numbers from east of the Alleghenies and some directly from Ireland, Scotland, and Germany, and a sprinkling from other countries. From about 1792 to 1800 some settlers located in Beaver, Butler, and Armstrong Counties, but there was only a scant population here prior to 1800.[34]

The Scotch-Irish predominated among the pioneers of Beaver County, which they began to occupy in 1792 under an act passed in that year by the General Assembly "throwing open for settlement the superfluous land in the military tracts," though some squatters had doubtless located there before this time. Here as elsewhere in the region north of the Ohio and west of the Allegheny, settlement was retarded by the hostile attitude of the Indians until this territory was rendered safe for occupation by Wayne's defeat of the Indians in 1795 and by the Treaty of Greenville which followed. Thereafter settlement was more rapid, though much difficulty was experienced over land titles. In 1800 Beaver County was erected, being cut off from Allegheny County; its population at that time was 5,776.[35] In Butler County also settlement began in 1792, the immigrants coming chiefly from Westmoreland and Allegheny Counties, with smaller numbers from Washington and Fayette Counties and a few from east of the mountains. Here again the majority of the pioneers were Scotch-Irish, though there were numerous Germans. Its settlement was slow until 1796, but thereafter proceeded at a more rapid pace. When separated from Allegheny County in 1800, it

34. Rupp, op. cit., 48.
35. T. F. Gordon, A Gazetter of Pennsylvania, Part II, 28; Burrowes, op. cit., 286.

numbered 3916 inhabitants.[36] The pioneers of Armstrong County were mostly Scotch-Irish and Germans, many of whom came from Westmoreland County and others from the more thickly settled districts of near-by counties.[37] It appears probable that the Scotch-Irish comprised the majority of the pioneers in this county, but the sources of information are not such as to warrant positive statement in this regard.

Indiana County, erected in 1803 from parts of Westmoreland and Lycoming Counties, was settled chiefly by the Scotch-Irish, many of whom came from the Cumberland Valley. Their first settlement was made in 1772 in the vicinity of the present town of Indiana, but immigration was slow until Wayne's victory over the Indians in 1795 rendered the region safe for occupation.[38] Other early settlements in the county were made along the Conemaugh River, Black Lick Creek and its branches, and in the southern part of the county; and, at a later date, in the "Mahoning Country" in the northern part of the county. The pioneers, who came principally from the Cumberland Valley and were nearly all Scotch-Irish Presbyterians, "came with their Bibles, their Confession of Faith, their catechisms, and their rifles," as was their custom.[39] The first settlement in the county was in its southern extremity at the forks of the Conemaugh River and Black Lick Creek, in 1769. The next was in the vicinity of the present town of Indiana, being effected by Samuel, Fergus, and Joseph Moorhead, James Kelly, and Moses Chambers. Another typical Scotch-Irish settlement, made in 1792, was at Armagh in the southeastern extremity of the county in the center of a fine farming region.[40] Early Presbyterian churches founded by the Scotch-Irish in Indiana County were Bethel (1790), Ebenezer on Blacklick (1790), Armagh (1792), and Conemaugh Associate Reformed (1797 or before).[41] Thus it appears that by 1800 there were a number of thriving Scotch-Irish centers in the county.

36. Samuel Hazard, Register of Pennsylvania, IX, 386; Gordon, op. cit., 76.
37. Burrowes, op. cit., 267.
38. Burrowes, op. cit., 264-265.
39. Egle, op. cit., 793-794.
40. Ibid., 793, 796.
41. Hanna, op. cit., II, 106-107.

Cambria County, erected in 1804 from parts of Huntingdon and Somerset Counties, was a wilderness prior to 1790, when the first settlement was made by Captain Michael McGuire, an Irish Catholic, in the vicinity of the present town of Loretto; later, under the leadership of Gallitzin, Loretto became the center of a strong Catholic colony. The Germans, entering the county in 1791, eventually became the prevailing racial group, especially in its southern portion. The Scotch-Irish, Scots, and English settled in the northern part of the county, while the Welsh, the founders of Ebensburg and of Cambria Township, occupied the center in predominant numbers. Though well represented, the Scotch-Irish have always been a minority group in this county; the majority of them appear to have come directly from Ulster rather than from eastern Pennsylvania. But the Germans, many of whom were Mennonites, Amish, and Dunkers, came mostly from the German counties of southeastern Pennsylvania.[42] On the basis of the nomenclature of the tax lists from 1795 to 1815, it appears that the British element comprised about 40 per cent of the population of the county; the Welsh, 10 per cent; and the Germans, Swiss, Dutch, and French, about 40 per cent, while the remaining 10 per cent were impossible to classify. The Scotch and Scotch-Irish at this time are estimated at 30 per cent of the population, the Welsh at 10 per cent, and the English at 7 per cent.[43]

Scotch-Irish Settlements in Central, North Central, and Northeastern Pennsylvania

Central Pennsylvania might well be considered as including the counties of Centre, Juniata, Mifflin, Huntingdon, Blair, Clearfield, Clinton, Lycoming, Union, Snyder, and Northumberland.[44] Four of these—Blair, Huntingdon, Mifflin, and Juniata—have already been discussed in the preceding chapter in connection with the story of the occupation of the Juniata Valley, and are therefore dismissed from further consideration. Throughout Central

---

42. Charles B. Trego, *A Geography of Pennsylvania*, 206; Egle, *op. cit.*, 468-471; Burrowes, *op. cit.*, 231-233.

43. Kate Alletha Standish, *The Racial Origins of the Early Settlers of Cambria County, Pennsylvania* (Manuscript Master's Thesis University of Pittsburgh, 1934).

44. This division is purely arbitrary and for purpose of convenience.

Pennsylvania as a whole, the Scotch-Irish were the prevailing racial group among the pioneer settlers except in the counties of Union and Snyder, where the Germans predominated.

Though the southern half of Centre County was included in the Land Purchase of 1758 and could therefore be occupied legally after that date, it does not appear that settlers began to enter this region (then a part of Cumberland County) until 1765 or 1766. The upper part of the county was embraced in the Land Purchase of 1768, and there were no settlements in this area prior to that time. The first settlers in Centre County came from the Cumberland Valley and were chiefly Scotch-Irish, who located in the lower part of the county as early as 1766, if not in 1765. The pioneers in the northern portion of the county entered by way of Bald Eagle Valley in 1768 or 1769.[45] The pioneer settlements were made in the vicinity of the present town of Milesburg and in Penn's Valley, dating from about 1766. By 1776 there were well established settlements in these places; General James Potter, who discovered Penn's Valley, erected a fort there known as Potter's Fort, which was the principal nucleus of occupation of the valley.[46] Prior to the Revolution the Scotch-Irish were the prevailing racial group of Centre County, though there were a few Germans among the pioneers. During the Indian troubles of the Revolutionary period many of the inhabitants recrossed the mountains to present Cumberland and Franklin Counties, but most of them later returned.[47] After about 1790 the Germans became an increasingly important element of the population and are today probably the predominant racial group.

In Clearfield and Clinton Counties the Scotch-Irish were the most numerous element among the pioneers, with Germans the next largest group. The eastern part of Clearfield County was the first to be settled, the immigrants coming mainly from Centre County; in the southern and southeastern parts of the county, however, they came principally from Huntingdon County and from farther to the westward. Until about 1801, settlement was

45. Egle, *op. cit.,* 503-506, 515.
46. Burrowes, *op. cit.,* 214-215.
47. John Blair Linn, *History of Centre and Clinton Counties,* 14-15, 17-33, 41.

very slight, and even in 1810 the inhabitants numbered only some 900, though Clearfield had been erected as a separate county in 1804.[48] The settlement of Clinton County began in 1765, when some Scotch-Irishmen from the neighborhood of Carlisle, in Cumberland County, located in the vicinity of the present town of Lock Haven.[49] By 1768 there was a respectable number of settlers in this general locality, most of whom came from the Scotch-Irish centers to the southward. During the Revolution the inhabitants fled before the fury of the Indian attacks in a mass movement known as the "Big Runaway," which occurred in 1778; later, however, nearly all of them returned.[50] The northern part of this county was not secured from the Indians until the Land Purchase of 1784. The tax lists of 1783 show that the residents were mostly Scotch-Irish, with a few English and a handful of Germans. Settlement proceeded slowly for many years, and Clinton was not organized as a separate county until 1839, being taken from parts of Centre and Lycoming Counties.[51]

The Scotch-Irish were but sparsely represented in the population of Union and Snyder Counties, where the Germans were the prevailing group. The lower part of Union County, which was cut off from Northumberland County in 1813, had a few scattered settlers along Penn's Creek as early as 1754, but in 1755 they were driven off by the Indians in the ravages following Braddock's defeat, and permanent settlements did not get well under way in this county until 1769. The first settlers were Scotch-Irish and Germans who located along the Susquehanna at the mouth of Penn's Creek and Buffalo Creek. Eventually the Germans came to be much the largest racial group in this county, where but few Scotch-Irish settled, except in the very beginning.[52] Snyder County, which was formed from the southern half of Union County in 1855, received a few Scotch-Irish pioneers along

48. L. C. Aldrich, *History of Clearfield County, Pennsylvania*, 57-64, 82-83; Burrowes, *op. cit.*, 235.

49. J. F. Meginness, *Otzinachson, or a History of the West Branch Valley*, 97.

50. Egle, *op. cit.*, 574-576.

51. Linn, *op. cit.*, 477, 481-482.

52. Egle, *op. cit.*, 1110-1111; Trego, *op. cit.*, 358; Burrowes, *op. cit.*, 217-218.

Penn's Creek in 1769, but this county, being mostly German, has never been Scotch-Irish territory.[53]

The pioneer settlers of Lycoming County were chiefly Scotch-Irish; later these were joined by some English Quakers from southeastern Pennsylvania and by Germans, and still later by English settlers from New England, New Jersey, and New York, thus giving the county a very mixed population by 1840. When this region was opened up to settlement east of Pine Creek by the Land Purchase of 1768, many Scotch-Irish from the Cumberland Valley poured into it and occupied the choice lands along the West Branch of the Susquehanna.[54] There being some doubt as to whether the fertile strip of territory lying between Lycoming Creek and Pine Creek was included in the purchase of 1768, the provincial government forbade settlements west of Lycoming Creek in order to keep peace with the Indians. Nevertheless, this desirable district was occupied by Scotch-Irish squatters in considerable numbers prior to the Revolution, and these were later given preëmption rights on account of their patriotic services during the war. At the time of the "Big Runaway" in 1778 a large part of the West Branch Valley was evacuated following the Indian massacre, but the settlers later returned. After the Land Purchase of 1784, settlement proceeded rapidly, especially above Lycoming Creek.[55]

In the North Central counties of McKean and Potter, especially in the latter, the Scotch-Irish were sparsely represented from the beginning. A large part of present McKean County was owned by a group of capitalists residing in Philadelphia, under whose auspices the first settlement was made in this region at Ceres about 1807 by an Englishman named King. Owing to its inaccessibility, there were no important settlements here until about 1816, when the proprietors opened roads to stimulate immigration. The pioneer settlers in this county were Scotch-Irish and

53. Burrowes, op. cit., ibid.; Egle, op. cit., 1072.
54. Sherman Day, Historical Collections of the State of Pennsylvania, 448; Meginness, op. cit., 160; Trego, op. cit., 291; Burrowes, op. cit., 222, 225-226.
55. Smith's Laws of Pennsylvania, II, 195; Meginness, op. cit., 161-167.

English, the former coming from eastern Pennsylvania and from the settlements along the West Branch of the Susquehanna, and the latter from New England and New York. Though the majority of the first settlers were Scotch-Irish, these were eventually outnumbered by the English as the prevailing racial group. There appear to have been no Germans among the pioneers of this county, which has never been German territory.[56] As in the case of McKean, a large part of Potter County was owned by Philadelphia capitalists and similar conditions obtained there. In 1809 a road was opened to induce settlers to locate in this region, but settlement proceeded slowly. In 1810 there were but twenty inhabitants, and in 1820 there were "only a few straggling settlements" containing about 186 people. The pioneers, who were located mostly in the northern part of the county, were practically all of English stock from New England and New York. A minority of the first settlers came from the older counties of Pennsylvania, and it is a fair inference that some of these were Scotch-Irish from the West Branch Valley, but this county was settled mainly by English immigrants. Between 1840 and 1850 a number of German and Irish immigrants coming directly from Europe settled throughout this region.[57]

Northeastern Pennsylvania[58] has never been Scotch-Irish territory. Among the pioneer settlers in the region as a whole the English were the prevailing racial element, with the Germans the next most numerous. There were, however, small numbers of Scotch-Irish among the first settlers throughout this area, particularly in Northumberland, Columbia, and Luzerne Counties. In Northumberland County the pioneers were the Scotch-Irish and English. Immediately after it was opened for settlement by the Land Purchase of 1768, many Scotch-Irish from the Cumberland Valley entered this county, being especially strong in the

---

56. R. B. Stone, *McKean, The Governor's County,* 33-35, 112.

57. Victor L. Beebe, *History of Potter County, Pennsylvania,* 39-40, 45, 48, 58, 119; Burrowes, *op. cit.,* 305.

58. The counties included in this term are Northumberland, Montour, Columbia, Sullivan, Luzerne, Lackawanna, Wyoming, Wayne, Pike, Monroe, and Susquehanna.

vicinity of Sunbury, though later outnumbered by the Germans.[59] Columbia County began to be settled in 1773, the pioneers being English and Welsh Quakers locating at Catawissa during the Revolution; but the Germans were the prevailing element among the early settlers, and Columbia became largely a German county. A few Scotch-Irish came from their early centers to the southward and from New Jersey, and there has always been a small minority of them in the county. The immigration to this region was slight until after the Revolution, when the Germans came in large numbers and prevailed as the majority group.[60] Luzerne County was first settled almost entirely by immigrants from Connecticut who were of English stock, though a few of the first comers were from southern Pennsylvania. Owing to special circumstances, Captain Lazarus Stewart and his company of Paxton rangers to the number of about forty, being a body of Scotch-Irishmen, removed from Dauphin County in 1770 and settled a large part of Hanover Township in Luzerne County. Outside of this settlement there were but few Scotch-Irish pioneers in Luzerne County, which was overwhelmingly English in its origin and long remained so.[61]

Elsewhere throughout Northeastern Pennsylvania the Scotch-Irish settlers were so few as to be negligible. Except for the present Northumberland and Columbia Counties, this whole territory was settled principally by people of English stock coming from New England, especially from Connecticut, which claimed this region under her charter of 1662. Here it may be noted that all the Pennsylvania counties bordering on the New York line were settled chiefly by immigrants from New England and New York, the large majority of whom were of English stock. There were scarcely any Scotch-Irish or Germans among the pioneers of this particular district except in Erie County. Very different from this, however, is the story of the settlement of Northwestern Pennsylvania, where the Scotch-Irish again play the leading rôle.

59. J. F. Meginness, "The Scotch-Irish of the Upper Susquehanna Valley," in Scotch-Irish Society of America *Proceedings*, 165; Burrowes, *op. cit.*, 181, 183.

60. J. H. Battle (ed.), *History of Columbia and Montour Counties*, Part II, 64-65, 105.

61. Stewart Pearce, *Annals of Luzerne County*, 101-107, 111-112, 116; H. B. Plumb, *History of Hanover Township . . . . in Luzerne County, Pennsylvania*, 144-145.

Scotch-Irish Settlements in Northwestern Pennsylvania

Except for those counties bordering on the New York line, Northwestern Pennsylvania[62] was settled principally by the Scotch-Irish coming either from their centers elsewhere in the commonwealth or directly from Ireland. Though the Scotch-Irish were the prevailing race throughout this area and were the most influential factor in its development, their settlements here are not so clearly traceable as were those in Southwestern Pennsylvania, nor was a similar reservoir formed to overflow freely and constantly to the westward. In fact, the expansion westward of the Scotch-Irish of Northwestern Pennsylvania was of no special significance. Hence this section has a less important bearing on the distribution of population throughout the country as a whole than was the case with the other principal centers of Scotch-Irish settlement in the commonwealth. Nevertheless Northwestern Pennsylvania, a large and progressive section, has played an important part in the history of Pennsylvania and of the country and merits greater attention than it has hitherto received at the hands of historians.

The settlement of this large area was retarded by troubles with the Indians, by the uncertainty of land titles, and by its inaccessibility. Its remote situation and inadequate transportation facilities rendered the marketing of products both difficult and expensive. Hence it was the last part of the commonwealth to be occupied, and it was not until the building of turnpikes, canals, and railroads had so far advanced in the eighteen-thirties and forties as to render its more remote portions accessible that it began to be settled rapidly. Parts of it were regularly listed as "frontier" in the census reports down to 1840, notably the present counties of Cameron, Elk, and Forest. The Pennsylvania frontier, so long in the process of being settled, finally disappeared in the eighteen-thirties. Settlement of Northwestern Pennsylvania may hardly be said to have begun prior to 1795, when this region was rendered

62. The term "Northwestern Pennsylvania" is here used to include the present counties of Lawrence, Mercer, Crawford, Erie, Venango, Clarion, Jefferson, Forest, Elk, Cameron, and Warren.

safe for occupation by Wayne's victory over the Indians and by the negotiation of the Treaty of Greenville promptly thereafter. Though this territory had been purchased from the Indians in 1784, they did not on this account cease from warlike incursions destructive of life and property.[63] The Indian menace to Northwestern Pennsylvania was removed effectually by the Treaty of Greenville, a circumstance which stimulated immigration into that area.

   In connection with the settlement of that portion of western Pennsylvania which lies north of the Ohio River and west of the Allegheny River and Conewago Creek, it is pertinent to take into consideration the so-called Depreciation Lands and Donation Lands throughout that territory. In anticipation of the extinguishment of the Indian title, the legislature by the Act of 1783 set aside the territory west of the Allegheny and north of the Ohio into two grand sections "intended as donations to the Revolutionary soldiers of the Pennsylvania Line, and for the redemption of the certificates of depreciation from the continental scale given to them for their pay." The purpose of this act was to comply with the original promise of a bonus to the soldiers. The Donation Lands, lying north of a line from Mogulbuhiton Creek above Kittanning and thence due west to the Ohio state boundary, included parts of the present counties of Lawrence, Butler, Armstrong, Venango, Forest, Warren, and Erie, and the whole of Crawford and Mercer Counties. The Depreciation Lands lay immediately south of the above line and included parts of the present counties of Allegheny, Beaver, Butler, Lawrence, and Armstrong. They were opened to settlement by Act of April 3, 1792, but, except for the choice locations, the sales were disappointing and were later suspended. The plan for disposing of the Donation Lands proved equally unsuccessful, since many of the tracts were left undrawn. Hence large sections which had been set aside for patriotic purposes were not disposed of, and much

---

63. Daniel Agnew, *History of the Region North of the Ohio and West of The Allegheny River*, 118.

of the land was occupied by squatters who eventually secured preëmption rights.[64]

The settlement of Northwestern Pennsylvania was further complicated, especially in regard to land titles, by the activities of several large land companies with vast holdings throughout this region. Though its operations were chiefly in New York, the Holland Land Company in 1793 acquired half a million acres in Pennsylvania in the present counties of Forest and Venango. The Pennsylvania Population Company also had about half a million acres, all of its holdings being in Pennsylvania and chiefly in Erie County. The North American Land Company held 625 tracts of 400 acres each, located in the counties of Beaver, Butler, Mercer, Crawford, Erie, Warren, and Venango. All these companies were led to engage in land speculation by the prospect of a large increase in the value of their holdings, but their ventures involved them in litigation with the actual settlers and in the end proved unprofitable, besides causing so much uncertainty over land titles as to retard settlement in Northwestern Pennsylvania.[65]

Lawrence County, as at present constituted, "was settled chiefly by the Scotch-Irish, or the descendants of that race, who migrated from the older counties of Western Pennsylvania, and some directly from Ireland itself." The pioneers came mostly from Cumberland, Franklin, Westmoreland, Fayette, and Washington Counties, with "a few from the States of Delaware, Maryland, and Virginia." Next to the Scotch-Irish, the Germans were the most numerous racial group; there were small numbers of English and Dutch.[66] The settlement of the county did not properly begin until 1795, and then proceeded slowly. Some squatters occupied tracts on the forbidden Depreciation Lands in 1784, but were driven off by General Harmar the following year. As a result of the throwing open to settlement of the superfluous land in the Donation Tract by the Act of 1792, there was a rush of

64. *Ibid.*, 117, 177-178; John E. Winner, "The Depreciation and Donation Lands," in *Western Pennsylvania Historical Magazine*, VIII, 3-4, 8.

65. Agnew, *op. cit.*, 128-133, 179; Elizabeth K. Henderson, "The Northwestern Lands of Pennsylvania, 1790-1812," in *Pennsylvania Magazine of History and Biography*, LX, 139-145, 159.

66. Egle, *op. cit.*, 855-866.

prospectors and landhunters to this region. Most of these did not immediately settle there, but marked the land for future settlement. These proceedings aroused the anger of the Indians, who rendered life and property unsafe for the next several years preceding the Treaty of Greenville, in 1795. Following the ratification of this treaty there was a great influx of settlers into Lawrence County as into all Northwestern Pennsylvania generally. The soldiers who had received grants of donation lands seldom attempted to occupy them, preferring to sell them "to relatives, acquaintances, or speculators."[67]

As in the case of Lawrence County, the majority of the early settlers in Mercer County were Scotch-Irishmen who came chiefly from the older settlements in Southwestern Pennsylvania and from North Ireland.[68] In 1850 Mr. B. Stokely, one of the pioneers in Mercer County, gave the following account of the early days in this county as he remembered them:

> "In the spring of 1797, as early as the middle of February, the county began to settle, so that in a few months the neighborhood began to assume the appearance of civilization. . . . The settlement at Cool Spring being among the very earliest in the county, it may be considered as begun in the spring of 1797, though many had made small beginnings in 1796, but had returned to the old settlements in the fall and back again in the spring."[69]

The early tax lists of Mercer County show an overwhelming preponderance of Scotch-Irish names, along with some English and a negligible number of Germans.[70] Later, however, there were many Germans and Irish entering the county, coming directly from abroad. Settlements in this region began about 1796, the earliest being in the forks of Mahoning, Shenango, and Neshannock Creeks.[71] In 1806 some settlements were made in the central part of the county in the vicinity of the present town of Mercer by

67. H. R. Johnson, *History of Neshannock Presbyterian Church*, 41-48.
68. J. G. White (ed.), *History of Mercer County, Pennsylvania*, 147-158.
69. *Memoirs of the Historical Society of Pennsylvania*, IV, Part II, 75-76.
70. J. Fraise Richard (ed.), *History of Mercer County, Pennsylvania*, 147-158.
71. I. D. Rupp, *Early History of Western Pennsylvania*, 49.

Scotch-Irish immigrants from Westmoreland, Washington, and Allegheny Counties, but here as elsewhere in Northwestern Pennsylvania settlement was retarded by difficulties over land titles.[72]

The first settlement in Crawford County was made on French Creek near the present town of Meadville in the spring of 1788 by David Mead and others, who came from the neighborhood of Sunbury on the Susquehanna. Despite trouble with the Indians, this proved to be a permanent settlement, whose numbers were increased by the coming of other settlers in 1793. The names of these pioneers indicate that they were of English stock for the most part, but the fact that the church established at Meadville in 1801 was Presbyterian indicates that some of the settlers here were probably Scotch-Irish. There was no considerable immigration into Crawford County until the cessation of Indian hostilities in 1795, and even then settlement was slow for some years by reason of the uncertainty of land titles and the inaccessibility of the region. In 1805, however, the United States Supreme Court having passed definitely upon the vexed question as to the respective rights of the land companies and the actual settlers, the uncertainty respecting titles was finally removed and thereafter immigration increased.[73] The pioneers in Crawford County were composed of Scotch-Irish, English, and Germans from the older counties to the southward and eastward, together with some English from New England and New York and a few Dutch.[74] The Scotch-Irish were undoubtedly a very substantial element of the population, but the evidence at hand does not show conclusively that they were predominant in the county, though they may have been. On the other hand, there are some indications that the English were in the majority, at least among the very early settlers.

The Scotch-Irish were well represented among the pioneers of Erie County. Coming mainly from Dauphin, Cumberland, Lan-

72. Burrowes, op. cit., 288.

73. Alfred Huidekoper, "Incidents in the Early History of Crawford County," in Memoirs of the Historical Society of Pennsylvania, IV, Part II, 115, 120-121, 126-127, 130, 160; Burrowes, op. cit., 279.

74. I. B. Brown, Early Footprints of Developments and Improvements in Extreme Northwestern Pennsylvania, 48-49, 64; Egle, op. cit., 602, 610.

caster, and Northumberland Counties, there appears to be no doubt that they comprised the majority element in this county until about 1805. Thereafter the English settlers hailing from New England and New York forged to the front as the most numerous racial element; there was, however, a strong minority German group, especially after 1825. The Scotch-Irish were particularly numerous among the early settlers of Mill Creek and Fairview Townships, where they were the prevailing racial element.[75] Like all the Pennsylvania counties bordering on the New York line, Erie County was settled chiefly by immigrants of English stock coming principally from New England and New York. The story of the early settlement of Warren County is similar to that of Erie County in that the principal racial groups among the pioneers were Scotch-Irish and English, the former prevailing in the beginning and the latter in the end. The Germans, almost wanting among the first settlers, came later in considerable numbers.[76]

The first settlers of Venango County were a small group of Scotch-Irishmen who located in the vicinity of the present town of Franklin, probably about 1790. Other settlers, mostly Scotch-Irish and English, followed from the middle counties and the Wyoming Valley, along with some coming directly from England. There were the usual disputes over land titles and the consequent retarding of settlement until the points at issue were decided by the United States Supreme Court in 1805, following which immigration was more rapid. In 1810 a few Germans settled in Reichland Township, but the German element was inconsiderable in the settlement of this county. It appears that the English eventually became the predominant group and so remained for many years.[77] In the adjoining county of Clarion a few individuals located here and there as early as 1792, but permanent settlement did not get well under way until 1800. The

75. Egle, *op. cit.*, 722-723.

76. *Ibid.*, 1134-1135; Burrowes, *op. cit.*, 311; J. S. Schenk, *History of Warren County, Pa.*, 127-30.

77. *Memoirs of the Historical Society of Pa.*, IV, Part II, 164-167; Sherman Day, *op. cit.*, 645.

pioneers came principally from Westmoreland, Centre, and Fayette Counties, and were prevailingly Scotch-Irish, though there were numerous Germans and some English among them.[78] Jefferson County began to be settled in 1797 by a small band of Scotch-Irishmen hailing from Dauphin County, and the Scotch-Irish continued to prevail. One of their early settlements was in the vicinity of the present town of Reynoldsville, where they were joined by a few Germans. The opportunities afforded by the lumber manufacture attracted some English from New England and New York, though these were but few in this predominantly Scotch-Irish county.[79]

As noted above, the Counties of Cameron, Elk, and Forest constituted the last frontier of Pennsylvania and had only begun to be occupied in 1840, though there were a handful of settlers prior to this time. A few adventurous souls located in Cameron County between 1809 and 1815, "hailing mostly from eastern and middle Pennsylvania, from the State of New Jersey, and from New England." Since they were principally Presbyterians and Baptists, it would appear that they were largely Scotch-Irish and English, though there were a few Germans among them.[80] A small group of settlers located in present Elk County about 1817. Their names indicate that they were prevailingly English, savoring strongly of Puritan antecedents.[81] The first permanent settler in Forest County was Eli Holeman, probably a New Englander, who was soon followed by Moses Hicks in 1805. Here again it appears that the pioneers in this county were chiefly of English stock coming from New England, though there was a German colony on "Dutch Hill," east of Tionesta.[82]

Thus it appears that except for those counties bordering on the New York line and for the sparsely occupied counties of Cameron, Elk, and Forest, Northwestern Pennsylvania was settled for the most part by the Scotch-Irish, with lesser numbers of English,

78. A. J. Davis (ed.), *History of Clarion County, Pa.*, 76-80; Egle, *op. cit.*, 553-554.
79. W. J. McKnight, *A Pioneer History of Jefferson County, Pa.*, 301; W. C. Elliott, *History of Reynoldsville and Vicinity*, 35; Burrowes, *op. cit.*, 271; Egle, *op. cit.*, 800-803.
80. Egle, *op. cit.*, 480-481.
81. *Ibid.*, 685-687.
82. *Ibid.*, 737-738.

Germans, and other racial elements.[83] True to their character and temperament, the Scotch-Irish ever sought the frontier, braving its hardships and dangers and loving the adventure that it brought. Their movement into Northwestern Pennsylvania largely spent itself before it reached the New York border, however, since they heard the call of the great West and hence did not establish themselves as firmly here as in the southwestern section of the commonwealth. When the West was being opened up for settlement, its fertile lands served as a magnet to attract them thither, just as at an earlier time thousands of them had migrated into the Valley of Virginia and the piedmont section of the Carolinas. Here again they showed that it was not their destiny to remain localized in Pennsylvania, but rather to spread all over the country and to make their influence felt far and wide.

83. S. J. M. Eaton, *History of the Presbytery of Erie*, 5-6; McKnight, *op. cit.*, 348.

6

The Pennsylvania Scotch-Irish of the Dispersion

It may not have been revealed to them that they as a people were not henceforth to live in distinct communities, but were to be dispersed throughout the country . . . . yet such was to be their destiny. JOHN STEWART

HAVING CONSIDERED the early settlements of the Scotch-Irish in the province, it would seem to be appropriate to describe another phase of settlement in which thousands of them were dispersed beyond the borders of Pennsylvania. Other racial groups, especially the Germans, shared with them in this migration, but not in such large numbers nor yet so far afield.[1] Among the Thirteen Colonies, Pennsylvania occupied a unique position as an early distributing center of population to the South and the West.[2]

CAUSES OF THE DISPERSION

The causes inducing the Pennsylvania Scotch-Irish to emigrate to other colonies, especially to the southward, may here be noted. By 1735, the advance guard of settlers, moving ever westward, had reached the foothills of the Alleghenies, and, being hindered by the mountain barrier, was deflected southward along the line of least resistance into the valleys of Maryland and Virginia and

1. The broader aspects of this subject are discussed by the author in his article entitled "Pennsylvania as an Early Distributing Center of Population," in *Pennsylvania Magazine of History and Biography*, LV, 134-169, of which large use is made in writing this chapter.

2. John Fiske, *Old Virginia and Her Neighbors*, II, 390-391; see also Fiske's *The Dutch and Quaker Colonies*, II, 329-30.

the piedmont region of the Carolinas.[3] The uplands of the South had not at that time been reached by the tide of settlers moving westward from the coast, and the vacant lands invited occupancy. It was easier to move down into the southern valleys than to cross the rugged mountain barrier into western Pennsylvania. Furthermore, prior to the Land Purchase of 1768, no land was offered for sale by the Proprietaries west of the Alleghenies. Even after the land in this region was put on the market, settlement was deterred by the inadequate military protection afforded by the provincial government to the inhabitants of the frontier. Again, the southern colonies had a much more liberal land policy than obtained in Pennsylvania; in 1732, lands could be secured in Maryland at less than one-third the cost in Pennsylvania, while the cost in Virginia and the Carolinas was nominal. With so many circumstances favoring emigration, it was inevitable that the movement over the border should begin. Having begun, it grew in volume until it reached large proportions, productive of important results. The conditions invited emigration, and nature had prepared routes which pointed the direction of travel.[4]

MARYLAND, VIRGINIA, AND WEST VIRGINIA

The first phase of the emigration of Pennsylvanians in any considerable numbers was the movement southward into western Maryland and the Valley of Virginia, the Scotch-Irish, with whom we are more particularly concerned, furnishing the largest number of emigrants. Although it was not until the 1730's that the Scotch-Irish trek southward became important, it appears that a few had settled near the present town of Martinsburg, West Virginia, as early as 1719 and had established soon thereafter the Presbyterian congregations of Falling Water and Tuscarora. The movement was in its early stages when Robert Harper, a Scotch-Irishman, settled at the junction of the Shenandoah and Potomac

3. Ellen C. Semple, *American History and Its Geographic Conditions*, 58-59; L. K. Koontz, "The Virginia Frontier, 1754-1762," in *J. H. U. Studies in History and Political Science*, Series XLIII, 206.
4. F. J. Turner, *The Frontier in American History*, 101; T. K. Abernethy, *Three Virginia Frontiers*, 60-61; A. Henderson, *The Conquest of the Old Southwest*, 10; Koontz, *op. cit.*, 207.

Rivers in 1734 and founded Harper's Ferry.[5] Relatively few Scotch-Irish settled in western Maryland and in the northern section of the Shenandoah Valley, these regions being occupied predominantly by the Pennsylvania Germans. Some of the company associated with Joist Hite in the settlement of Frederick County, Virginia, were Scotch-Irishmen, while other Pennsylvania Scotch-Irishmen were among the pioneers along the Opequon and in Winchester and vicinity. In fact, all through that portion of the Shenandoah Valley where the Pennsylvania Germans predominated would be found a respectable number of Scotch-Irish. Augusta, Rockbridge, and Botetourt Counties, Virginia, were settled principally by Scotch-Irishmen hailing from Pennsylvania, and here they planted their institutions as firmly as did the Germans in the northern part of the Valley. Among the first of this group to settle in Augusta County was John Lewis, from Lancaster County, Pennsylvania, who was soon followed by many others. The main sources of this emigration southward were the Cumberland Valley and the Scotch-Irish centers in the present Pennsylvania counties of Chester, Lancaster, York, and Dauphin. The Cumberland Valley in particular, where they were most numerous, was the very gateway to the South, and it was only natural that they should be the major group to follow it over the border into Virginia and the Carolinas.[6]

In 1736 Governor Gooch issued a patent to William Beverly, John Robinson, and John and Richard Randolph for 118,491 acres of land. This grant, embracing about one-fifth of the present county of Augusta, was soon taken over by Beverly individually and is known as the "Beverly grant." Settlement of the county now began in earnest and proceeded rapidly. As early as 1737, the settlers were present in sufficient numbers to enable them to form several Presbyterian congregations. Churches and schools

5. C. A. Hanna, *The Scotch-Irish*, II, 45.
6. R. R. Howison, *History of Virginia*, 172; W. H. Foote, *Sketches of Virginia, Historical and Biographical*, 106; Henry Howe, *Historical Collections of Virginia*, 451; Bolivar Christian, *The Scotch-Irish Settlers in the Valley of Virginia*, 9; S. S. Green, *The Scotch-Irish in America*, 9; J. C. Campbell, *The Southern Highlander and His Homeland*, 56.

multiplied, and a thrifty and intelligent community was planted.[7] When Philip Fithian preached at North Mountain meeting-house near Staunton in 1775, he found the people all Scotch-Irish, while the congregation was large and "genteel."[8] Rockbridge County, bordering Augusta on the south, was even more strongly Scotch-Irish than its neighbor. In fact, it has been called the most distinctively Scotch-Irish county in America, as it is one of the most strongly Presbyterian. Ephraim McDowell, who emigrated to this region from Pennsylvania in 1737, was one of the pioneers and was followed by a host of others. In 1736 Governor Gooch made a grant of 500,000 acres to Benjamin Borden on condition that he should settle one hundred families on it before receiving title, it being thought by his excellency that it was good policy to encourage the Scotch-Irish to settle west of the Blue Ridge as a means of protection of eastern Virginia against the Indians. The condition was met by Borden, who received title to the land in the fall of 1736. Some of the settlement under this grant, part of which was in Augusta County and the remainder in Rockbridge, was induced immigration direct from Ulster to meet the conditions under which the patent was issued. The main body of settlers in Rockbridge County, however, was that of the Scotch-Irish from Pennsylvania, whence a continuous stream poured until the Revolution. Nowhere in America today are the Scotch-Irish more strongly entrenched or their influence more clearly seen than in Augusta and Rockbridge Counties, Virginia. Educationally, this influence manifested itself in founding Washington and Lee University, which has been termed the "Scotch-Irish University of the South," while religiously it made this district one of the strongholds of Presbyterianism. Botetourt County, the next valley county to the southward, was only less strongly Scotch-Irish than were Rockbridge and Augusta, and was settled in much the same way by immigrants from Pennsylvania. As time passed, this region became itself a source of emigration of Scotch-Irish into the Caro-

7. J. L. Peyton, *History of Augusta County, Virginia*, 307-312; Abernethy, *op. cit.*, 56.
8. *Fithian's Journal, 1775-1776*, 139.

linas, Georgia, Tennessee, Kentucky, and the Old Northwest.[9] Thus it is seen that south of the German mass settlement in the northern part of the Shenandoah Valley was a still larger group of the Scotch-Irish, forming a compact and homogeneous settlement extending a distance of about ninety miles, occupying one of the most beautiful and fertile sections of Virginia and founding towns like Staunton, Lexington, and Fincastle.

Partly from Pennsylvania and partly from the older settlements in Augusta, Rockbridge, and Botetourt Counties, the Scotch-Irish spread farther down the Great Valley of Virginia into the present counties of Roanoke, Craig, Pulaski, and Wythe, and, at a somewhat later date, into the present Tazewell County and the extreme limits of Southwest Virginia. They also spread over the Blue Ridge into Piedmont Virginia, and over the Alleghenies into West Virginia. The swelling tide of emigration gathered force and rolled ever farther southward and westward.[10] It is not claimed that all the Scotch-Irishmen in the Valley of Virginia, or elsewhere in the colony for that matter, were immigrants from Pennsylvania, but only that a majority of them were. The movement from Pennsylvania which we have described was unquestionably a controlling circumstance in the settlement of a large area in the Old Dominion. When this area had itself become thickly settled, it sent forth many of the second and third generations to share in the occupation of the South and West, although the original impulse came from Pennsylvania.

The emigration of the Scotch-Irish from Pennsylvania to Maryland and Virginia was part of a larger movement which did not cease until it had gone far toward peopling the uplands of the South. The trail grows longer and more involved, but the source remains the same. Before proceeding with this phase of the sub-

9. W. C. Pendleton, *History of Tazewell County and Southwest Virginia,* 156, 407, 413, 420, 424, 432; Freeman H. Hart, *The Valley of Virginia in the American Revolution, 1763-1789,* 5-7; T. J. Wertenbaker, *The Old South,* 198; Scotch-Irish Society of America *Proceedings,* VII, 23-24, 201-202; Howe, *op. cit.,* 451-453; Peyton, *op. cit.,* 302; Foote, *op. cit.,* 105-106.

10. T. C. Anderson, *Life of Rev. George Donnell,* 14, 41-44; Stella H. Sutherland, *Population Distribution in Colonial America,* 200; D. Campbell, *The Puritan in England, Holland and America,* II, 483-485.

ject, however, attention is directed further to the settlements by the Pennsylvania Scotch-Irish within the bounds of the present state of West Virginia, whose settlement was not altogether in line with the main southern movement, but proceeded under somewhat different conditions. As the settlements in the Shenandoah Valley thickened, pioneers began to cross the mountains into West Virginia and to people the region drained by the South Branch of the Potomac, while others occupied the valleys of the New, the Greenbrier, and the Kanawha. Those entering by the South Branch of the Potomac, being largely the overflow from the Shenandoah Valley, settled in the present counties of Mineral, Hardy, Hampshire, Morgan, Grant, Tucker, and Pendleton. This movement, though not very large, had reached as far as the present Pendleton County by 1748.[11] In the New River region, settlement began somewhat later and received its initial impulse chiefly from the explorations of Christopher Gist, who traversed these wilds in 1750 and made a report which stimulated further emigration from the Valley of Virginia and from Pennsylvania. Among the pioneers was Andrew Culbertson of Chambersburg, Pennsylvania, who located in the present county of Summers in 1753. Other Scotch-Irish settlers entered this region by way of the Greenbrier and the upper reaches of the James River. In the district centering around Clarksburg, in the present Harrison County, there was an influx of settlers after 1774. In 1784 Alexander Parker, of Greene County, Pennsylvania, received a grant of land on which the present city of Parkersburg is situated.[12]

THE CAROLINAS

The emigration of Pennsylvanians into North Carolina, beginning about 1740 and getting well under way by 1750, continued in an increasing stream until the Revolution. Composed of Scotch-Irish, Germans, and smaller numbers of English and Welsh

11. J. M. Callahan, *Semi-Centennial History of West Virginia*, 16-18; R. E. Fast and H. Maxwell, *The History and Government of West Virginia*, 8-9; C. H. Ambler, *History of West Virginia*, 50-53.

12. W. E. DeHass, *History of the Early Settlement and Indian Wars of West Virginia*, 73-75; Callahan, *op. cit.*, 2, 18-19, 25-26, 38.

Quakers, it added a substantial element to the population of that colony. The Scotch-Irish, the largest single group in this immigration, came mostly from Pennsylvania, though many came from Virginia and some direct from Ulster. The numerous Pennsylvania contingent occupied a large area between the Catawba and the Yadkin. Glowing reports of the excellence of the climate and the fertility of the soil proved a sufficient inducement to undertake the long journey as to a land of promise. A goodly percentage of those entering North Carolina were Pennsylvania Scotch-Irishmen who had tarried a while in the Valley of Virginia, but, with the restlessness of their race, had again put on their traveling boots and sought new fields of endeavor.[13] Campbell describes this immigration as follows:

"This movement from Pennsylvania to the Carolina Piedmont commonly involved two or three generations of pioneers, each new generation moving on a journey farther into the wilderness. . . . In 1764 alone, over a thousand immigrant wagons are reported by Governor Tryon to have passed through Salisbury, North Carolina. To the southeast of the Blue Ridge, therefore, grew a second reservoir of population, fed not only from the north but from the south by later and lesser streams of transatlantic origin through the ports of Charleston and Wilmington. . . . The Carolina Piedmont was fed from many sources, the main stream flowing from Pennsylvania through the Valley of Virginia, while the lesser streams issued from the ports of Charleston and Wilmington."[14]

The Scotch-Irish settled in large numbers in the North Carolina counties of Granville, Orange, Rowan, Mecklenburg, Guilford, Davidson, and Cabarrus, and also in the extreme northwestern limits of the colony. In North Carolina, as in Virginia, they "tended to follow the valleys farther toward the mountains," while the Pennsylvania Germans were somewhat to the east of them.[15]

13. W. H. Foote, *Sketches of North Carolina*, 80, 188-189; G. G. Johnson, *Ante-Bellum North Carolina*, 8, 11; J. P. Arthur, *Western North Carolina*, 66; Hanna, *op. cit.*, 32-33, 38; Henderson, *op. cit.*, 10-11.

14. J. C. Campbell, *The Southern Highlander and His Homeland*, 25.

15. Jethro Rumple, *A History of Rowan County, North Carolina*, 27; Turner, *op. cit.*, 105; Foote, *op. cit.*, 309; Scotch-Irish Society of America *Proceedings*, I, 123-124.

The effects of the Scotch-Irish immigration upon the development of North Carolina were profound and lasting. Establishing schools and churches wherever they went, they exerted no slight influence in shaping the history of the colony and state. They founded the Presbyterian Church throughout an extended district of the province, and were mainly responsible for establishing Davidson College. At the close of the colonial era they were strongly entrenched, and were among the first to press farther west to settle the wilderness of Tennessee and Kentucky. One of the most celebrated of the early Scotch-Irish schools was the academy founded by the Reverend David Caldwell near the present city of Greensboro in 1787, and sometimes called the "Eton of the South." There appear to have been no organized Presbyterian congregations in North Carolina before the coming of the Scotch-Irish, who were the principal promoters of this denomination in the colony. Among the more noted Pennsylvania Scotch-Irishmen migrating to North Carolina was Hugh Williamson, author of the first history of the Old North State.

The emigration of the Pennsylvania Scotch-Irish to South Carolina was likewise considerable, but this time they were not accompanied by their German brethren, except perhaps a handful. Although some Scotch-Irishmen entered South Carolina through the port of Charleston, the majority of them came by the route through Virginia and North Carolina. Their first settlement was in the uplands known as "the Waxhaws" and "the Long Canes," whence they spread over a considerable area into the regions roundabout.[16] The advance guard, consisting of some six or seven families, arrived on the Waxhaw in May, 1751. About the same time, settlements were made by other Scotch-Irishmen from Pennsylvania on the western side of the Catawba on the waters of Fishing Creek; and between 1750 and 1756, eight or ten families from Pennsylvania settled on or near Fair Forest Creek. Prior to 1756 this immigration was small, but thereafter, and especially after 1760, it assumed large proportions and continued steadily until the Revolution, when it ceased. In 1783, however, it

16. C. K. Bolton, *Scotch-Irish Pioneers in Ulster and America*, 292; R. L. Meriwether, *The Expansion of South Carolina, 1729-1765*, 160.

was renewed, though with less strength. According to Ramsay, a thousand families arrived in the Piedmont region in 1763 alone, and this section became the most prosperous part of the colony.[17] As in the case of North Carolina, the uplands of South Carolina were settled in the first instance by immigrants from the North rather than by settlers moving westward from tidewater. Many also came from those parts of Virginia and North Carolina originally occupied by Scotch-Irishmen.[18] McCrady describes these early settlements as follows:

"The defeat of Braddock, July 9, 1755, threw the frontiers of Pennsylvania and Virginia at the mercy of the Indians; and these Scotch-Irish, thus exposed to the horrors of Indian war and without support from the wealthy Quakers of the East, abandoned Pennsylvania and came down, following the foot of the mountains, spreading themselves from Staunton, Virginia, to the Waxhaws, in what is now Lancaster County of this province. From this point they peopled the upper country of this state. . . . Around the old Waxhaw church . . . . was formed the settlement which gave tone and thought to the whole upper country of the state."[19]

From the Waxhaws the Scotch-Irish immigrants spread widely throughout the uplands of South Carolina, settling in considerable numbers in the present counties of Lancaster, York, Chester, Fairfield, Union, Newberry, Abbeville, and Edgefield; others settled in and around Spartanburg. They came in such numbers as to establish a social order of their own, distinct from that of the lower counties. Their influence upon the political, economic, religious, and cultural development of the Palmetto State was enormous. A case in point is that of John C. Calhoun, whose ancestors were Pennsylvania Scotch-Irishmen. Another eminent Scotch-Irishman of South Carolina was the historian David Ramsay, a native of Lancaster County, Pennsylvania. For many years the Scotch-Irish furnished a large proportion of the physi-

17. David Ramsay, *History of South Carolina*, I, 20-21; George Howe, *The Scotch-Irish and Their First Settlements on the Tyger River and Other Neighboring Precincts in South Carolina*, 10-14.

18. Ramsay, *op. cit.*, 207-210.

19. E. McCrady, *The History of South Carolina under the Royal Government*, 312.

cians, clergymen, lawyers, and schoolmasters of South Carolina, and made substantial contributions to her literature and general culture.[20]

From Pennsylvania came a few pioneers, chiefly of Scotch-Irish stock, to Georgia and the Old Southwest. Alabama, Mississippi, Louisiana, Arkansas, and Texas received a goodly number of their pioneer settlers from the Scotch-Irish of Virginia, the Carolinas, and Tennessee. These were in large measure the descendants of Pennsylvanians who had originally peopled the uplands of the southern seaboard states and may be regarded as being, in some sense, Pennsylvania Scotch-Irish of the dispersion.[21] The connection, however, is too slight to warrant extended treatment in the space at our disposal, nor is it proposed to follow the Scotch-Irish in all their wanderings.

TENNESSEE AND KENTUCKY

Of greater significance than in the case of the Old Southwest was the contribution made by Pennsylvania to the settlement of the New West, especially of Kentucky. Tennessee and Kentucky began to be peopled in the Revolutionary era, and, as the first states west of the Alleghenies to be settled, the story of their beginnings is replete with interest. Our theme has but slight direct bearing upon the early settlers of Tennessee, since Pennsylvania was not largely represented in the inrush of immigrants who laid the foundations of that commonwealth. Only a few of these pioneers came directly from Pennsylvania, although thousands of them were of the Pennsylvania Scotch-Irish stock which, in the preceding generation, had settled in Virginia and the Carolinas. When viewed from this angle, Pennsylvania's share in the settlement of Tennessee was considerable. Following the Battle of Alamance, many Scotch-Irishmen residing in the North Carolina uplands migrated to Tennessee and located on the Watauga and Holston Rivers. The present counties of Washington, Carter,

20. *Ibid.*, 313-318, 623-624; Scotch-Irish Society of America *Proceedings*, I, 125-126; R. H. Taylor, *Ante-Bellum South Carolina*, 1.

21. D. MacDougal, *Scots and Scots' Descendants in America*, 27-28; Scotch-Irish Society of America *Proceedings*, I, 126-129; Hanna, II, *op. cit.*, 32.

Sullivan, Greene, and Hawkins received Scotch-Irish settlers from Virginia and North Carolina as early as 1776. These settlements gradually extended for a distance of at least a hundred miles along the Holston, the Watauga, and the French Broad Rivers. In 1778, other Scotch-Irishmen were among the pioneers who had begun to settle the region around Nashville, far to the west of the Watauga settlement. The Scotch-Irish strain has always been an important racial element in Tennessee, and has been responsible for much of the progress of this state. If Tennessee was the daughter of North Carolina, it is likewise true that many of her sons were the grandsons or the great-grandsons of Pennsylvania Scotch-Irishmen.[22]

While Pennsylvania made but slight direct contribution to the settlement of Tennessee, this could not be said of Kentucky, since here her influence upon early settlement was of great significance. As early as 1750, a few explorers and hunting parties had penetrated the wilds of Kentucky, but important settlements in that region did not begin until 1775, when Boonesborough was founded and the Wilderness Road was begun. For some years this road was the only practicable route to Kentucky, and thousands of immigrants thronged it. Because of the danger incurred at the hands of hostile Indians in Ohio, the Ohio River route did not become popular until after the Revolution. Many Pennsylvania Scotch-Irishmen followed the long trail by way of the Valley of Virginia and the Wilderness Road leading to Kentucky, but the Virginians and North Carolinians constituted the bulk of this immigration, though here again, as in the case of Tennessee, many of these were the descendants of Pennsylvania Scotch-Irishmen of the preceding generation.[23] The initial movement from Pennsylvania was much larger by this route than by the Ohio River route,

22. W. R. Garrett and A. V. Goodpasture, *History of Tennessee,* 49; Theodore Roosevelt, *The Winning of the West,* I, 193-195, II, 267-268, 295; D. Campbell, *op. cit.,* II, 485; Abernethy, *op. cit.,* 52; J. W. Monette, *History of the Discovery and Settlement of the Valley of the Mississippi,* 265-270; Scotch-Irish Society of America *Proceedings,* I, 128, II, 151-161.

23. T. C. Cherry, *Kentucky, the Pioneer State of the West,* 59, 61-62; John Filson, *The Discovery, Settlement and Present State of Kentucky,* 39, 113-117; Thomas Speed, *The Wilderness Road,* 13, 22; W. A. Pusey, *The Wilderness Road to Kentucky,* 9, 13, 16, 51-52, 55; Roosevelt, *op. cit.,* II, 8-9.

but after the Revolution the situation was reversed and a far more numerous company of Scotch-Irishmen flocked into Kentucky by way of the Ohio River. Embarking either at Redstone Old Fort (Brownsville) on the Monongahela or at Pittsburgh, or in some instances at Wheeling, they went down the Ohio in canoes, pirogues, keelboats, and flatboats to Limestone (Maysville), and thence sought the interior of Kentucky, particularly the fertile bluegrass section. It appears that when Kentucky was admitted into the Union, about one-half of its inhabitants were from Virginia, the remainder coming chiefly from Pennsylvania, Maryland, and North Carolina. The immigrants from Pennsylvania are computed at approximately 15 per cent of the population in 1792, and of this number the Scotch-Irish furnished the largest percentage. If the Pennsylvania Scotch-Irish of the dispersion whose fathers and grandfathers had previously settled in the Valley of Virginia and in the uplands of North Carolina be considered, it would be found that they constituted a large proportion of the pioneer population of Kentucky, a goodly number of whose inhabitants are of Scotch-Irish ancestry.[24]

OHIO AND BEYOND

Pennsylvania Scotch-Irishmen furnished a large proportion of the pioneer settlers of Ohio in the rush to that region after the Revolution. The movement of Pennsylvanians across the Ohio River into the new Territory was much later than that which was directed to the South, and was somewhat later than that which had contributed to the settlement of Kentucky. The Scotch-Irish centers in Pennsylvania sent thousands of their sons into the fertile plains of Ohio between 1780 and 1830.[25] They had effected settlements on Mingo Bottom before 1780, and at the mouth of the Scioto River by 1785. In 1799 there was a rush of

24. L. Collins, *Historical Sketches of Kentucky*, 430-431; S. S. Green, *The Scotch-Irish in America*, 20; W. H. Perrin, J. H. Battle and G. C. Kniffin, *History of Kentucky*, 207-208, 226, 548, 552; Monette, *op. cit.*, II, 146, 194; Roosevelt, *op. cit.*, III, 95-98; J. C. Campbell, *op. cit.*, 34.

25. W. H. Hunter, "Influence of Pennsylvania on Ohio," in *Ohio Archeological and Historical Quarterly*, XII, 289, 294; R. E. Chaddock, *Ohio before 1850*, 32-33; C. A. Hanna, *Historical Collections of Harrison County, in the State of Ohio*, 43-44.

Scotch-Irish into Ohio from the Pennsylvania counties of Washington and Fayette, many of this particular group settling in Harrison County. About the same time, Major Stites led a colony of twenty-five persons from Brownsville into the Symmes Tract, where they founded the town of Columbia at the mouth of the Little Miami River. Following the War of 1812 there was a considerable influx of Scotch-Irishmen from Pennsylvania into Coshocton County, Ohio. The Scotch-Irish, in fact, were scattered all over eastern and Central Ohio, besides being largely instrumental in planting Butler, Warren, Preble, Darke, Greene, and Ross Counties in the southwestern part of the state as well.[26]

The influence of Scotch-Irishmen from Pennsylvania on the development of Ohio politically, economically, and socially was one of the most significant factors in the early history of that state. Among these were Jeremiah Dunlevy, the first judge; William McMillan, the first territorial delegate; and Jeremiah Morrow, the first state representative from Ohio, and one of its early governors and United States senators. Twelve natives of Pennsylvania, ten of whom were Scotch-Irishmen, were governors of Ohio prior to 1860. The majority of the members of the lower house of the Ohio Legislature in 1817 were men who had removed to that state from Pennsylvania. President McKinley and Senator Marcus A. Hanna, along with the mother of General Grant, were of Pennsylvania Scotch-Irish stock. Between 1827 and 1840, Pennsylvania immigrants continued to furnish a large proportion of the members of the Ohio Legislature, the percentage ranging in that period from 26 to 37, as compared with from 9 to 25 per cent from all New England, whose influence on Ohio was dwarfed by that of Pennsylvania. Of the ten Ohio counties named after Pennsylvanians, it appears that six were named after Scotch-Irishmen. Pennsylvania Scotch-Irishmen contributed powerfully to the religious and cultural development of Ohio, establishing many churches and schools. Among the leaders was

---

26. Hunter, *op. cit.*, 289, 302; W. E. Hunt, *Historical Collections of Coshocton County, Ohio*, 20, 177; Caleb Atwater, *A History of the State of Ohio*, 132; Hanna, *op. cit.*, 43-44, 59; W. H. Hunter, "Pathfinders of Jefferson County, Ohio," in *Ohio Archeological and Historical Quarterly*, XX, 38-39.

W. H. McGuffey, author of school readers and president of Athens University.[27]

To a less extent than was the case in Ohio, Pennsylvania Scotch-Irishmen participated in the settlement of Indiana and Illinois, and of the remaining states of the Old Northwest. Their influence was fairly strong in Indiana, where they were among the pioneers in settling Fayette and Rush Counties, but they were less noticeable in Illinois. Like the other states of the Union, Pennsylvania sent many of her sons to the Mississippi Valley and shared also in the general westward movement to the Pacific coast, where John W. Geary, a Pennsylvania Scotch-Irishman, was the first mayor of San Francisco.[28] It is not our purpose, however, to follow them so far afield, especially since the special significance of Pennsylvania as a distributing center of population to the South and West belongs to the earlier period which we have described, covering approximately a hundred years, from 1730 to 1830.

Significance of the Dispersion

The foregoing account of the Pennsylvania Scotch-Irish of the dispersion serves to illustrate further the restless temperament, migratory habits, and love of adventure of this racial group—characteristics which prompted them to move freely to any section where they thought they could better their condition. Not content to consider themselves fixtures in a given place merely because they happened to locate there in the first instance, they were ready to accept advantageous offers for their holdings and to move elsewhere if the prospect seemed inviting. It is true that at first they were inclined to be clannish, but this largely disappeared when once they had become identified with their new environment. Hence they were but little concerned with dwelling in distinct communities and seeking thereby to perpetuate a little Scotland on American soil. On the contrary, they became widely dispersed throughout the country. Such was their destiny and such in large part the secret of their great rôle in American his-

27. Hunter, *op. cit.,* 302-304, 307-308; Chaddock, *op. cit.,* 40-46, 69; Scotch-Irish Society of America *Proceedings,* VI, 116.

28. H. M. Tinkcom, *John White Geary,* 54.

tory. Their influence on American life was all the greater because they did not attempt to cling tenaciously to their Scotch brogue or to Old World traditions and customs. The loss to Pennsylvania occasioned by the emigration of so many of them to the South and West was the gain of the country at large, since wherever they went they contributed powerfully to the development of the districts to which they removed. With an estimated 10,000,000 people of Scotch-Irish ancestry in the United States today, there is no large area in the whole country which can be classed as a distinctively Scotch-Irish community, and who will say that it is not better so?

The continued emigration of the Pennsylvania Scotch-Irish to other parts of the country necessarily reduced their numbers correspondingly in this province and state, with the result that in some communities they became a minority where once they had been the prevailing element of the population. In the Cumberland Valley, for example, where they formerly comprised about 90 per cent of the population, they are now outnumbered by the Germans.[29] Various other Scotch-Irish communities in Pennsylvania underwent a similar transformation. In sketching the history of old Derry Presbyterian Church, once a famous Scotch-Irish congregation, Taylor speaks of the "all-prevailing pioneer spirit of their clan" which caused the depletion of the membership through the emigration of young and old to western Pennsylvania or to regions beyond the borders of the province. He further asserts that practically the whole Scotch-Irish colony located in the valley of the Conestoga migrated to Virginia and North Carolina between 1751 and 1789.[30] A similar fate befell the historic Hanover and Paxtang Presbyterian churches, and for the same reason. Egle refers to the "tumble-down church buildings with scarce a score of worshippers where a century ago were hundreds," and laments that all that is left to remind one of "the grand old landmarks of Scotch-Irish settlements" are the silent churchyards with their numerous tablets. The descendants of many of those whose names are on the tombstones are found no longer in this neighborhood, but dwell in cen-

29. John Stewart, "Scotch-Irish Occupancy and Exodus," in Kittochtinny Historical Society Papers, II, 19-20.

30. R. H. Taylor, Historical Sketch of Derry Presbyterian Church, 2, 9.

tral Ohio and Indiana.[31] These are but a few of the many examples that might be cited to show the effects of the emigration of the Scotch-Irish on various communities and churches in Pennsylvania.

Let it not be thought, however, that because of this dispersion only a remnant of the Scotch-Irish survived in Pennsylvania. After all, the majority of them did not emigrate to other colonies or states, and, if their numbers were depleted by removals, it is also true that they were augmented by new arrivals from Ulster throughout the whole of the eighteenth century, and to a less extent in the nineteenth and twentieth centuries. Hence it happened that, despite the great losses resulting to particular communities, the number of Scotch-Irishmen in Pennsylvania still remains impressive, being computed at approximately a million at the present time, and this commonwealth continues to maintain its ascendancy as the headquarters of the Scotch-Irish in America. Many of those who emigrated to the South and West had, in fact, never become firmly rooted in Pennsylvania, where they were sojourners rather than residents. In the outlying states to which they went, they added an intelligent, energetic, and resourceful element to the population, and many of these states would have had a history far less splendid had it not been for the deeds wrought in them by the Pennsylvania Scotch-Irish of the dispersion.

31. W. H. Egle, "Landmarks of Early Scotch-Irish Settlement in Pennsylvania," in *Scotch-Irish Society of America Proceedings,* VIII, 76-78; W. H. McAlarney (ed.), *History of the Sesquicentennial of Paxtang Church,* 45-46.

7

Politics, Law, and Government

We apprehend that as freemen and English subjects, we have an indisputable title to the same privileges and immunities with his majesty's other subjects, who reside in the interior counties of Philadelphia, Chester, and Bucks, and therefore ought not to be excluded from an equal share with them in the very important privilege of legislation. SCOTCH-IRISH MEMORIAL OF GRIEVANCES, 1764.

AMONG THE NOTEWORTHY characteristics of the Scotch-Irish is a genius for politics, law, and government. Their political influence has been large in the history of the nation in general, and of Pennsylvania in particular. Firmly rooted in this state as an important element of the population, their aptitude for politics has here had free play and has carried them far in the political life of the commonwealth. Despite their political propensities, however, they found upon their arrival that conditions in Pennsylvania were such as to preclude their becoming an important political factor in the province for a generation or more. They were the last of the major racial groups to arrive, and meanwhile the Quakers, massed in the three original counties of Philadelphia, Chester, and Bucks, had established themselves so firmly in control of the government that it was a practical impossibility to dislodge them, at least not without a long and bitter struggle. Again, the Scotch-Irish, being far out on the frontier, were at first too busily engaged in conquering the wilderness to devote much time to other matters. Furthermore, as the first line of defense against the savages, it fell to their lot to bear the brunt of the Indian wars. So full were their hands in attending to these concerns that they had small opportunity to engage in politics. Thus it was not until they had established themselves firmly on the soil and, increasing in numbers and resources, had created in the backwoods the ordered institutions of civilized life, that they became a potent influence in public affairs.[1]

SCOTCH-IRISH VERSUS QUAKERS

The significant entry of the Scotch-Irish into Pennsylvania politics dates from about 1744, but especially from the time of the French and Indian War, the issues of which crystallized them into a political party in opposition to the existing order of things. From the beginning they came into conflict with the Quaker government, and the history of Pennsylvania politics from 1755 to 1776 is largely the story of the struggle between them and the Quakers, whose policy they opposed at every point. Temperamentally and politically these two groups were the antipodes of each other, the Scotch-Irish being self-assertive and combative while the Quakers were retiring and pacific. For their personal character, religious toleration, and humane laws the Quakers deserve the applause of posterity, but from the standpoint of party politics they were a narrow, self-centered, illiberal group shrewdly shaping the government to their own ends. Although outnumbered in the province by 1720 and comprising only one-fifth of the population in 1755,[2] they so manipulated affairs as to build up a nice little Quaker oligarchy effectually controlling the government in their own interest with slight regard for the rights of others. This system of minority rule was especially resented by the Scotch-Irish, who found themselves discriminated against by the Quaker assembly. Hence they constituted the principal opposition party, committed to the overthrow of Quaker domination in the province.[3]

Hardly had the Scotch-Irish arrived on the scene, when the Quaker government, scenting a conflict from afar, sought to repress them in every possible way, which policy served only to make them more determined to assert themselves. At first they had to

1. F. D. Stone, "First Congress of the Scotch-Irish in America," in *Pennsylvania Magazine of History and Biography*, XIV, 70.
2. William Smith, *A Brief Review of the Conduct of Pennsylvania for the Year 1755*, 53.
3. C. H. Lincoln, *The Revolutionary Movement in Pennsylvania*, 26.

fight almost alone, but with the passing of time they received some aid from the Anglicans and the Germans in the issues presented in the colonial wars; and still later, on the eve of the Revolution, from the radical Whigs of eastern Pennsylvania. A practical and sagacious people, they took a realistic view of government, especially of the Indian menace. Gradually they formulated a political program such as they conceived to be adapted to the needs of the province in general and of themselves in particular. Mindful of their exposed position on the frontier, they stood stoutly for military preparedness and for a strong policy in relation to the Indians, about whom they had no illusions. Incensed at being deprived of their rightful share in the government, they demanded equality of representation in the assembly on the basis of population, and an equal distribution of the burdens and benefits of government. These demands the dominant Quaker party refused to grant. Reduced to its last analysis, the fundamental issue between the Scotch-Irish and the Quakers was whether Pennsylvania should be a democracy or an oligarchy. On American soil, at least, there could be but one outcome of such a controversy.

The first serious clash between the Scotch-Irish and the Quaker government was over the question of military preparedness, now brought to a head by the French and Indian War. This war found Pennsylvania defenceless in the face of the enemy, and with a pacifist Quaker assembly upon whom rested the responsibility for measures of defense. But with the war at their very doors, the assembly adopted a do-nothing policy. Meanwhile, following the defeat of Braddock, a mob of savages was turned loose upon the province to pillage and massacre the frontier inhabitants, who besieged the government with petitions for protection.[4] With unbelievable negligence, however, the Quaker assembly failed to meet the emergency. Instead of arming for the fray, they expended their energies in petty squabbles with the proprietaries and in seeking to conciliate the Indians whose hands were red with the blood of the frontiersmen. What was wanted and what the Scotch-Irish demanded was not talk with folded hands, not temporizing with

4. *Penn MSS.*, Official Correspondence, IX, 208; *Peters MSS.*, VI, 14; *Colonial Records of Pennsylvania*, VI, 130-131, 533.

murderous savages, but soldiers, forts, munitions, and war to the knife against the invaders of their homes and firesides. To these demands the Quakers turned a deaf ear, thereby abdicating the responsibilities of government and signing their own political death warrants. Far removed from the scene of warfare, secure in their own persons and property, they displayed an amazing indifference to the persons and property of the imperiled frontiersmen.[5]

As pacifists attempting to run the government in time of war, the Quakers were in an impossible position. The "Holy Experiment," now subjected to its first real test, broke down under the pressure of the French and Indian War. With the Quakers composing a constantly dwindling percentage of the population, their system would have collapsed eventually anyhow, but its downfall was hastened and rendered inevitable by the war. The demand of the Scotch-Irish for military preparedness and for a strong Indian policy now had behind it a majority of the people, including not only most of the frontier Germans but of the non-Quaker English of eastern Pennsylvania as well. A numerously signed petition was sent to England demanding the expulsion of the Quakers from the assembly, of which they comprised more than two-thirds of the membership. Finally, when the governor and his council declared war on the Indians and set a price upon their scalps, the Quakers, bowing before the storm, began to retire from the assembly, and their places were filled by those who had no scruples in voting war measures or in fighting the savages.[6] The influences which compelled the retirement of the Quakers from the assembly in 1756 committed the government to a vigorous policy, and thereafter Quaker views on war ceased to be a significant factor in Pennsylvania history.

The retirement of the Quakers from the assembly was but partial and temporary, however, and though they disclaimed responsibility for provincial policy thereafter, they continued, after the lapse of a few years, to compose a large part of its membership and to be influential in the government down to the Revolution. Even those members who were not Quakers came principally from the

5. G. A. Cribbs, *Frontier Policy of Pennsylvania,* 42, 46, 71.
6. Isaac Sharpless, *A Quaker Experiment in Government,* Pt. 2, 9.

three original counties where this sect prevailed and were dependent upon Quaker support for election. The assembly continued to be controlled by the "Quaker party" and to carry out Quaker policies, in the main, from 1764 to 1776. Furthermore, once the French and Indian War was over, the Germans generally returned to their political alliance with the Quakers, leaving the Scotch-Irish to fight their battles against great odds.[7]

With the renewal of Indian barbarities during Pontiac's War, the questions at issue between the Scotch-Irish and the Quakers were revived and accentuated. The depredations committed against the frontier settlers at this time were even more distressing than those following Braddock's defeat, and the inhabitants were compelled to flee for their lives to the more settled parts of the province. The savages, plundering and massacring, advanced far into the interior, but the assembly, again under the control of the Quaker party, adopted a policy of appeasement toward the Indians. By this time the Scotch-Irish, thoroughly enraged over the scalping of their wives and children, had arrived at the conclusion that the only good Indian is a dead Indian, and resolved upon their extermination wherever found. Under these circumstances they committed the so-called Conestoga Massacre in December 1763, exterminating the Conestoga Indians in Lancaster County to the number of twenty. This they did upon discovering evidence that these Indians, though seemingly friendly, had rendered secret aid to those perpetrating the massacres roundabout. Though this act cannot be justified, there were extenuating circumstances which might well be taken into account before passing a too hasty judgment upon the small body of Scotch-Irish rangers residing in Paxton (Paxtang) township in Dauphin County and known as the "Paxton boys," who were responsible for it.[8] It was one of the by-products of the Indian wars and one of the fruits of a mistaken Indian policy upon the part of the assembly. Had the assembly responded promptly and vigorously to the appeals of the frontiersmen for military protection, it would never have occurred.

7. Lincoln, *op. cit.*, 37.
8. Thomas Barton, *The Conduct of the Paxton Men, Impartially Represented*, 8-12, 18-22, 29-30.

When the Scotch-Irish borderers learned that the assembly, while failing to protect the frontier, had taken the Indians of the Lehigh Valley under its protection, they were thoroughly incensed. About two thousand of the frontiersmen had been killed in Pontiac's War, and as many more had been forced to flee to the eastward. "The frontier people of Pennsylvania," says Parkman, "goaded to desperation by long-continued suffering, were divided between rage against the Indians and resentment against the Quakers, who had yielded them cold sympathy and inefficient aid."[9] At various places on the frontier, indignation meetings were held denouncing the provincial authorities in general and the Quakers in particular. The Scotch-Irish were especially outraged because the provincial government had taken under its protection at Philadelphia 140 Indians. Now plainly in a rebellious frame of mind, the Scotch-Irish not only appointed delegates to seek redress of grievances but decided upon a display of armed force accompanying the delegation. Hence, to the number of some five or six hundred, they began their march on Philadelphia in February, 1764.[10]

As the frontiersmen approached Philadelphia a feeling of genuine alarm pervaded the city, and great preparations were made against an attack. The aid of the British regulars was sought while a volunteer army, consisting of six companies of infantry, two companies of cavalry, and a battery of artillery, was quickly enlisted and the quarters of the Indians were fortified with earthworks and cannon. Even the Quakers, "prepared like *Spartans brave,* striding forth with Gigantic Pace to defend their laws and liberty," took up arms in the emergency.[11] Meanwhile the Scotch-Irish, ignorant of the elaborate preparations made to receive them, came steadily on. Intending to enter Philadelphia, but finding the ferries on the Schuylkill guarded and the city defended by a superior force, they halted at Germantown, six miles away. At this juncture Governor John Penn, filled with forebodings, appointed commissioners to

9. Francis Parkman, *History of the Conspiracy of Pontiac*, 295.

10. *Ibid.*, 308; *An Answer to the Pamphlet entitled the Conduct of the Paxton Men, impartially represented*, 3.

11. *An Historical Account of the Late Disturbance between the Inhabitants of the Back Settlements of Pennsylvania and the Philadelphians*, 4.

enter into negotiations with them. Having discovered the hopelessness of attempting a forced entrance into the city, they contented themselves with the appointment of a committee to prepare a memorial of grievances to be presented to the provincial authorities.[12]

This memorial, drawn up by Matthew Smith and James Gibson, was an able document couched in temperate language. Entitled *A Declaration and Remonstrance of the distressed and bleeding Inhabitants of the Province of Pennsylvania,* it was presented to the commissioners on February 13, 1764, and may be taken as a true statement of the grievances of the Scotch-Irish and of other frontiersmen who shared their views at the time.[13] Aware of the fact that they had been roundly censured for the part that a few of them had taken in the Conestoga Massacre and for their march on Philadelphia, they undertook to justify their conduct by explaining the circumstances prompting these acts. The "Declaration" then goes on to express dissatisfaction that nothing was done to rescue the whites in captivity to the Indians, who were openly caressed while at the same time the frontiersmen were compelled to flee for their lives. The Quakers are further roundly accused of seizing the reins of government and establishing a political tyranny in Pennsylvania.[14]

The second part of the Memorial is termed a "Remonstrance," and is addressed particularly to Governor Penn and the assembly in behalf of the then frontier counties of Lancaster, York, Cumberland, Berks, and Northampton, being five of the eight counties of the Pennsylvania of that day. Among the grievances for which redress was demanded, the first and most important was the inequality of representation in the assembly; the others dealt with the military and Indian policies of the government. They declared it to be oppressive and unjust that the five frontier counties, "contrary to the Proprietor's Charter and the acknowledged principles of common justice and equity," were allowed only ten representa-

12. Parkman, *op. cit.,* 314-16.

13. The *Remonstrance* was presented to the Council February 13, 1764; the *Declaration* had been presented to the governor previously. See *Colonial Records of Pennsylvania,* IX, 138-142.

14. *Ibid.,* 4-8.

tives in the assembly whereas the three counties of Philadelphia, Chester, and Bucks were given twenty-six.[15]

The remonstrance inveighs against the policy and acts of the provincial government with reference to the Indians, denouncing in particular the taking under government protection of the 140 Indians then lodged in the barracks of Philadelphia and demanding their expulsion from the province. It further declares it to be contrary to sound policy to permit any Indians to live within the inhabited parts of the province while engaged in an Indian war, and demands a reward for Indian scalps. Complaint is made that many Quakers, without authorization and as individuals only, had repeatedly appeared at conferences where treaties were being made and "openly loaded the Indians with presents," thus causing them to despise the whites. Such action is claimed to be at the root of many of the calamities which the inhabitants had suffered, and it is demanded that "no private subject hereafter be permitted to treat with or carry on a correspondence with our enemies."[16] Such were the principal grievances of the Scotch-Irish. Instead of taking the memorial seriously and doing something to relieve the distresses of the frontiersmen, the Quakers resorted to abuse and ridicule and there followed a pamphlet war pitched on a low plane.

The pamphlet war was ushered in by Franklin, who, as a politician, espoused the cause of the Quakers, upon whose support he relied to further his political career. He promptly published a pamphlet entitled *A Narrative of the Late Massacres, in Lancaster County, of a Number of Indians, Friends of this Province, by Persons Unknown,* in which he gave a very one-sided and prejudiced account of the Conestoga Massacre. For this he was applauded by the Quakers, but he overreached himself and lost his seat in the next assembly. That the object of this publication was political he admitted in a letter to Lord Kames.[17] Franklin's *Narrative* was challenged, however, by the Reverend Thomas Barton, rector of the Episcopal church at Lancaster, who was better acquainted with the circumstances than Franklin could possibly have been. Though

15. Matthew Smith and James Gibson, *Declaration and Remonstrance,* 9-12.
16. *Ibid.,* 16-18.
17. W. H. Egle, *History of Pennsylvania,* 120.

not a Scotch-Irishman, he came to their defense in a letter to a friend in Philadelphia under date of March 17, 1764 (later published in pamphlet form) entitled *The Conduct of the Paxton-Men, impartially represented: with some Remarks on the Narrative.* After quoting at length from the Scotch-Irish memorial, Barton goes on to say that nine-tenths of the inhabitants of the back counties are in sympathy with the Scotch-Irish and either tacitly or openly support them. Attributing the attack of the Quakers upon the frontiersmen to fear of losing their power, he describes the Conestoga Indians as "a drunken, debauched, insolent, quarrelsome crew," of whose treachery in the late war there were undoubted proofs. He is outraged that the Quakers should express more sympathy for the death of "a few savage Traytors than ever they expressed for the Calamities of their Country, and the murders of their Fellow-Christians," and that they should take up arms to protect the savages while doing nothing to protect the settlers on the frontier.[18]

Barton's plea for the frontiersmen was answered by an anonymous writer upholding the Quaker view and belaboring the Paxton men in a lengthy pamphlet entitled *An Answer to the Pamphlet entitled the Conduct of the Paxton Men, impartially represented.* One of the significant signs of the times, as seen in this reply, was the insistence of the Quakers and their apologists upon designating their opponents as "Presbyterians," or rather in the use of the terms "Scotch-Irish" and "Presbyterians" interchangeably—a custom followed generally thereafter by the Quakers and their partisans until the end of the provincial period. The author of the reply to Barton not only uses these terms interchangeably, but implies that the contest between the Quakers and the Scotch-Irish ("Presbyterians") was a struggle between these two groups with the former in the role of St. Michael and the latter in the role of the dragon. Such also was the attitude of the other pamphleteers espousing the Quaker side of the controversy.[19] It appears, however, that no slight part of the Quaker pamphlet war-

18. Thomas Barton, *op. cit.,* 8-9, 17-18, 21-22, 30.
19. *An Answer to the Pamphlet entitled the Conduct of the Paxton Men, impartially represented,* 10, 28.

fare on the Scotch-Irish was motivated quite as much by political considerations as by outraged sentiments regarding the Conestoga Massacre and the march on Philadelphia. It was easy to becloud the issue of equality of representation in the assembly by seeking to overwhelm the Scotch-Irish with abuse for the Conestoga Massacre.[20]

The pamphlet war did not cease until some fifty or sixty pamphlets had appeared, the Quaker party ignoring the main questions at issue and seizing upon the Conestoga Massacre as a weapon with which to belabor the Scotch-Irish, who were not at all fooled by these tactics. On the other hand, the Presbyterians of Philadelphia and vicinity, along with most of the Episcopalians, championed the cause of the frontiersmen, pressing home the grievances of the Scotch-Irish as presented in the memorial. Neither side minced words, but it would appear that, when the pamphlet war was over, the Scotch-Irish supporters had the best of the argument and had succeeded in placing the Quaker party on the defensive. The Scotch-Irish themselves now found full vent for their feelings in heaping upon the Quakers the contempt which they had long felt for this sect, maintaining that people who held such principles could not at one and the same time be sincere in their religion and yet take part in politics; and that such as did take part were therefore hypocrites.[21] They claimed also that the Quakers had shown their political ineptitude in loading the Indians with presents and leading them to despise the whites at the very time when every consideration of sound policy called for relentless war against them. On the other hand, an anonymous pamphleteer, writing in the Quaker interest, not only maintains that the Quakers are the ones who ought to run the government, but makes light of the Scotch-Irish grievances, especially of their demand for a fair representation in the assembly, the political implications of which are intolerable to him.[22]

The Quakers were much twitted for taking up arms and for allowing their meeting-house to become a rendezvous for military

20. E. H. Baldwin, "Joseph Galloway, the Loyalist Politician," in *Pennsylvania Magazine of History and Biography*, XXVI, 180; Barton, *op. cit.*, 9.

21. S. G. Fisher, *Pennsylvania, Colony and Commonwealth*, 249.

22. *A Looking Glass for Presbyterians*, No. I, 5-9; No. II, 16.

purposes at the time of the Scotch-Irish march on Philadelphia. That they had done this was common knowledge. Some of them had worked on the fortifications hastily thrown up to defend the city, while others had shouldered muskets and breathed out fire and vengeance against the "banditti," even going so far, it is said, as to declare that it would be a good thing if every Scotch-Irishman in the province were killed.[23] That they were ready to slay the Scotch-Irish on the one hand and to protect their murderers on the other was a point of view which the frontiersmen would naturally resent. In their turn, the Scotch-Irish were strong in the belief that the progress of the province would best be served by the elimination of the Quakers, at least politically. One Quaker apologist asserts blandly, "I think the *Presbyterians* have been the Authors and Abettors of all the Mischief that's happened to us as a people"—a strange assertion, certainly, in view of the fact that the Presbyterians (Scotch-Irish) had been forced to submit to Quaker domination of the government from the beginning. The Quakers, however, like others who have long been in control of the government, had come to believe that they had a proprietary right to sit in the seat of power and had habitually regarded the demands of the frontiersmen as mere presumption, not to be taken seriously. Nevertheless, the possibility that the Scotch-Irish and their allies might wax strong and seek to overthrow the Quaker oligarchy was very disturbing to the complacent Quakers, who were resolved to exert themselves to the utmost to prevent it.

The Quakers erred in asserting that it was only the Scotch-Irish who had grievances against the provincial government and against the Quakers as its controlling force. John Harris, the founder of Harrisburg and one of the most substantial men in the province, may be taken as representing the view of the English settlers on the frontier. His sympathies were all with the Scotch-Irish, whose grievances he identified with those of the frontiersmen in general In a letter to Colonel James Burd he stoutly champions their cause, declaring that the people would not suffer their liberties and privileges to be taken from them and "if no Redress is Got in this

<hr/>

23. Parkman, *op. cit.*, 315; *The Conduct of the Paxton Men Impartially represented*, 9-12; *An Historical Account of the Late Disturbance* . . . , 4; Fisher, *op. cit.*, 241.

Province, perhaps his Majesty and Parliament may be apply'd to, in a short time."[24] That the cause of the Scotch-Irish was more widely supported than the Quaker pamphleteers and historians would have us believe, may be further seen in a letter of Governor John Penn to his Uncle Thomas in England, under date of June 16, 1764. After stating that the sympathies of the majority of the people were with the frontiersmen, he declares that it was impossible for this reason to apprehend any of the perpetrators of the Conestoga Massacre, or to secure a magistrate to try them even if arrested.[25] After having issued two proclamations denouncing the Paxton men and having exerted himself to have them brought to trial, he finally became convinced that it was impossible to secure their persons and decided to drop the matter, saying, "I am sure there is not enough force in this Government to take any one of them."[26]

It appears that the Scotch-Irish memorial exerted considerable influence upon many people in eastern Pennsylvania who had hitherto paid little attention to conditions on the frontier. The non-Quaker population of Philadelphia and vicinity now realized for the first time the devastating effects of the Indian wars upon the backwoodsmen and the justice of their claims to a greater share in the government.[27] Although the Scotch-Irish did not at this time secure their immediate objectives, they made it exceedingly uncomfortable for the Quaker party, which was placed increasingly on the defensive. Furthermore, it became evident that the frontiersmen were a factor to be reckoned with in the future and that they would not submit indefinitely to be ruled by an eastern oligarchy constituting a minority of the population of the province.

THE STRUGGLE FOR EQUALITY OF REPRESENTATION IN THE ASSEMBLY

As indicated above, one of the major issues of politics in provincial Pennsylvania from 1755 to 1776 was the question of equality

24. *Papers of the Shippen Family: Correspondence*, VI, 95.
25. Penn MSS., *Official Correspondence*, IX, 238.
26. *Ibid.*, 252.
27. *A Dialogue containing some reflections on the late Declaration and Remonstrance of the Back-Inhabitants of the Province of Pennsylvania*, 2.

of representation in the assembly, which the Scotch-Irish and other frontiersmen demanded and the Quaker party opposed. In 1755 the assembly contained thirty-six members, of whom the Quakers, comprising only about one-fifth of the population, numbered twenty-six.[28] Hitherto the Quakers had had everything their own way, but now the Scotch-Irish, aroused by their danger and sufferings, began to organize themselves into a party to seek the removal of the injustices to which they had long been subjected. According to Provost William Smith, head of the College of Philadelphia, writing in 1755:

"There is not perhaps a more flagrant piece of iniquity subsisting among any free people, than the manner in which this province is represented in assembly. We have eight counties and out of thirty-six members, the three older counties, where the Quakers are settled, return twenty-six of this number. The other five counties, settled with people of many other denominations, especially Presbyterians from the North of Ireland, send only the ten remaining members among them. This was the policy of the Quakers at the first erection of the last five counties; by which means, together with their artifices with the Germans, the Quakers are always a vast majority in the assembly, although they are not near one-fifth of the people of the province. . . .

If this piece of iniquity is not speedily redressed, it will be productive of much confusion and ill-blood among ourselves. The Scotch-Irish in particular think that the Quakers have a secret satisfaction in seeing their increasing multitude thinned and beggared in the back counties."[29]

While the Germans of eastern Pennsylvania were in alliance with the Quakers, there were many of these on the frontier who shared the views of the Scotch-Irish with reference to military protection and other matters, especially during the Indian wars. In December, 1755, for example, the Germans brought from a distance of sixty miles the bodies of some of their neighbors who had been massacred by the Indians and placed them at the State-House door, "cursing the *Quakers'* principles, and bidding the Assembly behold the Fruits of their Obstinacy, and confess that their pre-

28. Sharpless, *op. cit.,* 74-75.
29. William Smith, *op. cit.,* 52-54.

tended Sanctity would not save the Province without the use of Means; and at the same time threatening, that if they should come down again on a like Errand, and find nothing done for their protection, the Consequences would be fatal."[30]

The failure of the Scotch-Irish to secure redress of grievances at the time of the presentation of their memorial in 1764 did not deter them from continuing the fight for a just representation in the assembly. Rather, they were encouraged by the support received in the pamphlet war, and from this time forth they became more politically minded and more determined than ever not to relax their efforts until the issue was decided. No matter how much the Quaker party might try to obscure the issue, there could be no doubt that their whole endeavor was to remain entrenched in power by denying to the majority of the inhabitants equality of representation in the assembly. A clear view of the case is presented by a pamphleteer of the time, as follows:

> "For my part I am persuaded that Quaker politicks, and a Quaker faction, have involv'd this province into almost all the contentions and all the miseries under which we have long struggled.
>
> There can never be a greater cause, perhaps no other cause of tumults and complaints in any government, than the people conceiving that unjust laws are imposed on them, and that measures are pursued to which they did not consent. This is the very case with the majority of this province. They are deprived of their share in legislation, and yet cannot prevent, because they are not fairly represented in the Assembly."[31]

Throughout this whole controversy the Scotch-Irish and their supporters repeatedly attributed all their woes to the lack of a fair representation in the assembly. Since they could get no satisfaction from the party in power, they were fast coming to the point where they were ready to join in a movement to overthrow the whole existing political order, peaceably if they could, forcibly if they must. They had also discovered that their sympathizers were more numerous than they had supposed and that, if all the dissatisfied elements of the population could be united, their cause was by no

30. *Ibid.*, Postscript.
31. *The Plain Dealer: or a few Remarks on Quaker Politics*, 3-5.

means hopeless.[32] In 1770 the pressure on the assembly caused it to make some slight concessions in the matter of representation; Berks and Northampton Counties were each allowed an additional member. A further concession was made in the erection of three new counties—Bedford (1771), Northumberland (1772), and Westmoreland (1773), each of which was given one member of the assembly. This did not improve matters much, however, since care was taken that the three original counties should continue to elect a large majority of the assembly.[33]

In the spring of 1776 the assembly, now tottering under the blows administered to it by the radical Whigs of the Revolutionary era and anxious to preserve its own existence if possible, passed a measure providing for seventeen additional members, of whom four were from the city of Philadelphia and thirteen were from the western counties. Even this reapportionment, however, gave the original counties (including the city of Philadelphia) a majority of two, and the goal of the Scotch-Irish was still unattained. This tardy and partial justice failed to stem the tide of revolution which was about to engulf the old order, whose days were numbered.[34] Events moved rapidly in 1776. The conservative and vacillating assembly failed to keep pace with public opinion and rapidly lost the confidence of the people. The revolutionary Provincial Convention of 1776 framed a new state constitution, which sounded the death knell of the Quaker party and of the eastern oligarchy of which it was the controlling element. At long last, the Scotch-Irish had come into their own. Rising to the occasion, they seized with a firm hand the helm of government and, as the dominant force politically, steered the ship of state through the troubled waters of the Revolution. The new constitution, which embodied their demands, remedied all the injustices under which they had groaned, providing for equality of representation in the assembly and for universal male suffrage. Pennsylvania had now become a genuine democracy.

32. Lincoln, *op. cit.*, 54, 109, 113.
33. *Ibid.*, 52.
34. *Votes and Proceedings of the House of Representatives of the Province of Pennsylvania*, VI, 683; J. Paul Selsam, *The Pennsylvania Constitution of 1776*, 100.

The Movement for the Abolition of the Proprietaryship

Another issue over which the Scotch-Irish and the Quakers locked horns was that of the abolition of the proprietaryship. This movement, the object of which was to convert Pennsylvania into a royal colony, was favored by the Quaker party in general, though a few of them refused to support it; but the Scotch-Irish and their eastern allies—the Episcopalians and the Presbyterians of Philadelphia and vicinity—were strongly opposed to it. Parties were formed on new lines, known as the Proprietary and the Anti-Proprietary. The Anti-Proprietary party was composed principally of the Quakers and their German allies, though the Quakers were the controlling factor and shaped the policies of the party. After Thomas and Richard Penn forsook the Church of their father and became Anglicans, the Quakers turned against them, partly for this reason and partly because the Penns resisted taxation of their estates and controlled the whole executive administration through the appointment of judges and members of the council, coupled with secret instructions to the deputy governors. The Germans, without political background and untrained in the ways of practical politics, had from the beginning followed Quaker leadership. Furthermore, many of them, like the Quakers, were noncombatants, and practically all of them had imbibed in the homeland a wholesome distaste for military service. They did not concern themselves greatly about the proprietaryship, but took their cue from the Quakers, with whom they were accustomed to make common cause on most political issues.[35]

The Proprietary party, embracing the Episcopalians and Presbyterians in the east and the Scotch-Irish in the west, favored the retention of the proprietaryship. The Scotch-Irish and the Presbyterians, though not caring for the Episcopalians or for the Penns, were drawn into an alliance with them through a common dislike of the Quakers, whose pacifist policy they detested. Furthermore, the Scotch-Irish were bitterly hostile to the British Government and therefore favored a continuance of the proprietaryship rather than the conversion of the province into a royal colony, ac-

35. W. F. Dunaway, *History of Pennsylvania*, 144.

companied by an extension of the powers of the Crown. As between the Penns and the King, the Scotch-Irish thought the Penns the lesser of the two evils.[36]

These party alignments, dating from about 1755, continued for twenty years, the Quaker-German Anti-Proprietary party being arrayed against the Scotch-Irish- Anglican- Presbyterian Proprietary party on practically all major issues. Franklin, as a practical politician, regularly affiliated with the dominant Quaker party, of which he was one of the leaders. In 1757 he was sent to England by the assembly to appeal to the Crown for the right to tax the proprietary estates, and, after laboring patiently for two years, succeeded in his mission. The assembly, flushed with triumph, now sent him on a second mission to England with a petition to the Crown to convert Pennsylvania into a royal colony. The excitement caused by the discussion and passage of the Stamp Act, however, rendered it inexpedient for Franklin to present the petition, it now appearing that this was no time to enlarge the powers of the Crown. Hence the petition was never presented, and Pennsylvania continued to be a proprietary province until it was changed into an American Commonwealth in 1776. Thus the Scotch-Irish and their allies won a victory on this issue, though it was due to fortuitous circumstances which no one had foreseen.[37]

The Scotch-Irish and the New Political Order

The Quaker party, as noted above, did not represent the sentiment or speak the mind of the majority of the population of the province, but maintained itself in power by resorting to shrewd political devices. In so doing they offended not only the Scotch-Irish, but also the disfranchised lower and middle classes of Philadelphia and, to a certain extent, the frontier Germans, all of whom were interested in democratizing the government. On the eve of the Revolution a movement developed aiming to overthrow the oligarchy and to establish a new political order in Pennsylvania. This movement was actively stimulated by the continental Revo-

36. W. Roy Smith, *Sectionalism in Pennsylvania during the Revolution,* 210; Sharpless, *op. cit.,* 101-102.

37. Smith, *op. cit.,* 211.

lutionary movement leading to war and independence. While the Revolutionary movement was developing on a national scale between 1774 and 1776, there was a parallel movement within the province to overthrow the existing provincial government.[38] As time passed, the provincial government was increasingly subject to attacks by the dissatisfied elements of the population, who united their forces in a common cause. The continental Revolutionary movement against Great Britain led to new party alignments in Pennsylvania. Besides the chronic causes of discontent to which attention has been called, there was now added the more immediate dissatisfaction of the radical Whigs, who were displeased with the conservatism of the assembly on the eve of the Revolution. Its hesitant attitude and dilatory tactics brought it into disfavor with militant whigs like Franklin, Rittenhouse, Reed, Bryan, and McKean. Hence this group united with the Scotch-Irish and other dissatisfied groups to form the radical Whig party, whose objectives were not only to bring Pennsylvania into line with the continental Revolutionary movement, but to democratize the provincial government as well. This party was opposed by the moderate Whigs like Dickinson, Mifflin, Morris, and Wilson, who favored resistance to Great Britain but were unwilling to go as far and as fast as the radical Whigs in promoting aggressive measures. In time, the radical Whigs became known as the Constitutionalists and the moderate Whigs as the Anti-Constitutionalists. The Scotch-Irish, almost to a man, espoused the cause of the radical Whig party, furnishing its principal following and leadership throughout the Revolutionary struggle.

The actual means by which Pennsylvania was transformed from a proprietary province into an American commonwealth was the new political organization developed by the Scotch-Irish in alliance with the eastern radical leaders of the continental Revolutionary movement. This extralegal organization, consisting of the committee of safety, the provincial and county committees of correspondence, and the provincial conventions, supplanted the regular provincial government by absorbing its functions. The final act in

38. Lincoln, *op. cit.,* 241; Selsam, *op. cit.,* 93-96.

this drama was the calling of a provincial convention to meet in Philadelphia on May 20, 1776. While engaged in framing a state constitution, the convention proceeded to assume control of affairs as if the regular proprietary government had never existed, arrogating to itself the executive, legislative, and judicial functions of government. As its last and most important act, the convention framed the Pennsylvania Constitution of 1776, thereby throwing the whole power of government into the hands of the radical Whigs (Constitutionalists) and sounding the death knell of the oligarchy which had ruled Pennsylvania. By virtue of its new Constitution Pennsylvania became one of the most democratic states in the Union.[39]

With the overthrow of the proprietary government, there was an immediate and marked decline in the political influence of the Quakers—a result which was hastened and intensified by the Revolution. The termination of Penn's charter ended their influence as a political force in the commonwealth which they had founded and nourished through its formative years. The victory of the Scotch-Irish was complete, and they became the dominant force in the new government. They were the backbone of the militant Whig party—the party of action, demanding war and independence. Prompt in decision and bold in action, their time had now come and they made the most of it. That their methods were sometimes violent and their acts not always wise must be admitted, but it must also be conceded that at a time when others were vacillating and dilatory, they were resolute and energetic, raising their standard as a rallying point for the Revolution and remaining true to their objectives until independence had been won.

The most masterful and influential figure in the state government during the Revolution was Joseph Reed, a Scotch-Irishman, who led the Constitutionalist party and ruled with a strong hand as President of Pennsylvania from 1778 to 1781. He served on the committee of correspondence, in Congress, and in the continental army, but declined a brigadier-generalship and also the office of Chief Justice of Pennsylvania. After a stormy and picturesque ca-

39. Selsam, *op. cit.*, 183-189.

reer, this ardent patriot and dynamic leader died in 1784 "literally worn out in the service of his country." Another outstanding Scotch-Irish leader in the state politics of the period was George Bryan, Vice-President and President of Pennsylvania. Rising to prominence in state politics during the Revolution, he was one of the most active leaders of the Constitutionalists, and it was mainly through his efforts that the act for the gradual abolition of slavery was passed in February 1880.[40] Sharpless, a Quaker historian, has this to say about the Scotch-Irishman in the Revolutionary era:

"He now had a popular and winning cause which would draw to his side many of the Germans who had hitherto been Quaker allies. He could be avenged for inequitable representation. His militant spirit could find all the vent it needed . . . With the aid of the nonvoting population of Philadelphia he turned out the assembly, and, through improvised councils, seized the reins of government. He overthrew the charter of William Penn . . . . and adopted a new constitution. . . . He penalized loyalists and disfranchised neutrals to his heart's content, and reveled in the undisputed possession of all the rights for which he had been working for many years."[41]

Following the Revolution there was a political reaction which placed the Anti-Constitutionalists in power. The Constitutionalists were essentially the party of war and Revolution, but had always represented a minority as compared to the moderate Whigs and loyalists, and had been able to control the government in the Revolutionary era only because of their aggressiveness as the party of action. Now that the war was over, other forces began to assert themselves and gained the supremacy. With the election of John Dickinson to the Presidency of the Supreme Executive Council in 1781, the Constitutionalists suffered a defeat and thereafter the tide turned definitely against them. The new State Constitution of 1790 was the work of the conservatives, who regarded the Constitution of 1776 as erring on the side of too much democracy.[42] However,

40. S. G. Fisher, *The Making of Pennsylvania*, 178.
41. Isaac Sharpless, "Presbyterian and Quaker in the Revolution," in *Journal of the Presbyterian Historical Society*, III, 211.
42. H. M. Jenkins (ed.), *Pennsylvania: Colonial and Federal*, II, 113-121.

the Scotch-Irish were active in this period under the leadership of William Findley, Robert Whitehill, and John Smilie. In the fight over the ratification of the Federal Constitution in Pennsylvania, they were largely Anti-Federalists, though Thomas McKean favored ratification.

It has been customary for historians to describe the Whiskey Insurrection as a distinctively Scotch-Irish movement, whereas such was not the case. This rebellion was an uprising of the people of the four western counties of Fayette, Westmoreland, Washington, and Allegheny, whose population was by no means exclusively Scotch-Irish, although it is true that this racial group comprised a majority of the people throughout this region. In proportion to their numbers, however, other racial groups were no less active in the insurrection than were the Scotch-Irish, this being especially true of the leaders in the movement. Among those figuring most prominently in the rebellion were Bradford, Holcroft, and Parkinson, who were English; Brackenridge, who was a Scot, but not Scotch-Irish; Herman Husband, who was German; David Phillips, who was Welsh; and Albert Gallatin, a moderating influence, who was French-Swiss. By reason of their greater numbers, however, it was to a considerable degree a Scotch-Irish uprising.[43]

Political Influence of the Scotch-Irish

Space is lacking to call the roll of the host of Pennsylvania Scotch-Irishmen who have distinguished themselves in state and national politics, but a few of the most noteworthy may be listed. In the colonial period James Logan was long the most influential political leader in the province. At various times he held the offices of provincial secretary, commissioner of property, mayor of Philadelphia, acting governor, and chief justice of the province. In the Revolutionary era, James Smith, George Taylor, and Thomas McKean were members of the Continental Congress and signers of the Declaration of Independence, besides rendering other valuable services to the patriot cause. Charles Thomson was secretary of the Continental Congress, and was held in high esteem for his services

---

43. S. G. Fisher, *The Making of Pennsylvania*, 177.

to the Revolution.[44] As has been noted, Joseph Reed and George Bryan were outstanding leaders of the state government as Presidents of Pennsylvania in this period. In the post-Revolutionary period, William Findley, Robert Whitehill, and John Smilie were well out in front as representatives of the ideals and objectives of the frontier democracy.

It is apart from our purpose to deal at length with the activities of the Scotch-Irish of Pennsylvania in the nineteenth and twentieth centuries, but it may be said that throughout this whole period they have been a dominant force in the politics of the commonwealth. Since the creation of the office of governor by the Constitution of 1790, the Scotch-Irish, though at all times outnumbered by both the English and German elements of the population, have furnished twelve of the chief executives of the state, or more than one-third of the entire number.[45] With the passing of time their political genius attained its full outflowering, making them the most politically-minded group in the commonwealth. James Buchanan, who held the important offices of congressman, United States senator, minister to Russia, minister to Great Britain, Secretary of State, and President, besides being for many years the leader of the Democratic party in Pennsylvania, was the only Pennsylvanian to reach the White House. Among the cabinet members furnished by the Pennsylvania Scotch-Irish were William J. Duane, James G. Blaine,[46] John Armstrong, Franklin MacVeagh, Philander C. Knox, Jeremiah S. Black, and Andrew W. Mellon. Other Scotch-Irish political leaders and statesmen were William Maclay, Samuel Maclay, Matthew S. Quay, Robert W. Mackey,

44. According to Douglas Campbell, *The Puritan in Holland, England, and America,* II, 487n: "The Declaration of Independence, as we have it today, is in the writing of a Scotch-Irishman, Charles Thomson, the Secretary of Congress; it was first printed by Captain Thomas Dunlap, another Scotch-Irishman, who published the first daily newspaper in America; a third Scotch-Irishman, Captain John Nixon, of Philadelphia, first read it to the people."

45. The twelve Scotch-Irish Governors were Thomas McKean, William Findlay, David R. Porter, William F. Johnston, James Pollock, Andrew G. Curtin, John W. Geary, John K. Tener, Daniel H. Hastings, Edwin S. Stuart, Robert E. Pattison, and William C. Sproul. John S. Fisher was Scotch-Irish on the distaff side.

46. James G. Blaine was born and bred in Pennsylvania, the home of his ancestors, but removed to Maine when twenty-four years old.

A. K. McClure, George Logan, Thomas A. Scott, John W. Morrison, James Rose, Thomas H. Burrowes, Daniel Agnew, James Ewing, David Fullerton, and Andrew Gregg.[47] A survey of the politics of Pennsylvania since 1790 will show that the Scotch-Irish have held a disproportionate share of the more important political offices, thereby amply sustaining the assertion that throughout this long period they have been politically the most influential racial group in the commonwealth.

Lest the foregoing statement seem too sweeping, let the testimony of others be given to support it. Governor Martin G. Brumbaugh, an eminent Pennsylvania German, bears them this witness: "When the Revolutionary War came on and the Quaker retreated from his aggressive control of the government, it was the Scotch-Irish, backed by a large number of the Pennsylvania Germans, that leaped to the front, won the Revolutionary struggle, and organized the commonwealth of Pennsylvania, and to this day the Scotch-Irish have run Pennsylvania with Dutch aid."[48] Again, J. S. Futhey, historian of Chester County and a representative of the English element of the population, credits the Scotch-Irish of Pennsylvania with having furnished a majority of the legislators, as well as of those in other high official positions in the government.[49] Senator Boies Penrose, who was of Welsh ancestry, said in an address made in 1916: "Pennsylvania received within its borders more nationalities than any other state in the Union . . . but I say to you tonight . . . . that there is none of all those nationalities that has so contributed to the greatness of Pennsylvania as that peculiar Scotch-Irish people whom you represent here tonight."[50] Other evidence might be adduced, but the foregoing testimony from outstanding representatives of the German, English, and Welsh elements of the population will serve to show the historic dominance of the Scotch-Irish in Pennsylvania politics in the last century and a half.

---

47. But that it would be tedious, this list might be extended to great lengths.
48. Pennsylvania Scotch-Irish Society *Proceedings and Addresses*, XIX, 22.
49. Lancaster County Historical Society *Papers*, XI, 230.
50. Pennsylvania Scotch-Irish Society *Proceedings and Addresses*, XXVII, 47-48.

The Scotch-Irish and the Judiciary of Pennsylvania

The Scotch-Irish were even more predominant as members of the bench and bar than as politicians and statesmen. In no other profession did their genius express itself more brilliantly than in the law. Out of all proportion to their numbers, many of them occupied the highest judicial posts in the commonwealth. From the Revolution to 1900 there were fifty-four justices of the Supreme Court of Pennsylvania, of whom twenty-five were Scotch-Irish; and of the sixteen chief justices in that period, nine were of this racial group. John B. McPherson, in his article on "The Judiciary of the Commonwealth," written in 1899, says:

"In five of the counties—Juniata, Perry, Fulton, Butler, and Lawrence—the bench has been solidly Scotch-Irish. In ten others —Mifflin, Blair, Armstrong, Clarion, Westmoreland, Greene, Cameron, Franklin, Fulton, and Beaver—there has been one exception; while in eleven counties—Cumberland, Bedford, Somerset, Union, Snyder, Mercer, Jefferson, Washington, Fayette, Forest, and Indiana—the exceptions have been only two; and in Adams and Huntingdon, only three. In the remaining counties of this region the division has been more nearly equal; but be the majority large or small, it remains true that on every judicial roll in this great section (west of the Susquehanna), except in Lycoming, Elk, and Crawford, there is a majority of some size in favor of the Ulstermen. . . . In Allegheny the Scotch-Irish outnumber the others more than two to one, ten of the eleven judges now upon the bench being of this lineage. . . .

In brief, there have been 376 judges of the Common Pleas or Orphans' Court in Pennsylvania since 1791. Of this number 190, or more than 50 per cent belong to our stock in some degree. . . . Forty-five were on the bench of Philadelphia County. Adding the justices of the Supreme and Superior Courts that have not already been counted while in Common Pleas, brings the number of judges learned in the law since the Revolution to 438. Of this number, 223, or slightly more than half, are Scottish or Scotch-Irish in some degree, of whom only 14 were Scots." [51]

51. John B. McPherson, "The Judiciary of the Commonwealth," in Pennsylvania Scotch-Irish Society Proceedings and Addresses, XXVII, 47-48.

In Philadelphia and vicinity, in the Wyoming Valley, and in the counties bordering on New York, the judges were prevailingly of English ancestry, while in the German counties a majority were Pennsylvania Germans, but even in these localities many of them were Scotch-Irish. In the German counties there were, prior to 1900, some sixty-one judges, of whom twenty-five were Scotch-Irish, who were also largely represented in the counties bordering on Philadelphia.[52]

Of the chief justices of Pennsylvania the most renowned are Thomas McKean, John Bannister Gibson, and Jeremiah S. Black, all of whom were Scotch-Irish. Other Scotch-Irish chief justices of the commonwealth, hardly less distinguished, were Walter H. Lowrie, Daniel Agnew, James P. Sterrett, and James Thompson. There were many Scotch-Irish associate-justices of the Supreme Court of Pennsylvania, among whom may be mentioned George Bryan, John Ross, and George Chambers; and also a disproportionate number of president-judges.[53] Since 1900, the roll of Scotch-Irish judges has been still further greatly increased, many of this racial group sitting on the bench of Pennsylvania today.

52. *Ibid.*
53. *Ibid.*

8

The Scotch-Irish in War

They furnished some of the best soldiers of Washington. The famous Pennsylvania Line was mostly Irish. LECKY

SOLDIERLY QUALITIES OF THE SCOTCH-IRISH

THAT THE SCOTCH-IRISH have a genius for war has been abundantly proved on many a hard-fought battlefield. As their whole history shows, they came of fighting stock and the world well remembers their valiant struggle against great odds at Stirling and Bannockburn under the leadership of Wallace and Bruce. When the descendants of the heroes of Bannockburn migrated to Ulster, their native fibre was but strengthened by their experiences amid hostile surroundings in their new home. Here, at Enniskillen and Londonderry, they again showed the stuff of which they were made, especially in the defense of Londonderry against the overwhelming forces arrayed against them in one of the most famous sieges of history; and the whole world rang with their praise. It was ever their lot to struggle against hostile forces, whether on the Scottish border, or in Ulster, or on the American frontier; nor did they fail to meet unflinchingly every menace to their liberties, from whatever direction it might come.

From the beginning of their migration to Pennsylvania the Scotch-Irish "formed a cordon of defense around the non-fighting Quakers."[1] Constituting the outer fringe of settlement and constantly exposed to Indian ravages, they occupied a position of extreme danger. Thus they became familiar with danger, inured to

1. C. A. Hanna, *The Scotch-Irish*, II, 62.

hardship, and ready at a moment's notice to defend their firesides or to march against the enemy. In war, as in the chase, they were expert in the use of the rifle, which was so commonly employed that it was considered an essential part of household equipment.[2] Grown accustomed to war-alarms, they maintained a martial front, gained considerable military experience, and were seasoned by the very conditions of pioneer life for the hardships of the camp. Even the rude sports of the frontiersmen tended to toughen their physical fibre. Thus they constituted a group of men at once hardy and fearless, and capable of being quickly moulded into an efficient fighting force. In the hands of most men the heavy rifle of that day was cumbersome, but to the Scotch-Irishman it was a plaything which he handled with ease and skill.[3]

The usefulness of the Scotch-Irish as a shield against the Indians was early recognized by James Logan, who, though a Quaker, believed in defensive warfare. In a letter to James Steel, dated November 18, 1729, he says:

> "About this time [1720] a considerable Number of good Sober People came in from Ireland, who wanted to be Settled, at yᵉ Same time it happen'd that we were under some apprehensions from northern Indians of whose claims to the Lands on Sasquehannah I was not then sensible. . . . I therefore thought it might be prudent to plant a Settlemᵗ of fresh men as those who formerly had so bravely defended Derrry and Inniskillen as a frontier in case of any Disturbance. Accordingly the Township of Donegal was settled some few by Warrᵗˢ at the certain price of 10 pounds per hundᵈ but more so, without any."[4]

Himself a Scotch-Irishman, nobody knew better than James Logan the fighting qualities of his brethren from Ulster. Thus even from the beginning of their arrival in any considerable numbers, their services were in demand as a wall of defense between the

2. "Almost every soldier equalled William Tell as a marksman, and could aim his weapon at an opposer with as keen a relish. Those from the frontiers had gained this address against the savages and beasts of the forests." Cited by E. L. Parker, *The History of Londonderry, comprising the towns of Derry and Londonderry, New Hampshire*, 106.

3. "Their rifles were inordinately long and heavy, bored out of solid iron for small bullets of sixty to the pound, and carrying with precision up to eighty yards," says A. G. Bradley, "The Ulster Scot in the United States," in *Nineteenth Century*, LXXI, 1128-1129.

4. *Penn MSS.*, Official Correspondence, II, 101.

noncombatant Quakers and the Indians, and such they were throughout the whole provincial era. For this protection, however, they received scant thanks from the Quakers, as we have seen in the preceding chapter.

THE SCOTCH-IRISH IN THE FRENCH AND INDIAN WAR

The initial appearance of the Scotch-Irish on the battlefields of Pennsylvania was in the French and Indian War, which was the first experience of this province in actual warfare. The previous colonial wars had not seriously affected Pennsylvania, but in this war the situation was different. The struggle originated in Pennsylvania over the rivalry of the French and English for the possession of the Ohio Valley, and here occurred some of its most notable conflicts. In this war also the inhabitants of the province experienced for the first time the horrors of Indian massacres. It is apart from our purpose to go into the details of the French and Indian War, or of the other wars that followed, other than to call attention to the part played in them by the Scotch-Irish of Pennsylvania. In these conflicts of provincial and Revolutionary times, though themselves less numerous than the other major racial groups, they furnished by far the largest percentage of officers and troops of any of them. Partly because they were a practical people, partly because they came of fighting stock, and partly because of their post of danger on the frontier, they had always favored military preparedness in the form of militia, forts, and munitions. But unfortunately for them, as for the people at large, the shortsighted policy of the provincial government had left the inhabitants defenceless in the face of attack.

Of all the Thirteen Colonies, Pennsylvania alone was wholly unprepared for war. Having been ruled up to this time by Quakers, preparation for war had been consistently neglected, with the result that the province was peculiarly vulnerable to attack. Despite this fact, the assembly displayed an unwillingness to vote adequate supplies of men and money when war had actually begun and the savages were on the warpath. General Braddock, writing to Governor Morris from Williamsburg before his ill-fated expedition against Fort Duquesne was under way, expressed his astonishment at seeing "one of the Principal Colonies preserving a neutrality when his Majesties Dominions are invaded, when the Enemy is on the Frontier."[5]

The Indians, once friendly, had been alienated by the treatment accorded to them by the proprietaries, particularly in the notorious "Walking Purchase of 1737" and in the Albany Purchase of 1754. Gathered around their council fires in the depths of the forests, they rehearsed their grievances and swore revenge. Now, after a long peace with the whites extending over a period of seventy-four years, they donned their war-paint and allied themselves with the French, who promised them the restoration of their hunting grounds. The defeat of Braddock was the signal for turning loose upon the province a horde of savages bent upon massacre and pillage. The full fury of these attacks reached a climax during the months of September and October, 1755. The cabins of the settlers on the frontier were burned and many of their inhabitants were either massacred or captured and held for torture. Fleeing before the invaders, the suddenness of whose attack allowed no time to make a stand, they sought refuge in the eastern counties, while the assembly was besieged with petitions from the outlying districts for energetic measures of defense in view of the impending danger.[6] Marauding bands of savages, chiefly the Shawnees and the Delawares, continued their depredations on the more exposed sections of the province, inhabited mainly by the Scotch-Irish, throughout the winter of 1755-1756.

With war at their very doors and massacres of the inhabitants occurring daily, the ineptitude of the Quaker assembly may be seen from the following letter of Governor Robert Hunter Morris to General Shirley, November 6, 1755:

"Further intelligence that I have received from the Westward giving an Account of the destruction of some of our Inhabitants upon which I sent another Message to my Assembly but have no reason

5. *Penn MSS.*, Official Correspondence, VII, 9; His letter was dated February 20, 1755.
6. *Colonial Records*, VI, 680; *Penn MSS.*, Official Correspondence, VII, 151, VIII, 73; *The Pennsylvania Journal and Weekly Advertiser*, November 27, 1755; December 11, 1755; December 18, 1755; "List of Pennsylvania Settlers Murdered, Scalped, and taken Prisoners by the Indians, 1755-1756," in *Pennsylvania Magazine of History and Biography*, XXXII, 309-319.

to expect any aid from them as they tell me in Answer to my first Message that they propose to gain the Affections of the Indians now Employed in Slaughtering the People and are entering into an Enquiry what Injustice has been done them. Such a Conduct at this Time when hardly an hour passes without bringing some accounts of fresh Murders is to me shocking beyond parallel and argues a very great Indifference as to the Happiness or Misery of the People. In this Situation of Affairs without Men, Arms or Munitions at my disposal, I do not see how I can Protect the People or secure the Province from being laid waste unless you will supply me with Troops and money for that purpose; the former I have already applyed for and the latter I must now desire you will furnish me with."[7]

Replying from his headquarters at Albany, Governor Shirley explained his inability to furnish the desired aid on account of the great demands elsewhere, and took occasion to censure the assembly severely for its folly. He expressed himself as unable to understand how the assembly could be so utterly lacking "in their duty to his Majesty and a sense of the miseries of the people" as to refuse protection to the inhabitants.[8] Richard Peters, secretary of the province, was no less disgusted with the situation, and said in a letter to the proprietaries, November 25, 1775: "In the midst of all this misery, the citizens are doing their business as usual, without much seeming concern; they neither muster, arm, nor fortify nor make one effort for the Relief of the Back Inhabitants . . .; and this has much dispirited the country People."[9] Of all those who were aroused by the incompetence of Quaker government in the existing emergency, there were, however, none quite so much disgusted as its principal victims—the Scotch-Irish. Despite the massacres perpetrated by the Indians, the year 1755 closed without war being declared against them. The general sentiment of the people demanded a declaration of war, but the Quaker assembly held up its hands in holy horror at the suggestion and was all for peace at any price. Finally, Governor Morris, disregarding the remonstrances of the Quakers and acting on the advice of his council, proclaimed

7. *Penn MSS.*, Official Correspondence, VII, 151.
8. *Ibid.*, 153.
9. Rev. Richard Peters: *Letters to the Proprietaries of the Province of Pennsylvania, 1755-1777*, 19.

war against the Delawares and Shawnees and offered bounties for their scalps. Although the Quakers inveighed against these measures, they were soon to learn that the general body of the people would no longer tolerate their neglect in providing for the defense of the province. As we have seen, the Quakers now lost control of the assembly, and the government passed definitely out of their hands in 1756, never to be fully regained.

With the overthrow of the Quakers, energetic measures were taken to arm the province for war. Two hundred forts were erected on the frontier, and measures were adopted to supply men and money for defense. Moreover, the Scotch-Irish organized voluntary bands of frontiersmen, known as rangers, to defend their homes against the Indians whenever an emergency arose demanding prompt efforts for protection; they also furnished the larger part of the garrisons of the forts and the soldiers in the militia. From this time forth they became the deadliest foes of the savages, about whom they cherished no illusions. Others might seek to invest the Indian with romance and to descant at length upon the primal virtues of the "noble savage," but to the Scotch-Irishman he seemed bloodthirsty, cruel, and treacherous; and not without cause was he thus regarded. Witherow has summed up the Scotch-Irish view, as follows:

> "The Indian has a dislike, well-nigh unconquerable, to all labor; he can with difficulty be confined within limits. . . . He is usually, in his wild state, not generous, but savage, treacherous, and cruel . . . His method of making war is never open and manly. He skulks in ravines, behind rocks and trees; he creeps out in the night and sets fire to houses and barns; he shoots down, from behind a fence, the ploughman in his furrow; he scalps the woman at the spring, and the children by the roadside, with their little hands full of berries. He lounges about, idle and dirty, and forces the women of his tribe to do all the work. He is proud as Lucifer, and yet will beg like the lazzaroni."[10]

If to this general characterization of the Indian be added the many first-hand accounts of his actual performances, the Scotch-Irish point of view is readily understandable.[11] The Quakers and

10. B. J. Witherow, *The Insurrection of the Paxton Boys*, 645.
11. See Lazarus Stewart's account of Indian barbarities, cited by Witherow, *op. cit.*, 653.

the inhabitants of Philadelphia and vicinity in general, not being themselves in danger of being scalped by the Indians, displayed an amazing indifference to the dangers and sufferings of the frontiersmen. In view of the fact that the savages never got that far on their marauding expeditions, they felt secure in the possession of their lives and property. The Quakers in particular turned a deaf ear to appeals for protection, and talked about appeasing the Indians. To the Scotch-Irishman, this sounded like trying to pat a rattlesnake on the back when he was coiled to spring upon his victim; he was no appeaser. Having experienced the butcheries of the savages, he knew better. Nothing if not practical, he was convinced that the only way to bring the treacherous foe to lay down the hatchet was to knock some sense into his head with the butt of a musket, to treat force with force, to give him a sample of his own medicine, to carry the war into his haunts and to shoot him in his lair. At least that was the way he reasoned, and he did not greatly appreciate the attitude of those who, themselves immune from attack, assumed a self-righteous attitude and called him names. As for their policy of appeasement, he regarded it as the essence of asininity.

A weak point in the provincial method of warfare hitherto had been the failure to assume the offensive against the Indians. It was now proposed by the Scotch-Irish to carry the war into the enemy's country. The two chief strongholds of the savages in Pennsylvania were Kittanning on the Allegheny and Logstown on the Ohio. These places served as headquarters where they stored their plunder, kept their prisoners, and accumulated supplies of arms and munitions for their expeditions. It was decided to send an expedition against Kittanning, and Governor Morris selected Colonel John Armstrong, a Scotch-Irishman living at Carlisle, to raise a force for this purpose. Colonel Armstrong, who was the most distinguished soldier of provincial Pennsylvania, first came into prominence as the leader of the expedition against Kittanning; later, he was chosen to command the Pennsylvania militia in General Forbes's expedition against Fort Duquesne in 1758. In the Revolution he was the first brigadier-general to be appointed by Congress (February 29, 1775), and subsequently became major-general of the Pennsylvania militia. He served as member of Congress in 1779-1780, and again in 1787-1788. Armstrong County, Pennsylvania, was named after him.[12]

Colonel Armstrong's forces were recruited almost entirely from the Scotch-Irish of Cumberland, Lancaster, and Dauphin Counties, and his venture, which was the first attempt in Pennsylvania to assume the offensive against the Indians, was to all intents and purposes a Scotch-Irish expedition. Gathering about three hundred men at Fort Shirley on the Juniata in August, 1756, and advancing by rapid marches, Colonel Armstrong arrived within six miles of Kittanning on September 7. After sending out a reconnoitering party to gather information, he decided to attack at daybreak next morning. The Indians, taken by surprise, were decisively defeated. Having burned the village, Armstrong made no attempt to pursue the fleeing savages, but withdrew rapidly before they could rally and render his position hazardous. The destruction of Kittanning was a severe blow to the Indians, lowering their morale and causing them for a time to desist from further ravages. Their leader, one Captain Jacobs, was killed in the battle and several other important chieftains shared his fate.[13] More than fifty Indians were killed outright and others were wounded, while Armstrong's casualties were fewer than twenty. In his account of the battle to Thomas Penn, Richard Peters states that: "All their Council Belts were taken and brought here, their Magazine of Goods burned and all that they have got from the French for English Scalps were plundered by us and taken from them."[14] The whole province rang with the praises of Armstrong and his men. The editor of the *Pennsylvania Journal and Weekly Advertiser* declared that, "On the whole, it is allowed to be the greatest Blow the enemy received since the War began, and if well followed may soon make them weary of continuing it."[15] The alarm occasioned by Indian incursions subsided considerably thereafter, and the inhabitants felt a greater sense of security, which was increased by

12. J. W. King, "Colonel John Armstrong," in *Western Pennsylvania Historical Magazine*, X, 129-144.

13. *Colonial Records*, VI, 257-263; *Penn MSS.*, Official Papers, VIII, 165, 185.

14. *Penn MSS.*, Official Papers, VIII, 185.

15. Edition of September 23, 1756.

the measures taken by the new non-Quaker assembly to raise a militia and to build forts at intervals along the frontier from the vicinity of Easton to the present Fulton County near the Maryland line. Thenceforth, except for a few spasmodic raids by irresponsible Indian bands, there were no important attacks by the savages during the remainder of the war, insofar as Pennsylvania was concerned.

Meanwhile, under the leadership of William Pitt, the British bestirred themselves for a more vigorous prosecution of the war on all fronts. To relieve Pennsylvania, Maryland, and Virginia from Indian depredations and to drive the French out of Pennsylvania, the British high command decided to attempt the capture of Fort Duquesne and, in the fall of 1758, appointed General John Forbes to lead an expedition against that strategic stronghold. General Forbes's force numbered about 6000 men, composed of some 1600 British regulars besides colonial militia, chiefly from Pennsylvania, Maryland, and Virginia. The Pennsylvania militia numbered 2700 men under the command of Colonel Armstrong, while Washington commanded the remainder of the militia. Here again the Scotch-Irish furnished the greater part of Pennsylvania's contingent mustered for this expedition,[16] which resulted in the capture of Fort Duquesne and the expulsion of the French from Pennsylvania. Though the war was later brought to a triumphant conclusion on other fronts, this terminated the struggle insofar as fighting on Pennsylvania soil was concerned. The French, expelled from the Forks of the Ohio, were forced to evacuate the forts at Presque Isle, Le Boeuf, and Venango, and their flag disappeared permanently from Pennsylvania. The English now occupied these forts and held them as lonely outposts in the forest. Along Forbes's Road they held also the two small forts of Ligonier and Bedford, between Fort Pitt and Carlisle.

From the foregoing account of the French and Indian War it will be noted that the Scotch-Irish were not only the greatest sufferers at the hands of the Indians, but also that they furnished the leadership and were the backbone of the resistance offered by Pennsylvania to the enemy in the conflict. This they did despite

16. *Penn MSS.*, Official Correspondence, IX, 124.

the fact that their numbers were not one-fourth the population of the province.

THE SCOTCH-IRISH IN PONTIAC'S WAR

Although the Treaty of Paris, concluded between France and England in 1763, seemed to give promise of a long peace for the Thirteen Colonies, in reality it proved to be merely the signal for a new Indian outbreak with its accompanying barbarities. The cession to the English of all the Indian lands in the territory of the French caused an uprising of the savages more terrible than anything that had gone before. Hardly had the ink dried on the treaty when Pontiac's War began. Pontiac, an able chieftain of the Ottawas, headed a formidable confederacy of the Indian tribes in a desperate attempt to drive the whites back to the sea. With the utmost ferocity the enraged savages attacked the British forts, capturing all the most important ones except Fort Detroit and Fort Pitt. The weak garrisons at Presque Isle, Le Boeuf, and Venango were surprised and captured, and the forts demolished. Fort Bedford and Fort Ligonier, weakly protecting the long line of communications between Fort Pitt and the East—and even Fort Pitt itself—were in imminent danger of capture. So unexpected was the uprising that the settlers on the frontier were wholly unprepared to meet it, and fled for their lives to the eastern settlements. Shippensburg alone was crowded with 1500 fugitives, and Carlisle and other places were filled with them. The depredations committed against the frontiersmen were of the most distressing nature. The savages, plundering and massacring the inhabitants, burning their cabins and destroying their crops, advanced almost to Carlisle, where "every Stable and Hovel in the Town was crowded with miserable Refugees, who were reduced to a State of Beggary and Despair."[17] Circumstantial stories were told of men tortured and burned over a slow fire, of a schoolmaster and nine of his pupils killed and scalped, of a woman roasted, and of men's eyes pierced with awls and their bodies left with pitchforks sticking in them.[18]

17. *Pennsylvania Gazette*, July 28, 1763; August 4, 1763.
18. Witherow, *op. cit.*, 651-653.

Meanwhile Fort Pitt was invested and all communication with the East was cut off. General Amherst, in command of his Majesty's forces in America, commissioned Colonel Henry Bouquet to march to the relief of the beleaguered garrison. Colonel Bouquet, a capable soldier and a seasoned veteran of many campaigns, set out from Carlisle July 23, 1763, with his little army of about five hundred regulars and some Scotch-Irish rangers from Lancaster and Cumberland Counties.[19] Having advanced to within twenty miles of Fort Pitt, he encountered the Indians, who dropped the siege in order to waylay him. Here was fought the Battle of Bushy Run, the most important battle against the Indians in the history of Pennsylvania, resulting in a decisive victory for the British forces. This engagement turned the tide against the savages, and the settlers gradually returned to their devastated homes and their interrupted activities.[20] Small bands of Indians continued their raids during the winter of 1763-1764, but these were never so extensive nor so disastrous as the earlier attacks. Meanwhile, however, the frontiersmen had organized themselves into bands of rangers, and invariably routed such Indian forces as attacked them. The blood of the Scotch-Irish was up and, hardened by their experiences, they pursued the savages and shot them without mercy wherever they found them.[21]

Following the Battle of Bushy Run, Colonel Armstrong collected a force of about three hundred Scotch-Irishmen from the vicinity of Shippensburg, Bedford, and Carlisle, organized them into companies under Captains Laughlin, Patterson, Bedford, Crawford, and Sharp, and led them in an expedition against the Indians at Muncy and Great Island. Assembled at Fort Shirley on the Aughwick, the expedition started on September 30, 1763, and advanced rapidly against the savages. On their arrival at Muncy, however, it was discovered that the Indians had deserted their settlements in this vicinity some days earlier, and no engagement was fought. Nevertheless, an Indian village was demolished, and at Great Island a large quantity of grain and other provisions

19. *Frontier Forts of Pennsylvania*, I, 485.
20. T. F. Gordon, *History of Pennsylvania*, 401-403.
21. *Ibid.*, 404.

was destroyed.[22] This expedition had a salutary effect upon the minds of the Indians, gave the settlers in that region a greater sense of security, and still further enhanced the reputation of Colonel Armstrong and his Scotch-Irishmen as redoubtable Indian fighters. It served also to emphasize again the wisdom of attacking the savage in his lair, and to show him that this was a game at which two could play; it was now his turn to feel insecure in the possession of his life and property. Always fond of hunting, the Scotch-Irish were now getting around to the point where they considered hunting the savages as the most exciting sport in which they had ever engaged.

Two Scotch-Irish Presbyterian ministers figured prominently in the Indian wars. In 1755 Reverend John Steel, pastor of East and West Conococheague Presbyterian churches (now Greencastle and Mercersburg, respectively), organized a company of rangers and, being unanimously elected captain, was commissioned the following year by the provincial government. He was ordered by Governor Morris "to take post at McDowell's Mill upon the road to Ohio, which you are to make your headquarters and to detach patrolling parties from time to time, to scour the woods in such manner as you shall judge most consistent with the safety of the inhabitants." Fort Steel, or "Rev. Steel's Fort," erected in 1755 on the south side of Conococheague Creek, shortly after Braddock's defeat, was well known in the Indian wars.[23] An even more renowned border captain was Reverend John Elder, pastor of Derry and Paxtang churches. He organized a daring band of rangers, composed mostly of members of his congregations and known as the Paxton Rangers or Paxton Boys. Ranging the settlements from the Blue Mountains to the Susquehanna River, they gave a sense of security to the inhabitants of that region and were a terror to the Indians. Both of these famous organizations were composed of Scotch-Irishmen recruited from the present Cumberland, Franklin, Lancaster, and Dauphin Counties.

22. Francis Parkman, *History of the Conspiracy of Pontiac*, 285; *Pennsylvania Gazette*, October 13, 1763, and October 20, 1763.

23. *Frontier Forts of Pennsylvania*, I, 548-549; I. H. M'Cauley, *Historical Sketch of Franklin County, Pennsylvania*, 119.

Under the command of Colonel Elder were three companies of rangers commanded by Captains Lazarus Stewart, Matthew Smith, and Asher Clayton, organized at the outset of Pontiac's War, in which they played a conspicuous part. According to Egle, "The Paxtang rangers were truly the terror of the Indians; swift on foot, excellent horsemen, skillful in pursuit or in escape, dexterous as scouts, and expert in manoeuvering."[24]

In Pontiac's War, as in the French and Indian War, the brunt of the Indian attacks fell upon the Scotch-Irish, who furnished the only effective resistance to the savages offered by Pennsylvania in the struggle. The suddenness of the Indian attack left the frontiersmen no recourse in the beginning except to flee for their lives to the more settled parts of the province. Promptly thereafter, however, they proceeded to organize bands of rangers for their protection and, at the first good opportunity, marched against the enemy, as we have seen. The war was brief and but small opportunity was given to the inhabitants to organize forces for defense. The provincial government came tardily to the relief of the distressed frontiersmen by raising seven hundred recruits in the summer of 1763, but their main reliance was on their own right arm.

THE SCOTCH-IRISH IN THE REVOLUTION

The same fighting qualities and the same rough, hardy, outdoor life which had rendered the Scotch-Irish the recruiting ground for soldiers in the French and Indian War and in Pontiac's War found even greater play in the Revolution. They alone of the major racial groups had any unanimity of opinion respecting war and independence, and they alone appear to have had no Tories and no pacifists in their ranks.[25] With great enthusiasm they espoused the cause of the Revolution and marched with alacrity

24. W. H. Egle, *History of Pennsylvania*, 108-110.
25. W. E. H. Lecky, *A History of England in the Eighteenth Century*, II, 262; S. G. Fisher, *The Making of Pennsylvania*, 177. See also the poem of Mrs. Samuel Evans:

> "And when the days of trial came
> Of which we know the story
> No Erin son of Scotia's blood
> Was ever found a Tory."

to the battlefield. They did not love the English, who had oppressed them grievously in Ulster, which they left "with hearts
burning with indignation," and they asked nothing better than
an opportunity to avenge their wrongs.[26] According to Froude,
"The resentment which they carried with them continued to burn
in their new homes; and in the War of Independence, England
had no fiercer enemies than the grandsons and great-grandsons
of the Presbyterians who had held Ulster against Tyrconnell."[27]
This attitude of hostility toward England was increased by the
passage of the Stamp Act, the Townshend Revenue Acts, and the
Coercive Acts, with the result that the Scotch-Irish were in
thorough sympathy with the movement for independence, which
they were among the first to promote and which they consistently
supported with their best endeavors. The English racial group in
the province, with its large number of Quakers and Tories, was
divided on the issue of war and independence, as were the Germans with their noncombatant sects of the Mennonites, Amish,
Dunkers, and Schwenkfelders, but the Scotch-Irish maintained a
united and militant front throughout the struggle.

That the Scotch-Irish played a conspicuous rôle in the Revolutionary War is universally conceded. In England they were recognized as the head and front of the "Rebellion." Horace Walpole
rose in the House of Commons to say: "There is no use crying
about the matter. America has run off with a Presbyterian parson,
and that is the end of it,"[28] and Lecky informs us that "the
famous Pennsylvania line was mostly Irish."[29] Equally to the
point is the statement of Butler that, "It was the Presbyterians of
Ulster, driven from their homes by the mistaken religious and
economic legislation of the eighteenth century, who furnished the
backbone of the armies that put an end to the rule of England in

26. Lecky, op. cit., 262.

27. James Anthony Froude, The English in Ireland in the Eighteenth Century, I, 392.

28. E. C. McCartney, The Presbyterian Church in Western Pennsylvania, and the
Making of the Nation, cited on page 7. Attention is again called to the fact that the terms
"Presbyterians" and "Scotch-Irish" were used interchangeably by writers in colonial times,
when referring to America, as also were the terms "Scotch-Irish" and "Irish." At the
time of the Revolution there were about 70,000 Scotch-Irish in Pennsylvania, but only
about 5,000 Catholic Irish.

29. Lecky, op. cit., 262.

what is now the United States."[30] That the Pennsylvania Line of the Continental army was predominantly Scotch-Irish is seen from the fact that it was called by General Henry Lee "The Line of Ireland."[31] These statements are reinforced by Isaac Sharpless, the Quaker scholar and historian, who, in speaking of the part played by the Scotch-Irishman of Pennsylvania in the struggle, says: "He did not waver. He now had the chance for which he was waiting. . . . So far as Pennsylvania was concerned, the Revolution was three fourths at least a Presbyterian [Scotch-Irish] movement."[32] Throughout the country generally the Scotch-Irish rallied strongly to the patriot cause, especially in Pennsylvania, Virginia, and the Carolinas, but inasmuch as they were much more numerous in Pennsylvania than elsewhere, it followed naturally that this colony furnished more officers and soldiers of this racial strain than did any of the others. General Morgan's famous sharpshooters from Virginia were mostly Scotch-Irish, and at the decisive battle of King's Mountain the American army was composed almost entirely of them. The Scotch-Irish of Pennsylvania were superior to those found elsewhere in America only in numbers. Wherever found, they stood shoulder to shoulder in defense of American liberty, whether civil or religious, in the forum or in the field.

The general attitude of the Pennsylvania Scotch-Irish in the Revolution is shown in the two declarations made by them when the subject of independence was uppermost in the minds of the people, but before public sentiment in this province had fully crystallized on this issue. The first of these was the "Westmoreland Declaration." On May 16, 1775, a number of the inhabitants of Westmoreland County, being mostly Scotch-Irish, assembled at Hannastown (Hanna's Town),[33] the county seat, and adopted resolutions known as the Westmoreland Declaration, in which

30. William F. T. Butler, *Confiscation in Irish History*, 253.

31. Edward F. Roberts, *Ireland in America*, 32.

32. Isaac Sharpless, "Presbyterian and Quaker in Colonial Pennsylvania," in *Journal of the Presbyterian Historical Society*, III, 212; see also, Maude Glasgow, *The Scotch-Irish in Northern Ireland and in the American Colonies*, 305.

33. Hannastown at this time consisted of about thirty log houses, a court house, a jail, and a small fort.

they protested against the oppressive acts of Great Britain and expressed their willingness to oppose these with their lives and fortunes. The immediate occasion of these resolutions was the tidings of the battles of Lexington and Concord, which aroused the patriotic fervor of the people. The preamble recited that Great Britain was attempting to enslave the people of Massachusetts Bay; that there was reason for believing that the other colonies would share the same fate; that it was therefore the duty of all to resist this oppression; and "that for us, we will be ready to oppose it with our lives and fortunes. And the better to enable us to accomplish it, we will immediately form ourselves into a military body to consist of companies to be made up out of the several townships under the following Association of Westmoreland County." Five resolutions followed, in which those present pledged themselves to organize a "regiment or regiments"; to train themselves in military exercises; that "should our country be invaded by a foreign enemy, or should troops be sent from Great Britain to enforce the late arbitrary acts of its parliament, we will cheerfully submit to military discipline, and to the utmost of our power resist and oppose them" and would join any concerted plan for the defense of America. They declared that they did not desire "any innovation" but only the restoration of their liberties as they existed before the Stamp Act, and that when "the British Parliament shall have repealed their late obnoxious statutes . . . this our association shall be dissolved; but till then it shall remain in full force, and to the observance of it we bind ourselves by everything dear and sacred amongst men."[34]

Having adopted these resolutions, steps were promptly taken to organize a battalion of associators under the command of Colonel John Proctor; and, somewhat later, another battalion commanded by Colonel John Carnigan. The association thus formed did not serve as a regiment in the Continental Army, though many of the associators later saw service under Washington or against the Indians on the frontier. While these resolutions cannot be called a declaration of independence, they were

34. W. P. Breed, *Presbyterians and the Revolution*, 61-63.

"singularly bold and defiant" and virtually served an ultimatum on the British government that its authority would be resisted unless grievances were redressed.[35] No resolutions adopted in the country in 1775 went farther than these. It is not claimed that all the men gathered at Hannastown on this occasion were Scotch-Irish, but only that this racial group predominated in that region and that the Westmoreland Declaration is essentially a Scotch-Irish document, and that the militia companies formed under its stimulus were composed principally of Scotch-Irishmen.

Another episode illustrating the spirit of the Scotch-Irish in the Revolution is that known as "The Pine Creek Declaration," put forth by the "Fair-Play" settlers in present Clinton County. These were a group of Scotch-Irishmen who had settled as squatters without the bounds of the Land Purchase of 1768, on the West Branch of the Susquehanna above and below Pine Creek. They comprised "a set of hardy adventurers [who] seated themselves on this doubtful territory, made improvements, and formed a very considerable population," beyond the jurisdiction of the laws of the province. In this situation they formed a compact among themselves and established a tribunal known as the "Fair-Play System," which administered rude justice among the settlers of the community. Early in the summer of 1776 news penetrated to this remote settlement that Congress contemplated making a declaration of independence. These tidings were hailed with delight by the fair-play men, who decided to voice their approval of the movement for independence by endorsing it in a formal manner. Hence on July 4, 1776, they assembled on the banks of Pine Creek for this purpose, and, after a lively discussion, it was decided amidst great enthusiasm to approve the proposal then under discussion in Congress by a declaration of independence of their own. This was in the form of a set of resolutions absolving themselves from all allegiance to Great Britain, and declaring themselves to be henceforth free and independent. It was indeed a singular coincidence that this action was taken in the backwoods of Pennsylvania by a body of Scotch-Irishmen

35. *Ibid.*, 64.

on the outskirts of civilization, some two hundred miles from Philadelphia, on the same day that Congress adopted the Declaration of Independence, when neither party had any means of knowing what the other was doing. These men of the frontier not only declared their independence, but later rendered effective service on the battlefields of the Revolution. On December 21, 1784, the legislature of Pennsylvania recognized their services by granting them the right of pre-emption to the lands they had occupied before titles could be legally granted, as witness the following act of assembly:

> "And Whereas divers persons, who have heretofore occupied and cultivated small tracts of land, without the bounds of the purchase made as aforesaid in the year 1768, and within the purchase made, or now to be made [of 1784], have, *by their resolute stand and sufferings during the late war,* merited that those settlers should have the pre-emption of their respective plantations, it is enacted —That all and every person, or persons, and *their legal representatives,* who has, or have heretofore settled, on the north side of the West Branch of the Susquehanna, between *Lycomic* or *Lycoming* Creek on the east, and *Tyagahton,* or Pine Creek, on the west, as well as other lands within the said residuary purchase from the Indians, of the territory within this state . . . shall be allowed a right of pre-emption to their respective possessions, at the price aforesaid."[36]

One of the most famous regiments of the Pennsylvania Line was Colonel William Thompson's battalion of riflemen, composed mainly of Scotch-Irishmen. This regiment, the first to be enlisted under the authority of Congress, "formed the nucleus of the American army, absolutely loyal to the American cause, and knowing no fatherland but the wilderness." It was recruited in pursuance of two resolutions of Congress, adopted June 14 and June 22, 1775, authorizing the enlistment of nine companies of

36. Smith's *Laws of Pennsylvania*, II, 195; John Blair Linn, "Indian Land and its Fair Play Settlers, 1773-1785," in *Pennsylvania Magazine of History and Biography*, VII, 721; J. F. Meginness, *Otzinachson, or a History of the West Branch Valley*, 192-193; Egle, *op. cit.*, 919. The names of some of the settlers who were active in adopting the Pine Creek Declaration were: Thomas, Francis, and John Clark, Alexander Donaldson, William Campbell, Alexander Hamilton, John Jackson, Adam Carson, Henry McCracken, Adam Dewitt, Robert Love, and Hugh Nichols, but there were many others whose names are not available. See Egle, *op. cit.*, 919.

expert riflemen, which, as soon as the ranks were filled were to join the army at Boston. Seven companies of this regiment—the first, second, third, fourth, fifth, eighth, and ninth—were composed almost exclusively of Scotch-Irishmen; one, the seventh, was made up almost entirely of Germans from Berks County; and one, the sixth, recruited in Northampton County, was composed of a majority of Germans, with the remainder principally Scotch-Irish. The regiment as a whole was overwhelmingly Scotch-Irish, as were its commanders, chaplains, and most of its officers throughout the Revolution. It was commanded originally by Colonel William Thompson of Carlisle until his promotion to the rank of brigadier-general, when Lt.-Colonel Edward Hand succeeded to the command until he also became a brigadier-general. Other notable officers in this regiment were Colonel James Chambers of Chambersburg and Major Robert Magaw of Carlisle. This battalion became the Second Regiment of the Continental Line, and, after January 1, 1776, the First Regiment.[37]

This regiment was promptly raised, and arrived at Boston August 7, 1775. Thacher, in his Military Journal of the Revolution, under date of August 1775, comments on the appearance and marksmanship of this body of sharpshooters:

"They are remarkably stout and hardy men; many of them exceeding six feet in height. They are dressed in white frocks or rifle shirts and round hats. These men are remarkable for the accuracy of their aim; striking a mark with great certainty at two hundred yards distance. At a review, a company of them, while in a quick advance, fired their balls into objects of seven inches diameter at the distance of 250 yards. They are now stationed in our lines, and their shot have frequently proved fatal to British officers and soldiers who expose themselves to view at more than double the distance of common musket shot."[38]

Another regiment of Scotch-Irishmen raised under the authority of a resolution of Congress, adopted July 15, 1776, was the Eighth Pennsylvania. This regiment comprised seven companies from Westmoreland County and one from Bedford County. Its original

37. *Pennsylvania Archives*, Series II, Vol. X, 3-6, 39-41.
38. James Thacher, *Military Journal during the American Revolutionary War from 1775 to 1783*, 38.

purpose was to guard the western posts and to protect the frontier, but in the national emergency of 1777 it joined the Continental Army under Washington. The provincial Convention of Pennsylvania on July 20, 1776, recommended to Congress for field officers of this regiment, Colonel Aeneas Mackay, Lt.-Colonel George Wilson, and Major Richard Butler, and these recommendations were duly ratified and the commissions issued. The company officers of this regiment were named by the county committees of correspondence and were commissioned by Congress. That the regiment was overwhelmingly Scotch-Irish is evidenced by the roster of field and staff officers, non-commissioned officers, and privates. The celebrated Captain Sam Brady commanded a company in this regiment.[39]

There were thousands of other Pennsylvania Scotch-Irishmen serving in the Continental Army, these being so numerous that, as has been noted, "Light-Horse Harry" Lee called the Pennsylvania Line "the Line of Ireland," but it would carry us too far afield to attempt a detailed account of their exploits. As Lecky and other impartial historians assert without qualification and, in fact, as the rosters of the regiments will show, the majority of the officers and men in the Pennsylvania Line were Scotch-Irishmen. Sufficient evidence has been adduced, we trust, to show the conspicuous rôle played by the Scotch-Irish in the Revolution, as in the colonial wars preceding it. It seems fitting, however, to pass in brief review some of the outstanding Scotch-Irish soldiers Pennsylvania gave to the patriot cause in the mighty struggle for American independence.

Among the Pennsylvania Scotch-Irishmen who gained distinction in the Revolutionary War were Generals John Armstrong, William Thompson, Edward Hand, James Ewing, William Irvine, James Potter, Ephraim Blaine, Joseph Reed, and Andrew Porter. Attention has been called to General John Armstrong in connection with his exploits in the French and Indian War and in Pontiac's War, in the former of which he gained the title of "Hero of Kittanning" and commanded the Pennsylvania militia

---

39. *Pennsylvania Archives*, Series II, Vol. X, 641-669.

in Forbes's expedition against Fort Dequesne. In the Revolution he was commissioned brigadier-general by Congress March 1, 1776, but resigned his commission April 4, 1777, to become brigadier-general of state militia, of which he was later appointed major-general by the Supreme Executive Council of Pennsylvania. General William Thompson, a native of Ireland, was captain of a troop of horse in the French and Indian War and participated in Armstrong's expedition against Kittanning. He was commissioned colonel of the famous battalion of riflemen later known as the First Pennsylvania Regiment, but was promoted to the rank of brigadier-general on March 1, 1776. General Edward Hand, also a native of Ireland, was commissioned ensign in 1772 and accompanied his regiment to Fort Pitt, and, as noted above, was lieutenant-colonel and colonel of the battalion of riflemen. In 1777 he was promoted to the rank of brigadier-general. For a time he served as commandant at Fort Pitt; in 1783 he was brevetted major-general. General James Ewing began his military career as a lieutenant in the French and Indian War. From 1771 to 1775 he was a member of the assembly from Lancaster County, but on July 4, 1776, was chosen brigadier-general of Pennsylvania militia in command of the Second Brigade. In 1782-1783 he served as Vice-President of Pennsylvania.

General William Irvine, a native of Ulster, after serving for several years as a surgeon in the British navy, emigrated to Pennsylvania toward the close of the French and Indian War and practised medicine at Carlisle. Upon the outbreak of the Revolution he raised a battalion, later known as the Sixth Regiment of the Pennsylvania Line, of which he was commissioned colonel by Congress January 9, 1776. For conspicuous gallantry at the Battle of Monmouth, he was promoted in May, 1779, to the rank of brigadier-general in command of the Second Brigade of the Pennsylvania Line; in 1781 he was given the post of commandant at Fort Pitt, where he remained until the end of the war. He served as member of Congress in 1787-1788, and again in 1793-1795. He commanded the Pennsylvania militia in the Whiskey Rebellion. The Pennsylvania legislature rewarded his many valued services to the commonwealth by voting him a large tract of land on Lake Erie, known as "Irvine's Reserve."

General James Potter, a native of County Tyrone, Ireland, settled in Cumberland County, Pennsylvania, but in 1774 removed to Penn's Valley in Centre County. Beginning his military career as a lieutenant in Armstrong's expedition against Kittanning, he was promoted to a captaincy in 1759 and by 1764 had won a colonelcy in the Pennsylvania militia. He was chosen colonel of associators in 1776, and commanded the Northumberland County militia at the battles of Trenton and Princeton. In 1777 he was commissioned brigadier-general, and was present at the battles of Brandywine and Germantown. In 1780 he was elected a member of the Supreme Executive Council of Pennsylvania, becoming its vice-president in 1781. He served also as a member of the Council of Censors in 1784, and in May 1782 was commissioned major-general of Pennsylvania militia.

General Ephraim Blaine, grandfather of James G. Blaine, was a colonel in the Revolutionary War until promoted to the rank of commissary-general, his services being especially valuable during the terrible winter at Valley Forge. Joseph Reed, after serving for a time as Washington's military secretary, was promoted in 1776 to the rank of adjutant-general. Declining in 1777 a commission as brigadier-general, he devoted his great talents chiefly to civil affairs as President of Pennsylvania. Andrew Caldwell was for a time commander of the Pennsylvania Navy. General Andrew Porter was colonel of the Fourth Pennsylvania Artillery, and later became Major-general of Pennsylvania militia.

9

Economic Activities of the Scotch-Irish

They had exceedingly stiff and strenuous notions touching strict integrity in business transactions. J. W. DINSMORE

THE SCOTCH-IRISH have been an important factor in the economic life of Pennsylvania, as elsewhere throughout the country. In the colonial era, however, they were so busily engaged in establishing themselves in the wilderness that their genius for industry lacked adequate opportunity for expression. The more significant story of their achievements in trade, manufactures, and finance belongs to the later period, which is beyond the scope of our subject. Despite the early obstacles encountered, however, their contribution to the economic life of provincial Pennsylvania was by no means inconsiderable.[1]

FARMING

The principal economic interest of the Scotch-Irish in the colonial era, like that of the population generally, was farming. Since so large a proportion of them lived on the frontier, the type of agriculture associated with them in this period was that of pioneer farmers, and it is in this character that we shall discuss them. This does not mean to say, however, that the whole body of Scotch-Irish practiced the primitive husbandry of the backwoods. On the contrary, as time passed, many of them dwelling in the Cumberland Valley and in Chester, Lancaster, Dauphin, and North-

---

1. It is not claimed that the economic life of the Scotch-Irish as described in this chapter was much different from that of the other racial groups roundabout, but we do not, on this account, feel warranted in leaving untold an important part of the activities of the people we are describing.

165

ampton counties were skilful farmers. Here they lived comfortably in substantial stone houses with all the appurtenances pertaining to the most advanced agriculture of the times. They had fertile lands, commodious barns, good livestock, fences, and orchards, and were within reach of the Philadelphia market. Nevertheless, they represented a more highly developed stage of agriculture than that of their frontier brethren, who comprised the great majority of the Scotch-Irish in the early days. The frontier farmer labored under serious disadvantages, chief among which was his inaccessibility to market. An additional drawback was that he was subject to Indian depredations, to say nothing of the presence in large numbers of snakes and wild beasts and of the probability that a good part of his crops would be devoured by squirrels infesting the neighboring forest.

The securing of a farm in colonial Pennsylvania was a comparatively simple matter for an enterprising man, even if his means were small. For that matter, much land was occupied without being regularly purchased at all, either by merely squatting on it or else by military permit during the Indian wars. The proprietaries from time to time purchased land from the Indians and offered it for sale through the land office. Inasmuch, however, as settlement always proceeded westward in advance of the land purchases of the Penns, there were thousands of settlers who simply occupied the land without any right or title. Among the borderers west of the Alleghenies there grew up an irregular kind of title known as "tomahawk right," whereby a settler recorded his claim to a tract of land by deadening a few trees near a spring and cutting his initials in the bark of other near-by trees. Although this procedure was of no legal value, it was regarded by the backwoodsmen as establishing a priority of claim when applications were made later for warrants covering these particular tracts.[2] Thus, in one way and another, homesteads were acquired in the wilderness, varying in size from one hundred to three hundred acres, and occasionally larger; but whether secured by purchase or otherwise, the settler was confronted with the formidable task

2. J. S. Van Voorhis, *The Old and New Monongahela*, 13.

of clearing the ground, erecting his cabin, and working hard to make a living.

After securing a piece of land, the immediate task was to erect a log cabin, in which labor the pioneer was ordinarily assisted by the neighbors, as described in the succeeding chapter. Then began the arduous work of clearing the land, a process which started immediately but was extended over a period of years. When the emergency demanded hasty preparation for planting the crop, the method followed was to girdle the trees, thereby causing them to die, and the crops would be planted amidst the skeleton trees left standing. If, however, the trees were cut down, which was the usual practice, they were commonly left on the ground to become seasoned, when they were burned; but the brushwood was grubbed up. After the first rush of settlers to a new community had subsided, clearing the land became a somewhat standardized process accomplished by log-rollings, which were participated in by the neighbors. By means of a logging bee several acres could be cleared in a day. Grubbing, chopping, and logging bees were common, the neighbors helping each other in turn. After the pile of logs had been burned the debris was cleared away and the soil was made ready for the drag or the triangular harrow.[3] Once the land was cleared, the work of fencing began, a rail fence being constructed by degrees until eventually a good part of the farm was enclosed. The usual type was the worm fence made of rails, though in the more thickly settled communities in the late colonial era post-and-rail fences were sometimes found. Some farmers, probably as a makeshift, drove sticks close together into the ground to form a palisade fence. In the early nineteenth century, farmers on the frontier could engage rail-splitters at a cost of fifty cents a day and board.[4]

The original farm buildings, hastily built of logs, consisted of a cabin and a rude stable. Some years later, when the farmer had cleared a considerable portion of his land and had gotten it

3. W. J. McKnight, *A Pioneer Outline History of Northwestern Pennsylvania*, 217-218; G. D. Albert, *History of the County of Westmoreland, Pennsylvania*, 158; C. B. Johnson, *Letters from the British Settlement in Pennsylvania*, 56-57.

4. Albert, *ibid.;* McKnight, *ibid.*

into tillable condition, he effected substantial improvements on his property. Being now more prosperous, he built a better log cabin, erected a more commodious barn, built a springhouse, and completed his fencing operations; finally, he erected a good stone dwelling. His situation now resembled that of his brethren in eastern Pennsylvania, though a generation or more had elapsed before arriving at this condition. In Southwestern Pennsylvania, as on the frontier generally, this degree of prosperity would seldom be found until after the Revolution.

Methods of farming were crude, and the implements in use primitive. The plows had wooden mold-boards, the cutting edge of which was faced with a plain strip of metal. The first harrows were likely to be common thorn bushes cut from the woods, soon to be replaced by the triangular harrow with wooden teeth. Rollers were made from logs cut from large trees, serving but indifferently to crush clods and to compact the soil. It was long before wagons came into use on the frontier, sleds being the usual means of transporting heavy loads, even in summer. Harness was at first brought from the East, but when this wore out new gears were made from ropes, often replaced by raw deer thongs twined and twisted together and then dried.[5] Everything was done by the hardest manual labor. After the land had been plowed, harrowed, and rolled, the seed was planted by hand. Fortunately for the pioneer, the new ground was soft and easily turned up, though he was kept busy dodging the stumps and the heaps of stones piled up here and there. Corn was planted in hills and worked with the hoe, and other cereals were scattered broadcast by hand. Grass was cut with scythes; wheat and rye, with sickles. The threshing season lasted throughout most of the winter, being done at odd times when other work was not pressing. The usual method was with flails, though some farmers used horses to tread out the grain. After threshing, the chaff was winnowed from the grains by tossing the mixture in the air, either with a

5. VanVoorhis, *op. cit.*, 12; J. H. Bausman, *History of Beaver County, Pennsylvania*, 277.

pitchfork or with a winnowing fan.[6] The bottom lands, naturally the most fertile, were at first sown preferably in rye, due to the fact that the soil of the lowlands was "rank with poisonous vegetation" and was not regarded as adapted to wheat until it had been utilized for other crops; hence the higher land produced the best wheat in the beginning and was generally the first to be cultivated.[7]

Until farming had become well advanced, the main reliance of the family for food was corn rather than wheat. Corn was more readily harvested than other cereals, besides having the additional advantage of supplying food for stock. Furthermore, where mills were scarce it could be ground in handmills or converted into hominy by means of hominy-blocks. Corn-huskings were commonly resorted to as a means of getting large portions of the crop shucked for the winter. Harvesting the hay was a particularly laborious process. Since it was cut with the scythe, it required powers of endurance and entailed a heavy drain on the muscles of even the strongest men. Toiling from sunrise to sunset, the best workmen could cut from one-and-a-half to two acres a day. If the crop were large, neighbors helped each other in the hay-making season. There were no horse rakes in use, the work being done by hand, women often assisting in the fields.[8]

Stable manure was the principal fertilizer, its use differing little from modern practices. The supply at first was limited, however, because of the fact that the livestock was reared mostly in the open and the manure was wasted from neglect. By reason of the fertility of the virgin soil, the farmers grew careless and failed to appreciate the value of fertilization, with the result that the land tended to become exhausted and the yield was thereby reduced. For improving land, many farmers regarded with favor any substance rich in vegetable matter, such as mold from the woods, muck and peat from the swamps, sediment in ditches, and surface soil from ditch-banks. They also considered the burning of litter upon the farm as beneficial on account of the fertilizing

6. Albert, *op. cit.,* 165-166; L. Carrier, *Beginnings of Agriculture in America,* 177.

7. Albert, *op. cit.,* 158.

8. *Ibid.;* William Hanna, *History of Greene County, Pennsylvania,* 166-167; McKnight, *op. cit.,* 220-221.

value of the ashes. A popular fertilizer was soap ashes, which was the refuse after leaching for the manufacture of soap.[9]

Until they had become fairly well established as farmers the Scotch-Irish pioneers commonly possessed but one horse and one cow, but as they grew more prosperous the livestock increased. Swine and poultry multiplied rapidly, becoming quite numerous. Owing to the distance from market, it was long before an attempt was made to raise beef cattle, though sheep were somewhat plentiful. Stock was raised primarily for use on the farm rather than for sale. Due to improper housing and feeding, the horses and cattle were stunted in their growth; a gallon of milk a day was considered a good average for a cow. Many farmers had no cow-houses or stables at first, the livestock not infrequently roaming the woods the year around without shelter. A good part of their sustenance was derived from browsing on the tender boughs of the forest trees, especially of the birch and maple. Later, a barn was erected, as much for the purpose of protecting the stock from wild animals as of protection from the inclemency of the weather. Bells were hung on the necks of cattle and horses so that they might be located when wanted, as well as to warn the children when the cattle might be encroaching on the cornfield, which was often not enclosed.[10]

Lack of transportation facilities proved a serious handicap to the backwoods farmers. Overland transportation was restricted to short distances, since heavy farm products could not be hauled profitably to markets at a distance of more than sixty or seventy miles. Cattle, however, could be marketed by driving them longer distances, and this practice was resorted to by the farmers of the back country in post-colonial and early national times. In fact, there arose a class of drovers who made a business of driving cattle, sheep, hogs, and even turkeys, long distances to the eastern markets. Wheat, corn, and rye might be marketed by converting them into whiskey.[11]

9. Carrier, *op. cit.*, 271.
10. Albert, *op. cit.*, 158.
11. W. P. Schell, *The Annals of Bedford County, Pennsylvania*, 58-59.

MANUFACTURES

The manufactures of the Scotch-Irish pioneers were of the handicraft or domestic type generally found throughout colonial America. Of necessity the Scotch-Irishman living in the backwoods was a sort of Jack-of-all-trades. Not only were skilled mechanics few, but, even had they been numerous, money would have been lacking to employ them. Hence, in the first generation of settlement, the pioneer was his own shoemaker, tailor, blacksmith, and carpenter. In the handicraft stage of industry the family was thrown almost entirely upon its own resources, and the standard of living was adjusted to these conditions. The household must either make the things that were needed or go without them. The farm was to a great degree a self-sufficing economic unit, and was the scene of a great variety of activities in which all the family engaged. It was long before this domestic economy yielded either to specialists in the community or to itinerants going from house to house seeking work. Later on, when the community was more advanced, there arrived on the scene the village shoemaker, saddler, harness-maker, blacksmith, tinner, cooper and other craftsmen, but this was not until the settlement had passed from the strictly frontier stage to a more advanced civilization such as was found in the older settlements of the province.[12]

The principal homespun industries were the spinning and weaving of flax, wool, and hemp for clothing and for other household uses. Furniture, shoes, shoe-packs, moccasins, hats, caps, bedding, and implements of one sort and another were all made by the family. Other domestic industries were milling, bolting, distilling, soap-making, candle-making, leather products, brooms, baskets, and food products such as pickling, canning, preserving, and maple sugar.[13] Home manufacture of textiles was the most important single industry among the Scotch-Irish pioneers. Wool-carding was done by hand, and every family had a spinning wheel. Practically all the wearing apparel was homemade. The Scotch-Irish made quantities of linen, a branch of industry in

12. Malcolm Keir, "The Epic of Industry," in *Pageant of America*, II, 7, 17-19.

13. Victor S. Clark, *History of Manufactures in the United States*, 92-140; J. L. Bishop, *A History of American Manufactures from 1608 to 1860*, I, 339, 406, 420.

which they excelled, and produced a surplus for sale; the culture of flax was practically universal among them. There were spinning and quilting parties among the women, it being nothing uncommon for women to take their wheels to a neighbor's house, remain for supper, and then return home with their wheels under their arms.[14] The most common cloth in use was linsey-woolsey, with a linen warp and a woolen woof, and the favorite color was blue. Homemade dyes were obtained from indigo, copperas, walnut bark, oak bark, peach leaves, and madder, with alum as a mordant. Hats, caps, bonnets, and stockings were all handmade.[15]

An important early industry of the backwoods in which the Scotch-Irish engaged extensively was the making of maple sugar. When the sugar season was at hand, early in March, the equipment was assembled and the work began. About three hundred trees constituted the average sugar camp, and to boil the sap from that many trees required six kettles holding about twenty-two gallons each. The trees were tapped with an augur hole from one to two inches deep, into which was inserted a spile some eighteen inches long, two spiles being placed in each tree. The yield from a camp of this size filled thirty barrels and required steady boiling, employing six kettlers. The sap was boiled into a thick syrup, then strained while hot into a syrup-barrel. After settling, it was again strained and the syrup in the kettle was clarified with eggs beaten in skim milk. A barrel of sap ordinarily yielded from five to seven pounds of sugar, which was either made into cakes or "stirred off" into a granulated condition. The whole process required considerable skill to prevent the sugar from being burnt and thereby depriving it of its sweetness.[16]

Every family was its own tanner and shoemaker. A large trough sunk to the edge of the ground served for a tanning vat, and there was always on hand a plenty of bark obtained while clearing the land; this was made ready for use by pounding it, when

14. John M. Cooper, "The Scotch-Irish in the Cumberland Valley," in Scotch-Irish Society of America *Proceedings*, VIII, 295; McKnight, *op. cit.*, 415.

15. H. R. Johnson, *A History of Neshannock Presbyterian Church*, 73, 75; Albert, *op. cit.*, 157.

16. McKnight, *op. cit.*, 250-253.

dried, with an axe or mallet. As a substitute for lime, ashes were used for removing hair off the hide, and neat's oil or tallow for softening it. Currying was done with a drawing knife "with its edge turned." The leather thus made was coarse but substantial, and it was blacked when desired by applying to it a mixture of soot and hog's lard. Before the appearance of the itinerant shoemaker, the pioneer made his own shoes and moccasins.[17]

Though hampered by the inadequacy of his tools, the Scotch-Irishman developed considerable skill and ingenuity in woodworking. In the midst of the forest, wood was plentiful and was useful for manufacturing farming implements, furniture, and utensils of all sorts. The broad-axe, the frow, and the mallet were in constant use for making posts, rails, beams, clapboards, and puncheons; before the advent of the sawmill, ripsaws were employed in making boards. One of the most useful tools was the draw-knife, which was handy for making the major part of the wooden equipment such as churns, dashers, cheese hoops, flails, axehelves, splint brooms, dishes, and spoons, though the finishing process was by jackknife. Troughs, mortars, and large bowls were frequently made from heavy blocks of wood by burning. Cooperage, which later developed into an industry of itself, was at first carried on by the farmers themselves or by a few of the most expert of them, whose services were in constant demand for making barrels, tubs, and kegs for salt meat, cider, vinegar, and whiskey.[18]

Two characteristic frontier industries carried on by the women were candle-making and soap-making. Inasmuch as the houses were lighted by candles, it entailed no little labor to provide a supply to last through the winter. Wicks, made from tow, hemp, or cotton, after being tied to a candle rod, were dipped into a vessel containing hot tallow and then hung up to cool, this process being repeated until the candles attained the proportions desired. This primitive method was later superseded by the pewter or tin

17. Joseph Doddridge, *Notes on the Settlement and Indian Wars of the Western Parts of Virginia and Pennsylvania*, 143-144.

18. S. J. and E. H. Buck, *The Planting of Civilization in Western Pennsylvania*, 277-278; McKnight, *op. cit.*, 415.

candle mold, which produced from two to ten candles at a time; itinerant candle-makers, however, used larger molds. Candles were made not only from tallow, but also from beeswax and bayberry wax. Another characteristic woman's task was soap-making, the two essential ingredients of which were grease and lye. A supply of grease was accumulated from household cooking and from butchering, while lye was obtained by filling a barrel with wood ashes through which water seeped. The grease and lye were then placed in a large pot out of doors and boiled until the right consistency had been reached, when the product was removed and cut into such shapes and sizes as the housewife desired. A finer grade of soap for toilet purposes was made from bayberry wax.[19]

One of the principal industries of the Scotch-Irish was the distilling of whiskey, in which it appears that they were more largely engaged than was any other racial group, though they by no means had a monopoly in this industry. We are here concerned with the making of whiskey only from the standpoint of the economic life of the Scotch-Irish. On the frontier, distilleries were regarded as being just as much a necessity as gristmills and sawmills, and were far more numerous. In the four western counties which were the scene of the Whiskey Rebellion there were at that time about 570 distilleries, of which 272 were in Washington County alone.[20] In some communities one farmer in every five or six had a still and converted his own surplus grain and that of his neighbors into whiskey; if a neighbor brought his grain to the still to be manufactured into whiskey, he was charged a fixed part of the grain for each gallon of whiskey distilled. Since the use of whiskey was practically universal in those days, there was a great demand for it and the industry thrived, especially as it was the only way the farmers could dispose of their surplus grain. Stills were set up in the cellar of the house if it had one, but more generally in some near-by outhouse, and the same spring which

19. N. G. Parke, "Personal Knowledge of the Scotch-Irish," in Scotch-Irish Society of America *Proceedings*, VIII, 230; Clark, *op. cit.*, 440; Keir, *op. cit.*, 11-13.
20. VanVoorhis, *op. cit.*, 14.

supplied the springhouse furnished the worm-tub for the distillery.[21]

In provincial Pennsylvania the iron industry was but little developed in those districts where the Scotch-Irish predominated. Hence they did not figure conspicuously in the erection of forges and furnaces until the post-colonial period, when they were among the principal promoters of this industry in its two great inland centers of the Juniata Valley and the trans-Allegheny region of the Allegheny and Monongahela Valleys. Very little iron was in use among the pioneers of central and western Pennsylvania, and what articles of iron manufacture there were to be found in these districts were brought by pack horses from the eastern part of the province. In the national period, however, the Scotch-Irish were very active in the iron industry, particularly in Pittsburgh and the region roundabout.

TRANSPORTATION

Like other racial groups on the frontier, the Scotch-Irish were greatly hampered by the lack of adequate transportation facilities. Roads penetrated slowly into that region, and such of them as existed were well-nigh impassable, especially in winter. Communication with the older and more settled parts of the province was so difficult that the frontiersmen were isolated from the outside world, living largely unto themselves. Long after wagon roads had been opened in eastern Pennsylvania, the settlers farther to the westward had to content themselves with bridle paths along which they traveled on horseback and commonly conveyed the necessaries of life on pack horses. It was not until after the Revolution that wagons began to cross the Alleghenies into Western Pennsylvania.[22]

The first road to penetrate west of the Alleghenies was Braddock's Road, constructed in 1755 from Will's Creek (Cumberland), Maryland, to within seven miles of the Forks of the Ohio

---

21. James Veech, "The Secular History in Its Connections with the Early Presbyterian Church History of Southwest Pennsylvania," in *The Centenary Memorial of the Planting and Growth of Presbyterianism in Western Pennsylvania and Parts Adjacent*, 363-364; Samuel Wilkeson, "Early Recollections of the West," in *The American Pioneer*, II, 215.

22. A. B. Hulbert, *Pioneer Roads and Experiences of Travelers*, II, 25, 31, 39.

to enable General Braddock to advance to the attack of Fort Duquesne. This was a military road twelve feet wide and hastily made, and not very satisfactory for travel or traffic. The other principal road into the back parts of the province was Forbes's Road, built in 1758 by Colonel Bouquet to expedite the march of General Forbes against Fort Duquesne. This road extended from Raystown (Bedford) to Pittsburgh, connecting at the former place with the road to Philadelphia. From these two main highways, imperfect as they were, others even more unsatisfactory branched here and there to the chief settlements on the frontier. Even the best roads of that day were hardly passable, being full of stumps, fallen timbers, ruts, and bogs, which rendered traffic not only difficult but often dangerous. Carlisle was long the terminus of the wagon road, and from that point passenger traffic to the westward was by horseback, and freight traffic by pack horses. Travel over the mountains is described as being "little less than a continuance of miracles," some preferring to cross the Alleghenies on foot rather than to risk life and limb in a wagon.[23]

Prior to 1785, when freight traffic by means of wagons began to cross the Alleghenies at various points, freight was regularly transported over the mountains by pack horses, and pack-horse trains became a familiar sight to the inhabitants along the way. As many as five hundred pack horses were seen at Carlisle in one day, laden with freight bound for Fort Loudon, Bedford, Uniontown, Pittsburgh, and other points beyond the mountains. Sometimes a man could manage a pack-train of ten horses or more merely by the movements of his voice, riding either behind or before at will. Fifteen miles a day were accounted a good day's journey; all the harness that was needed consisted of a pack-saddle and a halter. Before the Conestoga wagons were introduced as freight carriers, shopkeepers would often organize a caravan and make the trip all the way to Philadelphia to lay in their yearly stock of goods. Until supplanted by canals and railroads, Conestoga wagons continued to be the principal means of transporting

23. Caroline E. MacGill, *History of Transportation in the United States before 1860*, 7, 51, 61; Elias Pym Fordham, *Personal Narrative of Travels*, 59, 68, 71-72.

freight to and from the frontier.[24] Whether by pack-horse trains or by Conestoga wagons, the cost of transportation was high. In 1784 the freight charges for goods from Philadelphia to Uniontown were five dollars per hundredweight. Even after the turnpikes were built, there was no cheap carriage for long distances, since high tolls were paid all along the line.[25]

From an early date rafting was carried on extensively on all the principal rivers of Pennsylvania, particularly on the Susquehanna, the Allegheny, and the Clarion Rivers and their tributaries. Representing many owners and employing a large body of men, the rafts carried large quantities of freight down stream in the spring season. They varied in size, but were commonly from 150 to 300 feet long and 24 feet wide. Beginning in 1782, when the first flatboat made the trip down the Ohio and the Mississippi to New Orleans, there was an increasing trade carried on by means of flatboats and keelboats. Many keelboats and flatboats were built at Pittsburgh, at Brownsville and other points on the Monongahela, and some even on the Youghiogheny, but the arrival of the steamboat on the "western waters" in 1811 gradually displaced this primitive river craft. Though the inhabitants of Western Pennsylvania continued to draw their supplies mainly by overland traffic from Philadelphia and Baltimore, they now shipped much of their produce down the Ohio and the Mississippi to New Orleans.[26]

TRADE

As noted above, trade was hampered on the frontier by the difficulty of reaching markets and by the high cost of transportation. Under such conditions business developed slowly and its methods were primitive. Trade with the Indians began promptly and flourished throughout the colonial era. Many of the most

24. Sherman Day, *Historical Collections of Pennsylvania*, 354; James Veech, *The Monongahela of Old*, 37.

25. James M. Swank, *Progressive Pennsylvania*, 103-104; Albert, *op. cit.*, 180; McKnight, *op. cit.*, 203, 381; Emory R. Johnson, *History of Domestic and Foreign Commerce of the United States*, I, 210, 218.

26. J. H. Walker, *Rafting Days in Pennsylvania*, 29-33, 50, 58-61; Isaac Weld, Jr., *Travels through the States of North America*, 66-67; Swank, *op. cit.*, 118-119.

prominent and adventurous of these traders were Scotch-Irishmen who had their headquarters in Donegal Township in Lancaster County. This Scotch-Irish settlement was a sort of nursery of Indian traders, who made long journeys into the wilderness, trading various kinds of merchandise for furs and skins, for which there was always a brisk demand abroad at good prices.[27]

Among the Scotch-Irish pioneers there was very little money in circulation, and transactions were ordinarily by barter. Lands were purchased in this way, and at the country stores goods were regularly exchanged for farm produce. Certain commodities had a standardized value for purposes of trade. Thus a bushel of salt, because of its scarcity and consequent high commercial value, was worth twenty bushels of wheat; other integers of value were a gallon of whiskey, a whiskey-still, a rifle, and a flask of powder. Business transactions on the frontier of Pennsylvania continued to be chiefly by barter until after the Revolution and, in remote sections of Northwestern Pennsylvania, until 1840 or even later. Many farms were exchanged for whiskey-stills, the net proceeds from the latter often exceeding in value those received from the farm in the course of a year. In the barter economy of the backwoods whiskey was the staple article of trade, other media of exchange being valued in accordance with the number of gallons, kegs, or barrels of whiskey they would fetch.[28]

The high cost of conveying goods long distances over bad roads raised the price of everything sold at the country stores, which played a great part in the economic life of the frontier. In every village was a storekeeper who carried a varied assortment of goods for which there was likely to be a demand. These he exchanged for practically everything in the way of produce that was offered by his customers. Having accumulated a great variety of these products from the farmers roundabout, he would engage the owner of a pack-horse train or of a Conestoga wagon to take them to Philadelphia or Baltimore, where he would sell them and use the proceeds to restock his shelves with a new load of merchandise. He acted, therefore, as a sort of middleman between the

27. I. S. Clare, *A Brief History of Lancaster County, Pennsylvania*, 26-28.
28. Albert, *op. cit.*, 166-169, 171-172.

farmers and the city merchants, serving the important function of affording a market for country produce. In view of the high cost of transportation, it was necessary for him to sell at a high profit in order to make a success of his business; hence he sold his goods at an advance of about 100 per cent on an average, and even then realized only a moderate profit.[29] In Northwestern Pennsylvania, the last frontier of the state, money was still scarce as late as 1840, and merchants were often compelled to exchange their goods for "boards, shingles, square timber, wheat, rye, buckwheat, flaxseed, clover seed, timothy seed, wool, rags, beeswax, feathers, hickory-nuts, chestnuts, hides, deer pelts, elderberries, furs, road orders, school and county orders, eggs, butter, tow cloth, and linen cloth."[30]

After 1790, Pittsburgh became the great emporium of trade west of the mountains, but other markets developed in the river towns down the Ohio and the Mississippi all the way to New Orleans. In the flatboat and keelboat era, and especially after the advent of the steamboat, the New Orleans trade grew steadily in importance. As the gateway of the West, Pittsburgh was strategically located for trade. In the summer season a great quantity of merchandise was brought over the mountains and stored there ready for shipment down the Ohio. This type of trade was well established by 1803.[31]

29. Johnson, *op. cit.,* 210.
30. McKnight, *op. cit.,* 414-415.
31. F. A. Michaux, "Travels to the West of the Alleghany Mountains," in Thwaites, *Early Western Travels,* III, 157-158; Wilkeson, *op. cit.,* 203.

10

Social Life And Customs of the Scotch-Irish

Tell me a tale of the timber-lands—
Of the old-time pioneers;
Somepin' a pore man understands
With his feelins's well as ears.
Tell of the old log house,—about
The loft, and the puncheon flore—
The old fi-er-place, with the crane swung out,
And the latch-string through the door.

JAMES WHITCOMB RILEY

THE SOCIAL LIFE and customs of the Scotch-Irish of colonial Pennsylvania were, for the most part, those prevailing on the frontier, and will be discussed from that point of view. This does not mean to say that all Scotch-Irishmen dwelt on the outer edge of civilization, but merely that they were characterized by the spirit of pioneering into the wilderness and that their social life reflected to an unusual degree the conditions obtaining in the American backwoods in the early days. By the close of the provincial period, their older settlements in eastern Pennsylvania had assumed the aspect of an ordered civilization, with substantial stone dwellings, churches, schools, and well-tilled farms, attended by a more gracious way of living conforming to the best standards of that day. This would not be true, however, of the great mass of the Scotch-Irish of this early period. They were, to be sure, not the only people on the frontier, but they were its most numerous and influential element, forming its backbone and setting its tone and direction. Theirs was the dominant strain in the blood of the pioneers engaged in transforming the backwoods into a civilized community.[1]

CHARACTERISTICS OF THE SCOTCH-IRISH

The characteristics of the Scotch-Irish were those of the Lowland Scots, modified and improved by their experiences in Ulster and especially by their changed environment in the New World, where their strong individuality exerted a profound influence in shaping the institutions of the country.

Physically, they were a tough and hardy breed, somewhat tall in stature, strong-boned, heavily-muscled, lean and sinewy. Broad-shouldered, robust, hard-handed and wiry, their physical vigor was such as to fit them for the tasks confronting them as pioneers. Hence they did not shrink from the heavy labor of levelling the forests, building their log cabins, and tilling the soil, or from the other hardships and privations of life on the frontier. Later, when the Indian wars began, their toughened physical fibre enabled them to endure with comparative ease the hardships of the march and of the camp.[2]

It is, however, by his mental and emotional qualities, his temperament and disposition, that the individuality of the Scotch-Irishman is most clearly expressed. He came of a strong-minded race, with no lack of common sense. That he was practical, level-headed, fearless, self-reliant, and resolute has never been denied. He was at once venturesome and cautious, taciturn to a fault, but speaking his mind freely when aroused. Serious in his outlook upon life, he nevertheless had a sense of humor, was fond of sports, and was by no means unsocial. Though ordinarily undemonstrative, his rough exterior often covered a great tenderness of feeling, and his love of family was deep, strong, and enduring. Steadfast and loyal, he was as hospitable to his friends as he was unrelenting to his foes. Prompt to resent an affront or to avenge an injury, his nature rebelled against anything that

1. Theodore Roosevelt, *The Winning of the West*, I, 125.
2. J. W. Dinsmore, *The Scotch-Irish in America*, 28-29; Charles McKnight, *Our Western Border*, 183-185; Daniel Agnew, "The Scotch-Irish of Pennsylvania," in Scotch-Irish Society of America *Proceedings*, II, 252; J. H. Keatley, "Scotch-Irish Conflicts," in *ibid.*, VI, 110.

savored of injustice or deceit, nor did he take kindly to restraint of any kind.[3]

That the Scotch-Irishman was uncommonly "set in his ways" may be illustrated by the prayer attributed to him, "Lord, grant that I may always be right, for Thou knowest that I am hard to turn." Tenacious of his opinions, as of his rights, he was but little given to yielding to his opponent in an argument. His enemies called him clannish, contentious, and hard to get along with, and it must be admitted that at times he could be very stubborn, not to say hot-tempered and combative. His thrift is proverbial, and it has been said of him, "The Scotch-Irishman is one who keeps the commandments of God, and every other good thing that he can get his hands on." Be that as it may, he was apt to do with his might what his hands found to do, with the result that he was remarkably successful in business.[4]

The Scotch-Irishman was a man of great force of character, albeit inclined to be dogmatic and inflexible in his views. His moral and religious convictions were an essential part of him, and he was prompt to establish churches wherever he went. He took his religion seriously, and not infrequently there was a touch of austerity about him. He was also a great believer in education, especially in a trained ministry, and was renowned for his achievements in this regard.[5] Once he had completed his initial task of conquering the wilderness, he became politically-minded and entered upon a great political career. In politics, as in religion, he was a strong partisan and hated like sin to make compromises with anybody or anything. The rather objectionable features of some of his qualities, especially his combative self-assertion, taciturnity, and stubbornness, became considerably toned down after he had passed from the frontier stage. Though still retaining the essential characteristics which made him a masterful figure in American life, he tended to mellow with the passing of time,

---

3. H. J. Ford, *The Scotch-Irish in America,* 539-540; J. Smith Futhey, "The Scotch-Irish," in Lancaster County Historical Society *Papers,* XI, 231; Dinsmore, *op. cit.,* 47-49; 56-57, 58, 61-62; W. H. McElroy, in Pennsylvania Scotch-Irish Society *Proceedings,* VII, 26; Carl Wittke, *We Who Built America,* 54.

4. R. E. Thompson, in Pennsylvania Historical Society *Proceedings,* VII, 26, 31.

5. E. Erskine, in *ibid.,* I, 35.

becoming broader in his outlook, more polished in his manners, and more gracious in his way of living. This "boulder of Scotch granite, overlaid and softened by the green verdure of Ireland" had its rough edges worn smooth by the contacts of a developing civilization.[6]

The Scotch-Irish women of Pennsylvania, as elsewhere in America, possessed the sterling qualities which made them an ornament to their sex. Their character and services were beyond all praise. They endured uncomplainingly the hardships of pioneer life, cradled a stalwart race, and contributed their full share to reclaiming the wilderness for the new civilization. Wise, virtuous, courageous, and energetic, they were true helpmeets of their husbands, patiently sharing with them the dangers and privations of frontier life. Physically well developed, their features indicated force of character rather than refinement of beauty. They were rather tall and strongly built, with fair complexions, light eyes, high cheekbones, and broad and high foreheads.[7] McCook, with sympathetic understanding, describes them as follows:

"Stalwart of frame no doubt they were, with muscles hardened under the strain of toil; hale and hearty, vigorous and strong, able to wield the axe against the trunk of a forest monarch or the head of an intruding savage; to aid their husbands and fathers to plow and plant, to reap and mow, to rake and bind and gather. They could wield the scutching knife or hackling comb upon flaxen stocks and fibers, as well as the rod of rebuke upon the back of a refractory child. They could work the treadle of a little spinning wheel, or swing the circumference of the great one. They could brew and bake, make and mend, sweep and scrub, rock the cradle and rule the household."[8]

Living in such an environment, the Scotch-Irish women were strong characters—self-reliant, resourceful, and loyal. Devout, patient, and cheerful in the midst of difficulties, they pursued the even tenor of their way, performing with efficient diligence the duties that lay nearest them.

6. J. H. Snowden, in Pennsylvania Scotch-Irish Society *Proceedings*, XXI, 11-12.
7. H. C. McCook, "Scotch-Irish Women Pioneers," in Scotch-Irish Society of America *Proceedings*, VIII, 83-85.
8. *Ibid.*

FRONTIER HOMESTEADS AND DOMESTIC ECONOMY

The life of the Scotch-Irish pioneers did not differ greatly from that of the other racial groups dwelling on the frontier, but, by reason of their greater numbers and more adventurous spirit, they have always been considered the typical frontiersmen of the colonial era, and their ways of living the most truly representative of the American backwoods in the early days.

The pioneer, bent upon establishing a home on the outskirts of civilization, was apt to be a young man in his twenties or thirties rather than in middle life. In some instances he made a special trip to the frontier to select a site for a home and then returned to the East to bring his family, but more often he started out for the wilderness with his family and a few household goods. He carried along a small supply of provisions, and supplied what was lacking by killing game along the way or by fishing in the mountain streams. Having selected a spot suitable for a homestead, his journey ended and the work of building a log cabin began. In this task he was assisted by the few neighbors, if any, in that remote district. After the frontier had become more thickly settled, however, and especially after the second generation reached maturity, house-raising became a sort of standardized system and a regularly organized activity on the frontier.[9]

A house-raising was commonly undertaken with the full cooperation of the neighbors, who gathered in a spirit of festivity as to a frolic. To erect a log cabin usually required but one day, though frequently it was preceded by a day spent in assembling materials and in clearing the site, generally near a spring; and was followed by having a neighborhood carpenter do finishing work around the door and window, and make a few rude articles of furniture. On the day appointed to raise the cabin, everybody in the neighborhood was present to lend a hand. Some felled the trees and cut them the lengths desired, while others were busily engaged in preparing puncheons for the floor and clapboards for the roof. The puncheons were made by splitting trees about eighteen inches in diameter and hewing the faces with a broadaxe, the

9. G. D. Albert, *History of Westmoreland County, Pennsylvania*, 154.

result being a "firm durable floor, which from dint of scrubbing and sanding, and from the incessant wear of the feet, became in time tolerably even and smooth."[10] The lower story was completed and ready for the joists by dinner time, when a substantial meal, prepared by the women folks, was eaten amidst great hilarity, especially as the host had not forgotten to bring along a jug of whiskey for his helpers. After dinner, the work proceeded without interruption until the cabin was completed, with ribs, roof, gable-ends and all. Meanwhile a "mortar hole" had been dug by a few of the men and clay secured for daubing the interstices of the building, while the boys were engaged in bringing water from the spring to mix it. It is now supper time, every one is tired, and there is less merriment than at dinner. Most of the men, especially the older ones, now start for home, taking with them their wives and children, their oxen, horses, and dishes. The young men, however, remain to daub the house with mortar made of clay and water, all the crevices being closed and the mortar smoothed over with wooden trowels. It is perhaps nine o'clock before the work is finished—a good day's work, and a fine example of the spirit of friendly neighborliness prevailing on the frontier.[11]

The early log cabins had only one room, with a loft above. Sometimes the loft was reached by a ladder from the outside, but generally by pins driven in the wall in the inside of the cabin. The door was hung on wooden hinges and was often made double, one above and one below, so that the upper part could be swung open to admit light, while the lower part was closed against the weather and intruding animals. A wooden latch was made to drop into a catch on the inside, and was manipulated by a latch-string, which, when drawn within, served as a lock. The fireplace was of generous dimensions, being commonly about ten feet wide. The single window was usually covered with oiled paper, admitting a dull, uncertain light. The construction of a huge chimney, made of stones, straw, sticks, and clay, completed

10. Albert, *op. cit.,* 155.
11. William Hanna, *History of Greene County, Pennsylvania,* 163-165; Albert, *op. cit.,* 155.

the cabin, and the work was left to dry for a few days, during which preparations were made for the housewarming.[12]

The furnishings of these humble homes were of the simplest kind imaginable; everything was crude and homemade. There would be a clapboard table, made of split slab and having four legs set in augur holes, some three-legged stools made in the same manner, and some shelves resting on pins driven into the back wall to be used for table ware. There might be a few pewter dishes, plates, and spoons, but more probably wooden bowls, trenchers, and noggins. On shelves near the fireplace were the pots and pans, skillets, pails, tin cups, and gourds. The bedstead consisted of a frame made by poles laid across rails resting in augur holes in the walls and in the notches of an upright post in one end of the room. On wooden pins over the fireplace rested the rifle, pouches, and powder-horn—indispensable parts of every Scotch-Irishman's equipment. Pegs were driven in various places around the walls, especially near the bed, for the display of the family wardrobe, the dresses of the women and the hunting-shirts of the men. The more of these there were on exhibition the greater the evidence of the prosperity of the family, and it appears that a secret pride was cherished in these displays.[13]

If, as was generally the case after the first inrush of settlers, the house-raising was for a newly married couple, it was customary for them to give a house-warming to the young people who had helped in building the cabin. Supper was served to the assembled guests, after which dancing was indulged in for a good part of the night. Relatives and friends of the young couple, among the older people, also were present in the earlier part of the evening, and entered sympathetically into the spirit of the occasion.[14]

A primitive log cabin such as has been described was usually occupied by the family for some ten or fifteen years, when it was likely to be replaced by a better log cabin made of hewn logs.

12. Joseph Smith, *Old Redstone, or Historical Sketches of Western Presbyterianism,* 95-96; W. J. McKnight, *A Pioneer Outline History of Northwestern Pennsylvania,* 224-225; Albert, *op. cit.,* 155-156.

13. A. J. Davis, *History of Clarion County, Pennsylvania,* 81.

14. Joseph Doddridge, *Notes on the Settlement and Indian Wars of the Western Parts of Virginia and Pennsylvania,* 137; Davis, *op. cit.,* 82.

The new cabin was a great improvement on the old, round logs giving way to hewn logs, clapboard roofs to shingles, puncheon floors to boards, wooden chimneys to stone, and greased paper to glass. Though most of the new cabins were but one and a half stories high and had but one room and a loft, some of the better class had two stories and four rooms. Stone houses represent an advanced stage of development, and, though the Scotch-Irish had these in plenty in eastern Pennsylvania, they do not appear to have been found on the western frontier until after the Revolution, and it was long after that time before they became at all general west of the Alleghenies. By degrees the pioneer extended his clearing, improved his dwelling and outhouses, increased the acreage of his crops, and at length found himself with a homestead in which he might take pride; but this transformation was accomplished only after much hard labor extending over a long period of years.[15]

The first stalls or stables for the stunted and scraggy stock were commonly constructed of chestnut saplings and were about six feet high. The interstices were ordinarily left open, and the roof was thatched with straw held in place by saplings and by placing large stones on the roof. Sometimes, however, the crevices were filled with straw and leaves, and the opening for the door was closed. A sty close by held a sow and a litter of pigs.[16]

The pioneers were a plain people, and home comforts and conveniences were few. It would be a mistake to assume that an advanced civilization, with its accompanying refinements, developed with any degree of rapidity on the frontier; life was primitive in the backwoods, and changes came slowly. Isolated, inaccessible, remote, with poor roads or none at all, communication with the east was slow and difficult, with the result that the frontiersmen lived a life unto themselves, pathfinders in the wilderness, laying the foundations on which a superior civilization was subsequently erected. A realistic approach to a study of life in the backwoods will conform much more closely to the facts in the

15. A. G. Bradley, "The Ulster Scot in the United States," in *Nineteenth Century*, LXXI, 1132.
16. Albert, *op. cit.*, 157.

case than a romantic account based on sentiment. Conditions of existence were hard, and not too lovely, while privations and discomforts abounded. That these were endured with patience and fortitude does not lessen the fact that they were ever present in this day of small things when civilization was in the making.

The domestic economy of the household centered around the wife and mother, whose duties were at once onerous and unending. She baked her own bread, and did the family cooking, washing, and sewing; she milked the cows and churned the butter; she picked, dyed, and carded the wool, broke and carded the flax, spun and wove the cloth, cut out the garments, and made the family wardrobe. Furthermore, she reared the children, taught them to read, and instructed them in the principles of Christianity. When anyone in the family was sick, she was the nurse and doctor, with home-made remedies of sulphate of iron, green copperas, bear's oil, snake root, and poultices. Mills were scarce and at first non-existent; hence if the housewife wished meal for johnny-cake or corn pone, she had to make it herself from corn ground on the hominy block or in the hand-mills. Cooking utensils were few and cumbersome, and there were no labor-saving devices to lighten her work, which was not confined entirely to the precincts of the cabin. She often worked the garden and roamed the woods in search of sassafras, sage, and mint to brew into teas. In summer, aided by the smaller children, she picked the wild fruits of the forest—blackberries, plums, cherries, haws, whortleberries, strawberries, and grapes. In autumn she laid in stores of hickory nuts and walnuts. In rush seasons she assisted in harvesting the crops, in burning brush and logs, and in gathering the fruits of the orchard. Supplies must be laid in to keep the family going through the long winter months, and she was kept busy drying apples, making oil from bear or opossum fat, hanging corn on the rafters to dry, and perhaps making corncob molasses. Her life was a ceaseless round of household duties and domestic cares, of loneliness and drudgery, often resulting in wearing herself out and becoming prematurely old. Moreover, she suffered much anxiety for fear that the rations would not last through the winter; that the wolves, or other wild animals, would destroy her loved ones if she ventured from home; or that the Indians would swoop down on the household with massacres, burnings, and widespread devastation. In emergencies, especially if her husband were absent in the wars, she learned to mold bullets and to use the rifle to defend her home and fireside from the savages. Her dauntless spirit rose with danger, and her heroism equalled that of her husband. The part played by the Scotch-Irish wife and mother in the life of the American frontier has never been adequately portrayed and perhaps could not be, so great it was and so sublime. On some towering mountain peak of Pennsylvania, the Commonwealth should erect to her a monument as a worthy memorial of her character and deeds.[17]

The customary fare of the Scotch-Irish pioneers included fried mush with wild honey, roasting ears and succotash, pone bread, johnny-cake, hominy, potatoes, turnips, wild fruits, game, and fish. Perhaps the most typical dish was pioneer porridge, consisting of mush and milk, although mush was frequently eaten with molasses, bear's oil, and the gravy of fried meat. A popular dish was hog and hominy, and another favorite was buckwheat souens. Every family had a garden, the vegetables most relied on being roasting ears, beans, squash, pumpkins, and potatoes. Johnny-cake and corn pone were the usual breads for breakfast and dinner, but the standard dish for supper was mush and milk. Doughnuts were much in evidence, and pies, especially apple pies, were in constant demand, though it appears that the latter were often made from dried apples. All sorts of wild fruits were gathered and eaten in season. Pork was the principal meat, but much game was found on the pioneer tables. Practically every Scotch-Irishman, trained in the use of the rifle from boyhood, was a skilled huntsman. He hunted deer, bears, rabbits, squirrels, wild turkeys, wild ducks, pigeons, and pheasants, relying strongly upon his rifle to keep the larder supplied with meat. He fished in the

17. H. R. Johnson, *A History of Neshannock Presbyterian Church*, 63-68; N. G. Parke, "Personal Knowledge of the Scotch-Irish," in Scotch-Irish Society of America *Proceedings*, VIII, 230; Samuel Wilkeson, "Early Recollections of the West," in *The American Pioneer*, II, 161, 205; F. L. Paxson, *History of the American Frontier*, 115; H. Calhoun, "Scotch-Irish Homespun," in Scotch-Irish Society of America *Proceedings*, IV, 195-197; H. C. McCook, in *ibid.*, VIII, 87-92; Albert, *op. cit.*, 157.

mountain streams for pike, bass, catfish, suckers, chubs, sunfish, trout, and eels. Beef, mutton, and lamb were seldom found on the tables of the pioneers, but hog-meat was common. In extremity, coons and opossums were eaten. Sweets were domestic and consisted of maple sugar, wild honey, and maple-molasses. Bee-trees were somewhat plentiful and often yielded from eight to twelve gallons of wild honey, the gathering of which became an art. The customary drinks were metheglin (a fermented liquor made of honey and water), small beer, cider, rye coffee, buttermilk, and sassafras, sage, mint, and fern teas, not to mention whiskey, which was in very general use among the Scotch-Irish as among all the elements of the population.[18]

The cooking was done in the large fireplace of the single room that served for living room, dining room, bedroom, and kitchen of the pioneer cabin. From a crane with a set of hooks, graduated in length, were suspended chains to hold the kettles for cooking the food. A few frying pans, skillets, and iron pots, and an open hearth served for the crude cooking equipment. Another part of the equipment in general use was a hominy block about three feet high, made of wood, with a hollow burned out at one end, wide at the top and narrow at the bottom, and a pestle to break up the corn.[19]

DRESS

The customary dress of a Scotch-Irish frontiersman consisted of a hunting shirt, woolen or leather breeches, cap, and moccasins. The hunting shirt, which was a sort of loose frock reaching half way down the thighs, had large sleeves and "the bosom of this dress served as a wallet to hold a chunk of bread, jerk, tow for wiping the rifle barrel, etc." It was made of coarse cloth or dressed deer skins, and the breeches or leggings were of like material. The belt, always fastened behind, held mittens, hatchet, hunting knife, bullet pouch, and powder horn. A heavy cape, often dec-

18. Joseph Smith, *op. cit.,* 97; W. J. McKnight, *op. cit.,* 226; A. S. Bolles, *Pennsylvania, Province and State,* II, 306-307; A. J. Davis, *op. cit.,* 82; E. Douglas Branch, *Westward: The Romance of the American Frontier,* 86; J. F. Stewart (ed.), *Indiana County: Her People Past and Present,* 20, 27.

19. Mary M. Sterrett, *op. cit.,* 16-18.

orated with a fringe of ravellings of different colors, was made of linsey-woolsey and hung down the back. The moccasins were made of a single piece of leather or untanned deerskin, and reached to the ankle. The frontiersman's garb, the most distinctive in the annals of American history, made him a picturesque figure. Continuing to be worn throughout the colonial era and beyond, it gave way slowly to other forms of clothing, the deerskin and linsey-woolsey hunting shirts being eventually supplanted by the wammus—a heavy-knit red woolen jacket, still worn by the older men down to the Civil War.[20]

The universal dress of the Scotch-Irish women on the frontier was a short gown and petticoat, made of wool for winter and of linsey-woolsey for summer. Wool hats or hoods were worn in winter, and sun-bonnets in summer; sometimes the headdress was simply a colored handkerchief, tied so that one point came down the back between the shoulders. The older ladies not infrequently wore full-frilled caps. A few of the more fortunate brought with them from beyond the mountains some finery, like a silk dress, carefully treasured for special occasions. Much later, calico became common for everyday dress, but this was regarded as very expensive, the price at first ranging from thirty to fifty cents a yard. Occasional relics of the old land and life, such as a ring, a pin or brooch, were more or less in evidence, though these were rare. Cloth was usually allowed to remain its natural color of gray, but was sometimes dyed red or green, the favorite colors. In winter the women wore shoe-packs or moccasins, but in summer they often went barefoot.[21]

Social Centers, Sports, and Amusements

The social centers of the Scotch-Irish of provincial Pennsylvania were the tavern, the cross-roads store, the mill, and the church.

20. Doddridge, *op. cit.*, 114-116; Joseph Smith, *op. cit.*, 97; H. R. Johnson, *op. cit.*, 72-73; James B. Finley, *Autobiography; or Life in the West*, 96-97; W. J. McKnight, *op. cit.*, 221; J. D. Schoepf, *Travels in the Confederation*, I, 238; Albert, *op. cit.*, 161; Thomas Creigh, *History of the Presbyterian Church of Upper West Conococheague*, 7-8.

21. H. Calhoun, *op. cit.*, 196; S. J. M. Eaton, *History of the Presbytery of Erie*, 19; Doddridge, *op. cit.*, 115-117; W. J. McKnight, *op. cit.*, 222; Finley, *op. cit.*, 97-98; Joseph Smith, *op. cit.*, 99; McCook, *op. cit.*, 85; Albert, *op. cit.*, 162; Mary M. Sterrett, *op. cit.*, 21-22.

Taverns in the early days served not only to provide food and shelter for travelers, but also were a sort of social club for the inhabitants of the village of the neighborhood generally. Here they gathered of an evening to while away an hour or two, to meet the neighbors, to patronize the bar, to hear the news and the neighborhood gossip, and to discuss happenings at home and abroad. Since newspapers did not circulate to any great extent on the frontier, the tavern became in a very real sense the news center of the community, the principal means of disseminating information from the outside world. Here, isolated communities heard with eagerness the tales of passing travelers. The tavern served also as a gathering place for local politicians, and was often the polling place at elections. Magistrates frequently held court there. The landlord was generally a man of consequence in the community, and exerted considerable political influence. In districts remote from the principal highways, however, taverns were not found; hence they played a relatively unimportant rôle in the life of most of the people on the frontier.[22]

Of greater significance as a social center in the early days was the crossroads store, one or more of which was to be found in every village, where the local merchant was a man of no slight importance. In rural communities practically all the business life of the times was concentrated in the country store, which not only furnished the neighborhood with merchandise, but also served as a market for country produce. In communities where taverns were not accessible, the neighbors were in the habit of gathering at the stores, where they sat on nail kegs and goods boxes, discussing politics, religion, crops, and local affairs generally.[23] To a less extent grist mills served as social centers, also. The miller, like the storekeeper, was a man of wide acquaintance and enjoyed a certain prestige in the community. Every farmer had to go to mill at rather frequent intervals, and, meeting there others bent on the same errand, lingered to talk over with his friends the neighborhood happenings. At both the store and the mill, house-raisings,

22. W. F. Dunaway, *History of Pennsylvania*, 329-330, 672-673; C. W. Dahlinger, *Pittsburgh; A Sketch of the Nineteenth Century*, 79, 81.

23. Dunaway, *op cit.*, 302-303.

corn-huskings, and log-rollings were often planned and the neighbors notified; perchance the forthcoming marriage of a son or daughter was published and everybody invited. Thus "norations" of one kind and another were circulated with comparative ease throughout the whole community. It is also probable, especially after the bottle had been passed around freely, that many tall stories were told in these social centers about the Indian wars, with their massacres, pillages, and burnings, together with the daring exploits and hairbreadth escapes of the participants, not to mention their adventures in hunting and fishing or their skill in shooting at marks or in wrestling.[24]

A social center of a different kind was the church, where men and women lingered in friendly conversation at "all-day meetings with dinner on the ground," discussing among themselves matters of common interest while youths and maidens wandered off to the near-by spring to enjoy each other's society in the recess of the dinner hour between the sermons. Where people came long distances over bad roads to "meeting," perhaps only once a month, and where opportunities for social intercourse were none too plentiful, they ordinarily made a day of it. Socially inclined and hungry for companionship in these sparsely settled communities, they naturally looked forward with interest to these periodical gatherings, which were well attended. Hence the church served the social as well as the religious needs of the people.[25]

The most popular sports of the Scotch-Irish frontiersmen were hunting, fishing, wrestling, foot-racing, jumping, throwing the tomahawk, and shooting at marks. Hunting and fishing were pursued partly as a pastime for the pleasure of it, and partly as a means of supplying the larder. In fall and winter they hunted deer; in winter and spring, bears and fur-skinned animals. Expert in the use of the rifle, they loved the excitements of the chase. The Scotch-Irish were skilled hunters, surpassing even their Indian foes in woodcraft, in trailing, and in artful strategy. Some of them, in fact, were attracted to the frontier "by their love of hunting and by a genuine attachment for the wild, unshackled scenes of

24. *Ibid.*
25. H. N. Potter, *One Hundred Years of Shenango Presbytery,* 13; Eaton, *op. cit.,* 20-21.

the ranger's life." [26] This latter type of huntsman, who was the exception and not the rule, is thus described by Schoepf as he saw them on the frontier in 1784:

"These hunters or 'backswoodsmen' live very like Indians and acquire similar ways of thinking. They shun everything which appears to demand of them law and order, dread anything which breathes constraint. They hate the name of a Justice, and yet they are not transgressors. Their object is merely wild, altogether natural freedom, and hunting is what pleases them. An insignificant cabin of unhewn logs; corn and a little wheat, a few cows and pigs, this is all their riches, but they need no more. They get game from the woods; skins bring them in whiskey and clothes, which they do not care for of a costly sort. . . . When they go out to hunt they take with them a blanket, some salt, and a few pounds of meal of which they bake rough cakes in the ashes; for the rest they live on the game they kill. Thus they pass 10 to 20 days in the woods; wander far around; shoot whatever appears; take only the skins, the tongues, and some venison back with them on their horses to their cabins, where the meat is smoked and dried; the rest is left lying in the woods. They look upon the wilderness as their home, and the wild life as their possession; and so by this wandering, uncertain way of life, of which they are vastly fond, they become indifferent to all social ties, and do not like many neighbors about them, who by scaring off the game are a nuisance besides. They are often lucky on the hunt and bring back great freight of furs, the proceeds of which are very handsome." [27]

The huntsman described by Schoepf was, of course, the extreme type of borderer, and their number was doubtless small, being found in the more mountainous and therefore less fertile districts, where farming was negligible. Nevertheless, every Scotch-Irishman on the frontier presumably was accustomed to the use of the rifle and employed it skillfully, whether in search of game or in defense of his fireside against the savages. Game was plentiful and many farmers subsisted through the winter largely on

---

26. Edwin MacMinn, *On the Frontier with Colonel Antes*, 270-271; J. H. Bausman, *The History of Beaver County, Pennsylvania*, 175; Winthrop Sargent, "The History of an Expedition against Fort Duquesne in 1755," in Historical Society of Pennsylvania, *Memoirs*, V, 86; Doddridge, *op. cit.*, 158; J. F. Stewart, *op. cit.*, 158; Bradley, *op. cit.*, LXXI, 1130.

27. Schoepf, *op. cit.*, 238-239.

bear-meat and deer-meat, which were considered necessaries on the border. If ammunition was scarce, it was considered unprofitable to hunt smaller animals, such as rabbits, squirrels, groundhogs, and raccoons, which were ordinarily caught in traps by boys or hunted with dogs.[28]

The amusements of the Scotch-Irish in the early days were simple and hearty—the natural, unrestrained diversions of the backwoods, boisterous rather than refined. The monotony of existence was varied by pastimes which, if few and primitive, were nevertheless adapted to the environment of the pioneers, wholesome in their nature and a source of relaxation and pleasure. A special feature of these diversions was that many kinds of labor were performed in a spirit of co-operative festivity regarded as frolics by the people of the community. Among these were house-raisings, log-rollings, wood-choppings, flax-pullings, corn-huskings, apple-cuttings, and quilting parties, which brought the people together and enlivened social intercourse; nor can there be any question that such gatherings not only exemplified the sociability and helpful attitude of the neighbors, but also that they were thoroughly enjoyed by those who participated in them. One of the most characteristic features of frontier life, they were entered into with zest and "a good time was had by all."

Then there were the friendly gatherings of the neighbors in each other's houses. They were a hospitable folk; the latch-key hung on the outside, and visitors were always welcome. Often, in the long winter evenings, a family would go over to visit a neighbor and "sit up till bedtime," which, however, in this case would not mean till the wee small hours of the morning, but till about nine o'clock. From her store the hostess would bring forth quantities of doughnuts, gingerbread, hickory nuts, sweet cider, and other simple refreshments; the elders would exchange ideas on congenial topics, and the children would play before the great open fireplace whose glowing embers lighted up the room. The men might indulge in a glass of whiskey, and there was sure to be laughter, jokes, and perhaps games. Because of the enforced

28. W. H. Egle, "The Scotch-Irish Pioneer Hunters and Scouts," in Pennsylvania Scotch-Irish Society *Proceedings*, XI, 46-47; MacMinn, *op. cit.*, 271.

cessation of labor in the fields, the winter was especially the season for social enjoyment. At a later stage of frontier life, when the people had become more settled in their habits, singing-schools, spelling-bees, and debating societies were community gatherings and helped to enliven the winter months.[29]

Cards, dice, backgammon, and other games of chance were seldom or never indulged in by the Scotch-Irish borderers, but dancing was a major amusement of the young people. This was in the form of reels and jigs; it does not appear that the cotillons and minuets of the eastern towns and cities had any vogue on the frontier, where all the amusements were of a rollicking, unconventional character, lacking in the formal etiquette prevailing farther to the eastward.[30]

A great event on the frontier was the muster of the militia, in which the social instincts of the people found further expression. This was a gala occasion occurring twice a year, in April and October, when the men gathered from far and near to receive a sort of training in the exercise of arms on the parade ground. The training, to be sure, was rather casual, but the social aspects of the muster were much enjoyed. Furnishing an opportunity for old friends to meet and greet each other, it was a sort of picnic for everybody, both officers and men. At these reviews, as on election day, another great occasion, the gathering was enlivened by pugilistic encounters, either for determining the physical prowess of certain renowned bullies of the community, or else for settling grudges of long standing between individuals. There was always plenty to eat and plenty to drink on these occasions, and no doubt some of the prowess exhibited was of the pot-valiant variety.[31]

No account of the social customs of the Scotch-Irish of the Pennsylvania backwoods would be complete if it failed to call attention to the prevalent use of whiskey throughout that area. Stills abounded in Southwestern Pennsylvania, where the use of whiskey was practically universal, not only among the Scotch-

29. H. R. Schenck, *History of the Falling Spring Presbyterian Church*, 17-19; Dinsmore, *op. cit.*, 186-188; William Hanna, *op. cit.*, 166-167; Davis, *op. cit.*, 85; Creigh, *op. cit.*, 9; McKnight, *op. cit.*, 230.

30. Stewart, *op. cit.*, I, 21; Doddridge, *op. cit.*, 158-160.

31. Stewart, *ibid.*; Dahlinger, *op. cit.*, 74-77.

Irish but among the other racial groups as well. The Scotch-Irish made more whiskey and drank more of it than any other group in this district, to be sure, but only because there were more of them; they had no monopoly on either its manufacture or its use. Storekeepers kept whiskey on their counters and sold it freely to thirsty customers, and it was of course found at all the taverns. Many of the farmers, having their own stills, had several barrels of it in their cellars or in outhouses near by. Some would drink it straight, while others drank it mixed with tansy, mint, or maple sugar. Drinking was taken largely as a matter of course, without prejudice to the character or standing of those who drank it. Its moderate use was thought to be beneficial rather than harmful, and it was regarded as a means of promoting neighborliness and sociability.[32]

Whenever a visitor called, hospitality and courtesy required the host to offer him liquor; not to have done so would have been a serious breach of etiquette. The custom of the country was to furnish whiskey in liberal quantities at all community gatherings, such as house-raisings, corn-huskings, and the like, to say nothing of supplying the laborers with it at harvest time, haying, and fruit-gathering. It was considered indispensable at weddings and funerals. Ministers drank it along with everybody else, and their influence was not impaired thereby—an indication that there was nothing disreputable about it in the minds of the people, unless it was taken to excess. It was the popular beverage of the back-woods and, as time passed, was fixed up in different forms, such as eggnog, apple toddy, and punch, hot or cold. Moreover, it was considered good as a medicine, a remedy for ague, rheumatism, snake bites, and for a score of other diseases.[33]

It must not be supposed, however, that the people were drunkards. In fact, it appears that there was probably less drunkenness on the frontier than there was in eastern Pennsylvania, where it was not unusual for young men to get drunk at the taverns or to

32. Albert, op. cit., 171.

33. Wilkeson, op. cit., II, 215; Veech, op. cit., 363; J. S. Van Voorhis, The Old and New Monongahela, 14; W. W. McKinney, "Eighteenth Century Presbyterianism in Western Pennsylvania," in Journal of the Presbyterian Historical Society, X, 103.

drink themselves under the table at weddings or at other social functions. Among the Scotch-Irish frontiersmen, drunkards were few and were generally despised by the people. There were no saloons on the frontier, and but few taverns, and drunkenness was not a characteristic of these people distinguishing them from those of other localities. Howbeit, the Scotch-Irish, though not a race of drunkards, undoubtedly did their full share of drinking, and it seems that they were able to stand up under it remarkably well.[34]

WEDDINGS AND FUNERALS

Weddings were events of unusual interest in the social life of the Scotch-Irish pioneers. Everybody in the neighborhood for miles around was invited, and everybody turned out for the occasion. There was more equality on the frontier than was found elsewhere, social rivalry and distinctions being practically unknown; hence parents seldom vetoed a marriage on the ground that their children were marrying their social inferiors. Where nobody was rich, a young man who was a suitor and a prospective son-in-law was not asked if he had any money; if he was industrious and of good character, he was deemed eligible. When young folks decided they wanted to get married, which was apt to be when they were around eighteen years of age, there was seldom any barrier in the way. Having set the day by mutual consent, great preparations were made for the wedding, which was to be no ordinary affair. The bride's mother had long been accumulating woolens, linens, and feathers for furnishing her daughter's cabin, and her father generally provided a horse and cow as the principal part of her dowry. The banns were published on two successive Sabbaths preceding the wedding, which was always celebrated at the home of the bride and was always in the daytime. On the morning of the wedding day, which was ushered in by the firing of rifle guns, the men gathered at the home of the bride and selected two of their best riders to "run for the bottle." The signal for the start of the race was the firing of a gun nearly a mile away, by the side of the road along which the groom's company was

34. Veech, *op. cit.,* 364; Wilkeson, *op. cit.,* 215; H. Hollister, *History of the Lacka-wanna Valley,* 142, 146-147.

to come. The winner of the race received from the groom the bottle and returned in triumph, followed by the groom and his party of relatives and friends on horseback.

The bottle is passed around and everybody takes a swig, the minister first. After the marriage ceremony every one kisses the bride. Then follows an elaborate dinner, bountiful rather than dainty, during which a festive spirit prevails, gradually reaching a climax in which there is the greatest hilarity, especially among the young men. After dinner, the remainder of the afternoon is spent in games and athletic sports until supper time. Supper over, the dancing begins and sometimes lasts all night, when the company departs. Two weeks later the neighbors gather for the house-raising, and a cabin is soon ready for the newly married pair. The house-warming, coming soon thereafter, completes the round of activities connected with the marriage, except that custom requires the bride and groom to make a formal appearance at church at the next regular service. The young couple, now left to themselves, begin life with little except strong arms and willing hands, as their fathers and mothers had done before them; but, full of hope and sustained by the buoyancy and confidence of youth, they face the future with undaunted faith and courage, thinking little and caring less about the hardships, dangers, and privations of their environment. It was the way of the frontier.[35]

Funerals were conducted with the utmost simplicity. There were no undertakers' establishments and no undertakers among the early Scotch-Irish borderers. When anyone died, a local carpenter would be engaged to make a plain coffin to order, and the expense was small; and this was the only expense. The neighbors dug the grave, furnished a wagon to serve as a hearse, and rendered all other needed services gratuitously. Funerals were almost universally held at the home of the deceased rather than at church, and this custom continued to be observed very generally even after churches had long been established in the community. Interment was usually in the family burying-ground in a near-by grove.[36]

35. William Hanna, *op. cit.*, 157-162; Dinsmore, *op. cit.*, 188-191; Doddridge, *op. cit.*, 128-129.
36. Dinsmore, *op. cit.*, 249-250.

With the passing of time, the social life and customs of the Scotch-Irish were greatly modified. As the frontier vanished and the refinements of civilization appeared on every hand, the descendants of the pioneers became more dignified in their bearing and more polished in their manners. Cultured gentlemen, they are accustomed to a gracious way of living. The Scotch-Irishman has not, nor has he ever had, an inferiority complex, and he stands abashed in the presence of no man. He is proud of the sturdy qualities of his ancestors and of the achievements of their descendants, and he considers the title "Scotch-Irishman" a sort of patent of nobility, or at the very least a designation of honor and a badge of respectability.

11

Religious Life of the Scotch-Irish

The practices peculiar to them as a class belong to their religious system, which was a culture and discipline whose effects upon American national character have been very marked. H. J. FORD

THE SCOTCH-IRISH were a very religious people, holding firmly to the tenets of their faith and promptly establishing churches in the wilderness. Believing in an educated ministry, their ministers were almost without exception trained men, well qualified to perform acceptably the duties of leadership.[1] The contribution made by this racial group to the moral and religious development of Pennsylvania is one of their outstanding achievements.

RELIGIOUS BACKGROUND OF THE SCOTCH-IRISH

The average Scotch-Irishman was a Presbyterian, as we would expect him to be in view of his European background. Scotland is prevailingly a Presbyterian country, and when the Lowland Scots migrated to Ulster they naturally established the Presbyterian Church strongly throughout that region, which became an important nursery of their faith. Upon coming to America, being well-grounded in their beliefs, they held to them no less firmly in the New World than in the Old. The mere crossing of the ocean did not effect any change in their principles; they brought their kirk with them into Pennsylvania as they had carried it into Ulster, and here they were intent upon maintaining their doctrines pure and undefiled.

1. C. P. Wing, *A Discourse on the History of Donegal and Carlisle Presbyteries*, 6; H. J. Ford, *The Scotch-Irish in America*, 415; A. Alexander, *Biographical Sketches of the Founder and Principal Alumni of the Log College*, 14.

Sandy might be a bit bigoted, to be sure, but he had the Scotch granite in his make-up; he was no reed shaken by the wind. A rather austere individual, he was somewhat stern and uncompromising. The iron had entered his soul when called upon to do battle against the injustices of Church and State in Scotland and Ulster, and it would take time to broaden and mellow him. Crude and narrow he might be, but he was never weak and vacillating. It was his habit to keep the Sabbath religiously and to instruct his children in the doctrines of the Westminster Confession and in the Shorter Catechism; this was a part of his inheritance, not to be regarded lightly. He was the principal founder of the Presbyterian Church in America, and made it the most numerous religious body in provincial Pennsylvania.[2] He established a Christian civilization in the wilderness and adorned it with his virtues.

The Scotch-Irish were overwhelmingly, though by no means exclusively, Presbyterian in their religious affiliations. It appears that fully 90 per cent of those found in Pennsylvania belonged to this denomination, and it is certain that wherever in the province they gathered in sufficient numbers to form group settlements, they invariably established Presbyterian churches.[3] Although as individuals they not infrequently united with other communions, it is impracticable to attempt to trace their religious affiliations with other bodies than the Presbyterian Church. As time passed and their contacts broadened, the Scotch-Irish became less exclusively Presbyterian than in the colonial era; many of the great leaders of other denominations and a goodly percentage of their membership are of Scotch-Irish ancestry, though less so in Pennsylvania perhaps than in other states of the Union. The Presbyterian churches of eastern Pennsylvania contained a larger percentage of communicants who were not Scotch-Irish than did those farther west, where the Scotch-Irish strain and influence were more pronounced.[4]

2. Charles Keith, *Chronicles of Pennsylvania*, II, 601; Ford, *op. cit.*, 285-286, 379.

3. J. G. Craighead, *Scotch and Irish Seeds in American Soil*, 280; D. H. Riddle, *The Scotch-Irish Element of Presbyterianism*, 14.

4. John Dalzell, "The Scotch-Irish in Western Pennsylvania," in Scotch-Irish Society of America *Proceedings*, II, 175; H. D. Funk, "The Influence of the Presbyterian Church in Early American History," in *Journal of the Presbyterian Historical Society*, XII, 60.

The Organization and Spread of Churches

The first Presbyterian church in Pennsylvania had its origin in the missionary labors of Francis Makemie, a Scotch-Irishman from County Donegal, Ireland. It appears that Makemie visited Philadelphia in 1692 and gathered a congregation of Presbyterians, who were organized in 1698 as the First Presbyterian Church of Philadelphia by Reverend Jedekiah Andrews. Although there were probably some Scotch-Irish among the charter members of this church, there is no evidence to show that they were a majority. The Second Presbyterian Church of Philadelphia was organized in 1743 under the leadership of Reverend Gilbert Tennent, and it is likely that a majority of its members were Scotch-Irish, as was its founder. By the close of the colonial era there were four Presbyterian churches in Philadelphia, where the Scotch-Irish had now become fairly numerous. They were also influential in the organization of the Presbytery of Philadelphia in the spring of 1706 and of the Synod of Philadelphia in 1717, when the first strong wave of Scotch-Irish immigration set in.[5]

After 1717, Presbyterian churches multiplied in the province in proportion as recruits from Ulster arrived. As a result of this immigration, churches were organized farther to the westward, where they became more numerous in the Cumberland Valley and beyond than in the vicinity of Philadelphia.[6] Inasmuch as there were some strong Scotch-Irish settlements in the present Chester, Lancaster, York, and Dauphin Counties, we find in these districts a number of early, historic Presbyterian churches such as Derry, Donegal, and Paxtang.[7] To trace the growth of Presbyterianism in colonial Pennsylvania is the work of the church historian and is apart from our present purpose. Since, however, the Scotch-Irish were so closely connected with this religious body, it seems advisable to give a brief survey of the organization and spread of the Presbyterian churches, which owed their origin and growth mainly

5. Guy S. Klett, *Presbyterians in Colonial Pennsylvania*, 38-43; White and Scott, *The Presbyterian Church in Philadelphia*, 3-4; Scharf and Westcott, *History of Philadelphia*, II, 1263.

6. Klett, *op. cit.*, 59, 68.

7. *Minutes of the Presbytery of New Castle*, I, *passim*; *Minutes of the Presbytery of Donegal*, I, 100, 127, 133.

to this racial group. Wherever the Scotch-Irish were the prevailing racial strain, there the Presbyterians were the predominant religious denomination, but elsewhere they were scantily represented.[8] Thus we find that in the Scotch-Irish settlements in Chester, Lancaster, and Dauphin Counties were located the early Presbyterian churches of Upper Octorara, Donegal, Pequea, Oxford, Middle Octorara, New London, Derry, Paxtang, Fagg's Manor, Chestnut Level, Forks of Brandywine, Hanover, Little Conewago, Leacock, and Muddy Run. In their settlements in Bucks County were Neshaminy, Deep Run, Newton, and Tehicken; in Northampton County, Mount Bethel and Allen Township; and in Montgomery County, Providence.[9]

When the Scotch-Irish crossed the Susquehanna into the Cumberland Valley, they founded numerous Presbyterian churches throughout this region, dating from about 1734. Among these were Silvers' Spring, Meeting House Spring (Carlisle), Big Spring, Falling Spring (Chambersburg), Upper West Conococheague (Mercersburg), Middle Spring, Rocky Spring, Stony Ridge Reformed, Lower Path Valley, Upper Path Valley, and Mossy Spring. In York and Adams Counties they founded the churches of Monaghan, Slate Ridge, Chanceford Reformed, Guinston Associate, Hopewell (Shrewsbury), Upper Marsh Creek, Lower Marsh Creek, Great Conewago, Round Hill, and Rock Creek Reformed.[10]

The Scotch-Irish were chiefly responsible for planting churches in the "back parts" of the province, as well as for fostering education throughout that region. Many historians, especially those writing in the Quaker interest, have been so concerned in portraying the Scotch-Irishman as a squatter, or as a rough, combative, unruly individual, as to overlook the fact that he was normally a devout Christian bent upon reclaiming the wilderness to the ways of civilization through the agency of churches and schools, and that, in his endeavor to achieve these objectives, he was notably successful. Moving ever farther out on the frontier, his trail was marked not

8. C. A. Hanna, *The Scotch-Irish*, II, 60-62, 103-104.

9. Hanna, *ibid.*; W. A. West, *Origin and History of the Presbyteries of Donegal and Carlisle*, 192-215; J. L. Ziegler, *History of Donegal Presbyterian Church*, 8-9.

10. Hanna, *ibid.*

only by the settlements he made and the villages he founded, but also by the Presbyterian churches he organized, making this denomination by far the most numerous and influential west of the Susquehanna, to say nothing of the considerable number of its adherents east of that river.

By 1750 the Scotch-Irish had begun to spread from the Cumberland Valley into the Juniata Valley, and here again, as soon as gathered in communities large enough to make it practicable, they founded churches, as was their custom. It was not, however, until after the French and Indian War that this region had received a sufficient population to enable it to plant churches. Among the Presbyterian churches organized by the Scotch-Irish in the Juniata Valley prior to the Revolution were Great Cove, Tyrone, Toboyne, Dick's Gap, Lower Tuscarora, Cedar Spring, Derry (in Mifflin County), Limestone Ridge, Middle Tuscarora, Frankstown, Upper Tuscarora, East Kishacoquillas, West Kishacoquillas, Fermanagh Associate, Tuscarora Associate, Sherman's Creek, Hart's Log, Cove Associate, Warrior's Mark, Lewistown, Dry Hollow, Huntingdon, Shaver's Creek, Sinking Valley, Shirley, and Bedford. These churches were located in the counties of Fulton, Perry, Juniata, Blair, Huntingdon, and Mifflin.[11]

Meanwhile the Scotch-Irish had crossed the Alleghenies and had begun to establish another great stronghold of their race in Southwestern Pennsylvania in the present counties of Westmoreland, Fayette, Washington, Allegheny, Greene, Beaver, and Indiana, founding many churches throughout this area between 1771 and 1798. When this process had been completed, the ultimate outcome was to make Pittsburgh the capital of American Presbyterianism. This may be illustrated by the following excerpt from an address delivered by Reverend Henry D. Lindsey, D.D., in 1913:

"Pittsburgh is Presbyterian through and through. Its very smoke has a bluish tinge. The man you meet on the street is a Presbyterian, and if not a Presbyterian he is a United Presbyterian, and if he is not a United Presbyterian he is an Associated Presbyter-

11. Hanna, *op. cit.*, 105-106; *Minutes of the Presbytery of Donegal*, II, 25, 48, 186-188, 201-208; III, 66, 69; Klett, *op. cit.*, 75, 82; *Fithian's Journal*, 1775-1776, 99-100.

ian, and if not an Associated Presbyterian he is a reformed Presbyterian, and if you have missed it all along the line he hastens to assure you that his father is a Covenanter."[12]

After making due allowance for the exuberance of the speaker, and not taking him any more seriously than he meant to be taken, one still gathers from his statement that the Presbyterians are a numerous and influential body in Pittsburgh, and this cannot be gainsaid. Not all of them, however, are of Scotch-Irish ancestry.

While the Scotch-Irish were advancing into Southwestern Pennsylvania, they were likewise spreading throughout Central Pennsylvania, where they planted pioneer churches between 1773 and 1800. Among these were Warrior Run, Chillisquaque, Northumberland, and Sunbury, in Northumberland County; Penn's Valley, Sinking Creek, and Lick Run in Centre County; Great Island in Clinton County; and Lycoming, Washington, and Pine Creek, in Lycoming County.[13] Into west central and northwestern Pennsylvania settlement proceeded slowly, hence the Scotch-Irish founded but few churches in that area prior to 1800; the first church they organized north of the Ohio was in 1797.[14] The region embraced in the original Presbytery of Erie comprised the territory north and northwest of the Ohio, where the settlers were prevailingly Scotch-Irish. In this district were founded prior to 1801 the Presbyterian churches of Cool Spring, Upper Salem, Rocky Mount, Amity, Morefield, Neshannock, and Fairfield, in Mercer County; Hopewell in Lawrence County; and Meadville and Sugar Creek (Cochranton) in Crawford County.[15]

MISSIONARY WORK ON THE FRONTIERS

With the organization of the Presbytery of Philadelphia in 1706, an effort was made to furnish ministerial supplies for neighboring destitute places. Numerous missionaries were sent out thereafter by the Presbyteries of Philadelphia, New Castle, and Donegal. As

12. Pennsylvania Scotch-Irish Society *Proceedings and Addresses*, XXIV, 17.

13. *Fithian's Journal*, 53, 59, 63, 67; J. Stevens, *History of the Presbytery of Northumberland*, 6-7; Hanna, *op. cit.*, 105.

14. H. N. Potter, *One Hundred Years of Shenango Presbytery*, 13.

15. S. J. M. Eaton, *History of the Presbytery of Erie*, 5-7, 16, 29-30; E. G. Trail, *First Presbyterian Church of Erie, Pennsylvania*, 7-14.

far as circumstances permitted, both the synod and the presbyteries supplied missionaries to the Scotch-Irish settlers of the backwoods. Ministers regularly serving in the more settled parts of the province were expected to do a certain amount of missionary work in the interior—preaching, catechising, administering the Lord's Supper, performing the marriage ceremony, and forming congregations. Supplications from the Scotch-Irish settlers on the frontier were constantly pouring into the presbyteries and the synod calling for ministerial supplies, and these requests were granted whenever possible. A special fund, known as a "fund for pious uses," was created and was maintained by collections from Presbyterian congregations, the object of which was partly to aid educational and charitable projects and partly to support the missionary undertakings in the destitute portions of the province.[16]

At first, in the absence of church buildings, worship was conducted in private houses or in the open air under the forest trees. When a congregation became sufficiently strong, it was organized as a church, a meeting-house was erected, and a burial ground was laid out in the immediate vicinity. As the community became more highly developed, the old log meeting-house was replaced by a frame or stone building. This process continued throughout the provincial period and indeed far into the nineteenth century until the frontier vanished. At the same time that the Scotch-Irish in their older settlements were living in progressive communities with well established churches worshipping in substantial buildings, the frontier settlers were being organized into churches under the guidance of missionaries supplied to them by the regular Presbyterian organization until they, in their turn, became self-supporting churches.[17]

The Scotch-Irish on the frontiers were mostly in poor financial circumstances and consequently were unable at first to raise sufficient funds to support ministers in their midst; hence they were dependent on outside aid. This was the day of small things, but the

16. *Records of the Presbyterian Church*, 8, 14, 419; *Minutes of the Presbytery of Donegal*, I, 262-263; Klett, *op. cit.*, 186-189, 192; *The Diary of Rev. John Cuthbertson, passim*.

17. Klett, *op. cit.*, 88, 92.

seed thus sown took root and resulted in a great spiritual harvest. Organized Presbyterianism in the East was kept busy meeting the unceasing demands for aid for the struggling communities on the frontier, and exerted itself, with considerable success, to meet the needs of the situation. Its efforts in this direction did not differ greatly from those of other denominations except that they had more particular reference to the needs of the Scotch-Irish, whereas those of the other religious bodies centered principally upon the English and German elements of the population. Presbyterian missionary effort was not confined exclusively to Pennsylvania, but extended as far as Virginia and North Carolina.

Character and Methods of the Frontier Churches

The Scotch-Irish were a church-going people, often riding or walking long distances to attend church services. Traveling in those days was by horseback, and the roads were rough. Eaton gives the following circumstantial account of how people went to church on the frontier of Northwestern Pennsylvania:

> "A family of six might be seen coming to church on two horses. The father would be mounted on one horse, with the oldest child behind him, and the third before him; whilst the mother would be on the other horse, with an infant in her arms, and the second in age behind her. Sometimes the mother and two children would be mounted on a solitary horse, while the father walked by her side with his coat hung over his arm. Young ladies often walked a distance of several miles to church, and in summer would carry their shoes in their hands until they approached the place of worship, when they would stop by the wayside and place them upon their feet, and be prepared to present a respectable appearance at the sanctuary."[18]

Church buildings were at first rude log structures, often built by the congregation in a single day, with no metal used in the whole building. They were commonly furnished with seats made of round logs, which sometimes lay on the ground, but ordinarily were raised to a suitable height by logs. These being hard and uncomfortable, the people would not infrequently rise and stretch

18. Eaton, *op. cit,,* 20.

themselves or walk about for a while to relieve their weariness. If the day were hot, men would leave their coats at home, and even the minister, when he had reached eighthly or ninthly and was warmed up by the exercise of speaking, might pause in his discourse to remove his coat. In winter, however, the churches were uncomfortably cold, there being no provision for heating them.[19]

Though the services in the frontier churches were invariably long and would be regarded today as an endurance test, they were submitted to with cheerful patience. They commonly began at ten o'clock or as soon thereafter as the congregation had assembled, and lasted well into the afternoon. The day's program consisted of two sermons, hymns and prayers, with a recess of about half an hour, during which the people ate the lunch they had brought with them. The older folks sat around discussing crops and the happenings of the neighborhood, while the young folks were apt to wander off to the spring near by and enjoy each other's society. At the expiration of the recess, the congregation reassembled for the afternoon service. There was never any hurry about anything; they had come to make a day of it and there was plenty of time. The sermons were long, as they were expected to be, often taking an hour and a half for delivery, and, as there were two of them, the congregation listened to three hours of preaching during the day. The minister, who was generally the only well educated man in the community, was held in great respect and proceeded deliberately from firstly to twelfthly, or thereabouts. Luther's advice to ministers to "rise up boldly, speak out loudly, sit down quickly" was observed by him only in part; he rose up with leisurely dignity, spoke out loudly only when warmed up to his subject, and sat down only when he was ready. He was not particularly emotional and was not given to "whooping it up and putting on the rousements." In the early days services were held once or twice a month —generally once a month on the frontier—and the people were hungry for the Gospel message, as well as glad of an opportunity to touch elbows after their loneliness in their isolated homes. "Going to meeting" was an event in their lives and they made the most

19. *Ibid.*, 18; C. E. McCartney, *The Presbyterian Church, Western Pennsylvania, and the Making of the Nation*, 5.

of it. They had come a long way to attend services and would have felt cheated if these were abbreviated. Long prayers were offered up by the elders, and long hymns or psalms were sung by the congregation. These, with the sermon, ordinarily consumed two hours or more at each service. On the other hand, there was no Sunday School, no Ladies Aid Society, no Mission Circle, no mid-week prayer-meeting, no young people's meetings, and no night services, so that the amount of time devoted to the church services weekly was no more than that given today by zealous church members. Sermons were delivered without the use of manuscripts, against which there was a strong prejudice in the backwoods.[20]

A special feature of the service was the singing, which was congregational and, except in the older settlements, without the use of an organ or other musical instrument, and there was no church choir. The service was led by the clerk, standing in front of the pulpit and facing the congregation. Generally it was "lined out" by the leader, though in some cases, where the hymn or psalm was familiar, it was simply announced and the congregation joined in the singing "with spirit and understanding." More commonly, however, it was lined out by the clerk, who announced the tune to be used. The lining out consisted merely in reciting one or two lines at a time before singing them. It appears that this custom arose partly from the scarcity of hymnbooks, and partly because some were unable to read, but long after these disabilities had been removed the custom continued in the rural districts because the people had become accustomed to it and liked it. This practice "became actually a matter of conscience with many of the old fathers, who insisted that the lining out was as much a part of worship as the singing and praying."[21] Furthermore, the Scotch-Irish Presbyterians were a conservative body and did not take kindly to innovations.

Of special significance were the semi-annual communion services, which usually lasted several days and were anticipated with great interest by the people, who came from far and near to attend

20. Eaton, *op. cit.*, 20-22; Roy H. Johnson, "Frontier Religion in Western Pennsylvania," in *Western Pennsylvania Historical Magazine*, XVI, 30.

21. Eaton, *op. cit.*, 21-22.

them. Many members from other congregations being present, the local church building would ordinarily be too small to accommodate them, and special arrangements had to be made for holding the service. Not infrequently in the summer season the service was held in the woods, a special stand being erected for the accommodation of the pastor and the visiting ministers. The hospitality of the local congregation was taxed to the utmost to provide food and lodging for the visitors, but no effort was spared to make them welcome. This hospitality was amply repaid when the members of the church now acting as host attended similar services in some other district. The ordinance was observed with the literal use of tables, and "tokens" were distributed to those entitled to them. The tokens were merely pieces of lead with the initial letters of the name of the church on them. This type of communion service, which played so large a part in the religious life of the early days, ceased to be observed when the necessity for it no longer existed.[22]

Scotch-Irish Religious Leaders

The Scotch-Irish ministers were not only the religious leaders of their communities, but also often the civil leaders as well. Many of the first ministers were graduates of the universities of Glasgow, Edinburgh, and Dublin, but later in the colonial era they were mostly graduates of Log College or of the College of New Jersey (Princeton), and of the academies at New London and Chestnut Level. Of the eighteen ministers attending the Presbytery of Donegal on the eve of the Revolution, at least fifteen are said to have been graduates of Princeton.[23]

The life of the Scotch-Irish ministers on the frontier was full of hardships cheerfully borne. They lived in log cabins and shared the inconveniences of the people generally. Most of them served several churches in widely separated communities and were compelled to spend much of their time on horseback, travelling back and forth over poor roads in all kinds of weather. Not only were their salaries small but even what was promised was slow in being paid, it being

---

22. *Ibid.*, 22-25, 67; Johnson, *op. cit.*, 29.
23. *Fithian's Journal*, xvi; J. W. Houston, "Early Presbyterianism in Lancaster County," in Lancaster County Historical Society *Papers*, 224.

not unusual for a congregation to be months and even years behind on salary payments, a good part of which was apt to be paid in kind rather than in money. Sometimes a preacher was engaged with the understanding that half his salary would be paid in cash and the remainder in country produce. Others were given a tract of land and a small cash salary of perhaps fifty to a hundred dollars for half their time.[24] In many instances they augmented their income by teaching school, generally in their own houses. Dr. John McMillan relates the circumstances under which he came to assume charge of the churches at Chartiers Creek and Pigeon Creek, accompanied by his bride, as follows: "We placed two boxes one on the other which served us for a table, and two kegs served us for seats, and having committed ourselves to God in family worship, we spread a bed on the floor and slept soundly till morning. We enjoyed health, the Gospel and its ordinances, and pious friends. We were in the place we believed God would have us be."[25] Though he was outstanding as a minister, his salary for many years amounted to about $260 annually, part of which was paid in cash and the remainder in kind. Among other things, he received in 1782 some tallow, a quire of paper, corn, and wheat.[26] In 1736 the Paxton Church arranged to employ Reverend William Bertram for half his time, his salary being paid half in money and half in hemp, linen yarn or linen cloth, at market price.[27]

Prominent among the Scotch-Irish ministers of provincial Pennsylvania were William Tennent and his three sons—Gilbert, Charles, and William, Jr. —, John Ewing, Samuel Blair, John Blair, Charles Beatty, Samuel Finley, Francis Alison, John Elder, Robert Smith, Joseph Smith, John Steel, John McMillan, Thaddeus Dod, Joseph Patterson, Elijah McCurdy, James Power, John King, and David Smith.[28] It is not feasible to describe the labors of all these ministers, but rather to select from them several of the most representative ones in different sections of the province. In

24. Johnson, *op. cit.*, 26.
25. Cited by McCartney, *op. cit.*, 11.
26. D. M. Bennett, "Concerning the Life and Works of the Reverend John McMillan, D.D.," in *Journal of the Presbyterian Historical Society*, XV, 218.
27. Alfred Nevin, *Churches of the Valley*, 72.
28. This list comprises only a few of the many that might be listed.

the Philadelphia area two of the most eminent of them were Gilbert Tennent and John Ewing, the former being the founder of the Second Presbyterian Church in that city in 1743 and for many years a conspicuous religious leader, whom George Whitefield declared to be one of the ablest preachers he ever heard. Reverend John Ewing, D.D., who was pastor of the First Presbyterian Church at Philadelphia from 1759 to 1802, was recognized on all sides as a man of exceptional attainments as a minister and educator; in 1779 he was chosen as the head of the newly created University of the State of Pennsylvania.[29]

Of far-reaching significance was the work of Reverend William Tennent, the founder of the famous Log College at Neshaminy in Bucks County and the pastor of the Presbyterian Church in that community. Another outstanding minister and educator of eastern Pennsylvania was Reverend Francis Alison, D.D., who was pastor of the Presbyterian Church at New London, and later became vice provost of the College of Philadelphia.[30] These two men were perhaps more celebrated as educators than as ministers, and are described at greater length in the chapter on education.

Farther to the westward in a region more typically Scotch-Irish were located John Elder, John Steel, and John King. Reverend John Elder, a native of County Antrim, Ireland, was pastor of the Presbyterian church at Derry from 1738 to 1791, and for a time of the Paxtang Church also. A graduate of the University of Edinburgh and a man of exceptional force of character, he was for many years an outstanding leader in his community—the present Dauphin County and the region roundabout. During the Indian wars he organized a band of rangers to protect the people against the savages. Commissioned captain by the provincial government and known as the "fighting parson," he was regarded as a wall of defense by the people, who loved and honored him both as a preacher and a soldier. Regularly during these trying times he would carry his rifle up the winding stairs and place it beside him

29. C. E. McCartney, "Period of the General Synod," in *Journal of the Presbyterian Historical Society*, XV, 27; Funk, *op. cit.*, 201, 204.

30. R. P. Dubois, *A Discourse on the Origin and History of the Presbyterian Church and Congregation of New London, in Chester County, Pa.*, 15-18; Alexander, *op. cit.*, 20-22, 30.

near the pulpit, while the other men stacked theirs under guard at the entrance to the church or hung them on the wooden pins around the interior of the building. The Paxton Rangers, whom he commanded, were made up chiefly of young men from the congregations of Paxtang, Derry, and Hanover, and were a gallant band of Scotch-Irishmen.[31] Reverend John Steel, another of the fighting parsons, was pastor of the church at Upper West Conococheague (Mercersburg), and also of the churches at Greencastle and Carlisle, in the Cumberland Valley. Resembling Elder in his intrepidity, he was not only "a good preacher and sound divine," but was a captain of provincial militia in the Indian wars and in the Revolution. On one occasion he led a band of a hundred men against the Indians.[32] Reverend John King, pastor of Mercersburg Presbyterian Church from 1768 to 1811, was an able and scholarly minister upon whom Dickinson College conferred the degree of D.D. in 1792, in which year he was elected Moderator of the General Assembly of the Presbyterian Church. He was also the author of several small publications which evidence his scholarly propensities.[33]

Until 1774 the Scotch-Irish settlers in Western Pennsylvania were dependent upon missionaries sent out by the Synod, but in that year Reverend James Power began the labors which were to result, in 1776, in his becoming the first Presbyterian pastor west of

---

31. R. H. Taylor, *A Historical Sketch of Derry Presbyterian Church*, 7-8; W. M. Downey, *History of Paxton Church*, 26-27.

32. Thomas Creigh, *History of the Presbyterian Church of Upper West Conococheague*, 24-27; D. K. Richardson, *The Presbyterian Church at Greencastle*, 12-13; Nevin, *op. cit.*, 80-81, 237.

In *Frontier Forts of Pennsylvania*, I, 553, we find the following reference to Mr. Steel: "At one time, it is stated, Rev. Steel was in charge of Fort Allison, located just west of the town, near what afterwards became the site of McCaulay's mill. At this time the congregation had assembled in a barn. . . .During this period, when Mr. Steel entered the church and took his place back of the rude pulpit, he hung his hat and rifle behind him, and this was done also by many of his parishioners. On one occasion, while in the midst of his discourse, some one stepped into the church quietly, and called a number of the congregation out, and related the facts of a murder of a family by the name of Walker by the Indians at Rankin's mill. The tragic story was soon whispered from one to another. As soon as Mr. Steel discovered what had taken place, he brought his discourse to a close, took his hat and rifle, and at the head of the members of his congregation, went in pursuit of the murderers."

33. Nevin, *op. cit.*, 106, 112-113.

the Alleghenies. In 1779 he entered upon his first regular charge as pastor of the churches at Sewickley and Mount Pleasant. A graduate of Princeton, he was well equipped for the ministry; energetic, zealous, and capable, he exerted a strong influence in his community. Along with John McMillan, Thaddeus Dod, and Joseph Smith, he was one of the founders of the Redstone Presbytery, which was organized on May 16, 1781, on the extreme frontier of the province.[34] The second and most famous of this group of Scotch-Irish founders of Presbyterianism in Western Pennsylvania was Reverend John McMillan, D.D., who was distinguished both as a minister and an educator. A man of great force of character and intellect, he became the leader among the ministers of his section, earning the title of "the Apostle of Western Pennsylvania." After receiving a thorough academic training at the classical schools of John Blair at Fagg's Manor and Robert Smith at Pequea, he entered Princeton College and pursued the regular course leading to graduation. Licensed to preach in 1774 by the Presbytery of New Castle, he spent the summer of 1774 and the following winter as a missionary in Western Pennsylvania. Ordained at Chambersburg in 1776, he returned to the Redstone region to become pastor of Chartiers and Pigeon Creek Presbyterian Churches in Washington County. For nineteen years he served these two churches, but thereafter gave his whole time to the Chartiers congregation. As a preacher, he was "strong, earnest, and sometimes eloquent, though without much pulpit action." He had a powerful voice, which could be heard distinctly by large crowds at camp-meetings in the open air no less than in church buildings. For more than half a century he preached the Gospel far and near, great spiritual awakenings attending his ministry. Their effects spread not only throughout Western Pennsylvania, but extended even to the settlements in Kentucky and Tennessee. His influence may be noted in the fact that he was Moderator of the Synod of Virginia in 1791 and of the Synod of Pittsburgh in 1803 and 1817. After a long and useful life he died on November 16, 1833, at the age of eighty-one.[35]

34. E. H. Gillett, *History of the Presbyterian Church in the United States of America*, I, 258-260.

35. J. F. Tuttle, *Presbyterianism on the Frontiers*, 8-9; W. B. Noble, *History of the*

Thaddeus Dod and Joseph Smith were the other two of that remarkable quartette of Scotch-Irish pioneer leaders who laid the foundations of Presbyterianism in Western Pennsylvania. Both were graduates of Princeton and both arrived early in the field. Dod came in 1777 and for a while engaged in missionary work, but in 1778 organized congregations at Lower Ten Mile and Upper Ten Mile, each being about ten miles from the village of Washington. These two congregations constituted one church organization, of which he was long the pastor. According to Tuttle, he was "winning in manner, imposing in person, powerful in thought, devoted in piety, impassioned in voice and action . . . at times overpowering in his discourses."[36] He was also an educator, being one of the principal founders of Washington Academy. Reverend Joseph Smith served as pastor of Lower Brandywine Presbyterian Church from 1773 to 1778, but in 1779 went to Western Pennsylvania to become pastor of the churches at Buffalo and Cross Creek, which he continued to serve until his death. It was said of him that he was "one of the most truly remarkable men that ever preached on any of the frontiers, not only in his piety and gifts as a preacher, but in the truly astonishing effects which often attended his ministry."[37]

The contribution of the Scotch-Irish ministers and churches to the moral and religious development of colonial Pennsylvania is impressive, being unexcelled by that of any other religious body. By the end of the provincial period the Presbyterians, whose growth was due largely to them, were the most numerous denomi-

---

Presbyterian Church at Fagg's Manor, Chester County, Pa., 28-29; C. E. McCartney, The Presbyterian Church, Western Pennsylvania, and the Making of the Nation, 5, 11.

The following story, which bears all the earmarks of authenticity and would be in accord with the customs of the frontier, is told of Dr. McMillan: He and Reverend Joseph Patterson, on their way to attend a meeting of the Presbytery at Pittsburgh, stopped at an inn to refresh themselves. "Two glasses of whiskey were set down and Dr. McMillan proposed a prayer and a blessing. Patterson's blessing was protracted, and McMillan, putting forth his hand, drained off first one glass and then the other. When the prayer was finally ended and Patterson, opening his expectant eyes, saw only two empty glasses, McMillian said to him, 'My brother, you must watch as well as pray.'" See C. E. McCartney, "John McMillan; The Apostle of the Gospel and Presbyterianism in Western Pennsylvania," in Journal of the Presbyterian Historical Society, XV, 129.

36. Tuttle, op cit., 6-8.
37. Tuttle, op. cit., 8.

nation in Pennsylvania, being particularly strong in certain parts of Chester, Lancaster, and Dauphin Counties; in the Cumberland Valley; and in Southwestern Pennsylvania. Thus it appears that, contrary to the impression conveyed by some writers who have not investigated the subject carefully, the Scotch-Irish were in fact conspicuous among the racial groups of Pennsylvania for their zeal and success in promoting the moral and religious welfare of the people.

12

Educational and Cultural Contribution
of the Scotch-Irish

The schoolhouse and the kirk went together wherever the Scotch-Irish frontier moved. The extraordinary zeal of this group for education is revealed in its emphasis on a learned ministry, in its founding of schools and colleges, and in its printing of catechisms and other books. CARL WITTKE

ELEMENTARY SCHOOLS

IN THEIR CONTRIBUTION to education in colonial Pennsylvania the Scotch-Irish were unexcelled, if indeed they were equaled by any other racial group. No less interested in establishing schools than in founding churches, we find these twin sisters of civilization advancing hand in hand into the frontier. The Scotch-Irish ministers being Presbyterians, the educational activities which they promoted were under the direction of that religious body. It appears that most of the Scotch-Irish ministers were more or less employed in teaching school and, in the event they were not teachers, were at least expected to have a general supervision over the instruction of the children of their congregations.[1]

As among the other racial groups of the province, the typical elementary school among the Scotch-Irish was the church school. In their case the distinguishing feature was found in the fact that the religious instruction given was according to the standards of the Presbyterian Church, especially in the insistence upon learning the Catechism as a regular exercise. Little was taught in these schools beyond the rudiments. Reading, writing, arithmetic, and

1. J. P. Wickersham, *A History of Education in Pennsylvania*, 105, 178.

spelling were the branches ordinarily studied. The Bible was the customary daily reader, and the Shorter Catechism was recited by all the school every Saturday morning.[2] The equipment of these early schools was exceedingly meager. Ordinarily the school buildings were rough log cabins, though in the older settlements these were gradually replaced by structures of hewn logs or of frame lumber. The furnishings consisted of benches made of split logs hewn to a proper thickness and supported by four legs, and tables of similar material. Pens were made of goose quills, but there were no blackboards, slates, or pencils. In the beginning the log churches served as schoolhouses, but when the people became more prosperous better church buildings would be erected and another building would be constructed on the church lot to be used as a schoolhouse.[3]

With the advance of the frontier into remote regions, it was found that the facilities afforded by church schools were inadequate to meet the needs of the pioneers. Not only were there districts in which there were no churches, and hence no church schools, but some churches, small and widely scattered, did not find it practicable to establish schools. Accordingly, it became necessary to organize another type of elementary school to supplement the work of the church schools. The new type of school which arose to meet these conditions was known as the "neighborhood school," and the Scotch-Irish were its principal promoters. These schools were of the nature of community enterprises, established by the voluntary efforts of the people to meet an urgent necessity. Although inadequately equipped and poorly taught, generally by itinerant schoolmasters, they met a real need in a thoroughly American way. As in the case of the church schools, those who were able to pay the tuition of their children were required to do so, but the children of the poor were admitted free.[4]

CLASSICAL SCHOOLS AND ACADEMIES

Through their church schools and neighborhood schools the Scotch-Irish contributed worthily to the development of elemen-

2. *Ibid.*
3. *Ibid.*, 108-109, 187-193.
4. Alfred Creigh, *History of Washington County, Pennsylvania*, 53; Wickersham, *op. cit.*, 180-184.

tary education in Pennsylvania, but they did not excel other racial groups in this regard. In secondary education, however, they were far in the lead of all other groups, as the record clearly shows.[5] In founding schools of a more advanced type they were motivated mainly by the desire to provide an educated ministry. The first of the schools of higher grade to be established in Pennsylvania by the Scotch-Irish was the celebrated "Log College" founded by Reverend William Tennent, Sr., at Neshaminy. This school was the first institution founded by American Presbyterians designed to educate young men for the ministry. Its founder, who was educated at the University of Edinburgh, was a scholar of exceptional attainments, being "skilled in the Latin language so as to speak it and write it almost as well as his mother tongue; a good proficient, also, in the other learned languages, and well read in divinity."[6] Emigrating from Ireland to Pennsylvania in 1718, he became pastor of the Presbyterian church at Neshaminy in 1726 and here continued until his death in 1743. His school, which was founded in 1726 or 1727, and of which he was the sole teacher, ceased to exist in 1742. He was aided by James Logan, secretary of the province, in securing fifty acres of land and a small sum of money. George Whitefield, who visited the school in 1739, says: "The place wherein the young Men study is in contempt called *the College*. It is a Log-House, about Twenty Feet long, and near as many broad; and to me it seemed to resemble the schools of the prophets. . . . From this despised Place Seven or Eight worthy Ministers of Jesus have lately been sent forth; more are almost ready to be sent, and a foundation is now laying for the instruction of many others."[7] Yet the Log College was not a school founded under ecclesiastical auspices, but was rather a private classical school established and maintained as a one-man institution primarily for the training of ministers. Not in any sense a college, it was an academy in which Greek, Latin, and the "arts and sciences" were taught, along with theology. Nevertheless it was of great significance as a nursery of

5. Wickersham, *ibid.*, 110; Guy S. Klett, *Presbyterians in Colonial Pennsylvania*, 199.
6. A. Alexander, *Biographical Sketches of the Founder and Principal Alumni of the Log College*, 13, 27; Elias Boudinot, *The Man in a Trance, or the Life of the Reverend William Tennent*, 9; *Logan Papers*, II, 80-81; *Logan Letter Books*, III, 204.
7. *A Continuation of the Reverend Mr. Whitefield's Journal*, 31, 44.

ministers and of other leaders, and as furnishing an example for the founding of other schools of similar type. Receiving no financial aid from the outside, it was supported entirely by tuition fees paid by students. Among its alumni were the following eminent ministers: Samuel Blair, John Blair, Samuel Finley, Charles Beatty, and John Rowland, of whom the first three were also distinguished educators. John Blair and Samuel Finley became presidents of Princeton; in fact, the Log College was the germ from which Princeton developed.[8]

Another famous school of the provincial era was Fagg's Manor Classical School, which was founded by Reverend Samuel Blair in Chester County in 1739. A native of Ireland and emigrating to America when a boy, Mr. Blair became pastor of the Presbyterian church at Fagg's Manor in 1739 and promptly established his school there. Like the Log College, of which it may be regarded as in some sense the successor, this school was designed primarily to prepare young men for the ministry. It probably closed with the death of its founder in 1751, but was reopened in 1757 by his brother, the Reverend John Blair, who continued to conduct it until his removal to Princeton a decade later to become professor of theology and moral philosophy.[9] Among its better known alumni were John Rogers, moderator of the first General Assembly of the Presbyterian Church in America; Robert Smith, founder of the Pequea Academy, John McMillan, outstanding minister and educator of Western Pennsylvania; and Samuel Davies, president of Princeton College.[10]

Not less renowned than Fagg's Manor Academy was Pequea Academy, founded by Reverend Robert Smith, D.D., a Scotch-Irish graduate of the Log College. Becoming pastor of the Presbyterian church at Pequea in Lancaster County in 1850, Dr. Smith opened his school there two years later. A distinguishing feature of this school was that it enjoyed a longer life than other similar

8. James Mulhern, *A History of Secondary Education in Pennsylvania*, 65, 67; E. R. Craven, "The Log College of Neshaminy and Princeton University," in *Journal of the Presby'n Hist. Soc.*, I, 314.

9. W. B. Noble, *History of the Presbyterian Church at Fagg's Manor, Chester County, Pa., 1730-1776*, 6-7; Mulhern, *op. cit.*, 68; Alexander, *op. cit.*, 295.

10. William B. Sprague, *Annals of the American Pulpit*, III, 304.

schools in the province; it continued under Dr. Smith's management for forty years. Like the school at Fagg's Manor, it was not only a preparatory school for Princeton, but also instructed in theology some graduates of Princeton—notably George Duffield, John McMillan, and Samuel Doak. Special emphasis was placed upon the study of Latin, Greek, and theology. It was not a one-man school, for Dr. Smith employed some of the most accomplished teachers of his day. The alumni included a number of men who attained distinction as ministers and educators, among whom were two of Dr. Smith's sons—Samuel Hope Smith and John Blair Smith, the former of whom became president of Princeton College, and the latter the president of Hampden-Sydney College and later of Union College. Among the teachers employed to assist Dr. Smith was James Waddell, the celebrated blind preacher and orator of Virginia, described in Wirt's *British Spy*.[11]

Reverend Samuel Finley, D.D., a native of County Armagh, Ireland, came to Philadelphia in 1743 and within a year became pastor of the Presbyterian church at Nottingham in Chester County, bordering on the Maryland line. Here he founded Nottingham Academy, and from 1744 to 1761 was engaged in preaching and teaching until elected to the presidency of Princeton College in the latter year. His school was noteworthy for the number of its eminent alumni, among whom may be mentioned Dr. Benjamin Rush and his brother, Judge Jacob Rush, James Waddell, Governor John Henry of Maryland, Governor Alexander McWhorter of New Jersey, and Governor Alexander Martin of North Carolina. After a fruitful career of seventeen years, Nottingham Academy closed its doors with the removal of Dr. Finley to Princeton.[12]

Numerous other Scotch-Irish schools were founded upon the initiative of Presbyterian ministers as purely private ventures supported by the tuition fees of students. While these did not achieve the celebrity of those mentioned above, they all served a useful

11. Jacob N. Beam, "Dr. Robert Smith's Academy at Pequea," in *Journal of the Presbyterian Historical Society*, VIII, 150-153; Futhey and Cope, *History of Chester County, Pa.*, 303.

12. J. H. Sheppard, "Irish Preachers and Educators in the Early History of the Presbyterian Church in America," in *Journal of the American Irish Historical Society*, XXIV, 168-169; Mulhern, *op. cit.*, 67, 71; Klett, *op. cit.*, 205.

purpose in giving better instruction than that afforded by the elementary schools. After Princeton had become firmly established as the Presbyterian college of the Middle Colonies, the emphasis was chiefly upon preparing students for that institution. Among these schools were Sampson Smith's academy at Chestnut Level, Henry McKinley's Academy at Carlisle, John King's Classical School at the Conococheague Settlement, James Latta's Classical School at Chestnut Level, Upper Octorara Classical School, Alexander Dobbin's Academy at Gettysburg, John Roan's school at Neshaminy, and the classical schools near Bath in Northampton County and at Strasburg in Lancaster County.[13]

A different type of school from those described above was that founded by the Presbyterians in the Scotch-Irish settlement at New London in Chester County. This school, known as the New London Academy, was under ecclesiastical control and grew out of the academy founded by Dr. Francis Alison in 1744. Dr. Alison, a native of County Donegal, Ireland, was educated at the University of Glasgow. Around 1835 he emigrated to Pennsylvania at the age of thirty and became a tutor in the home of Samuel Dickinson, the father of John Dickinson, where he taught the future author of the *Farmer's Letters,* along with several other boys. In 1737 he became pastor of the Presbyterian church at New London, where he bought a farm and started a school, which was at first a purely private enterprise. Among its alumni were John Ewing, James Latta, and Matthew Wilson, ministers; Charles Thomson, Secretary of the Continental Congress; Hugh Williamson and David Ramsay, historians of North Carolina and South Carolina, respectively; and Thomas McKean, James Smith, and George Read, signers of the Declaration of Independence.[14] In 1743 the Synod of Philadelphia began to consider the advisability of establishing under ecclesiastical control a school for the education of ministers,

13. H. D. Funk, "The Influence of the Presbyterian Church in Early American History," in *Journal of the Presbyterian Historical Society,* 184-185; Mulhern, *op. cit.,* 115; Klett, *op cit.,* 206-207; W. F. Rutherford, "Notes and Queries," in *History of Paxtang Presbyterian Church.*

14. J. W. Weidman, "Rev. Francis Alison, D.D., and Classical Education in Pennsylvania," in *Scotch-Irish Society of America, Proceedings,* IX, 109-111; Sheppard, *op. cit.,* XXIV, 164-165.

and in the following year approved a plan for this purpose. Dr. Alison's school was chosen as the one best suited to the requirements of the Synod, and it was agreed to take it under synodical control. The agreement provided that free instruction should be afforded "in the Languages, Philosophy, and Divinity to all who chose to attend," and that the school should be supported by contributions from the churches composing the Synod. Dr. Alison was appointed master of the school, with the privilege of choosing an usher to assist him.[15] This arrangement continued from 1744 to 1752, when Dr. Alison removed to Philadelphia to assume charge of the academy connected with the College of Philadelphia, where he became vice-provost and professor of moral philosophy in 1755. After his removal, Reverend Alexander McDowell was placed in charge of the school at New London. How long the Synod continued to support McDowell is not clear, though probably not beyond 1758, in which year Princeton became the authorized school of the Synod and was thereafter the recipient of the funds for the education of Presbyterian young men entering the ministry.[16] Dr. Alison labored as minister and educator in Philadelphia for more than a quarter of a century, gaining distinction in both fields. Princeton and Yale conferred upon him the degree of A.M., and the University of Glasgow conferred on him the degree of D.D., he being the first American to be so honored by a European university.[17]

SCOTCH-IRISH CLASSICAL SCHOOLS AND ACADEMIES IN WESTERN PENNNSYLVANIA

Late in the colonial era, Scotch-Irish ministers began to found schools of academic grade beyond the mountains. Three of the most eminent of these were Thaddeus Dod, John McMillan, and Joseph Smith, all of whom taught school in Washington County,

15. *Records of the Presbyterian Church,* 175-176; Richard Webster, *History of the Presbyterian Church in America,* 468.

16. *Records of the Presbyterian Church,* 224; Klett, *op. cit.,* 212-13. When Dr. Alison's school was moved to Delaware, the Synod established a similar school at Chestnut Level under the care of Reverend Sampson Smith. See Mulhern, *op. cit.,* 80-81.

17. Sheppard, *op. cit.,* 165; Alexander, *op. cit.,* 115, 116; Webster, *op. cit.,* 441.

Pennsylvania. Reverend Thaddeus Dod, who was pastor at Ten Mile in that county, erected a school building on his farm and taught the classics and mathematics for several years until the sale of his farm led to the transference of his students to the school of Reverend Joseph Smith. Mr. Smith, who was pastor at Buffalo, opened a school there in 1785 in his own home and conducted it successfully for several years until failing health compelled its discontinuance.[18] Another Joseph Smith, the grandson of the pastor at Buffalo, in writing about the early Scotch-Irish ministers of Western Pennsylvania, says:

"They also cooperated with their people in organizing schools; and in most cases took them under their own care, becoming teachers themselves, or providing adequate instructors. This may have been, possibly, in some cases with a view, in part, to eke out a scanty support. . . . Almost coeval with their settlement west of the mountains, these ministers got up schools near their dwellings. As such dwellings would generally be as near the center of their congregations as practicable, this location of the school houses would be most convenient to their people."[19]

In the provincial era Dr. John McMillan was the foremost educator of Western Pennsylvania. His log-cabin academy at Chartiers was contemporary with those of Dod and Smith, but outlasted them and was of greater significance. Beginning in 1782, it continued until 1791, when he turned over his students to Canonsburg Academy. He gave instruction not only in Greek and Latin, but in theology as well. Though giving up his academy, he continued to teach theology for many years—to the graduates of Canonsburg Academy, to the students of Jefferson College, and, in some instances, even to graduates of Princeton College. He is said to have trained not less than one hundred students for the ministry alone, besides others distinguished in other professions. Twenty of the early ministers of the Presbytery of Erie received their theological training

18. C. E. McCartney, *The Presbyterian Church, Western Pennsylvania, and the Making of the Nation*, 6; Wickersham, *op. cit.*, 113.
19. Joseph Smith, *History of Jefferson College: Including an Account of the Early Log-Cabin Schools, and the Canonsburg Academy*, 6.

under him.[20] A large majority of the young men entering the ministry on the Pennsylvania frontier during the first generation of settlement received their theological training under his direction.[21]

Meanwhile, with the growth of population in Western Pennsylvania, it was felt that the time had now arrived when the educational needs of that region could not be met by individual enterprise, but required the associated effort of all the friends of education in that area. At least this was the way that Messrs. McMillan, Dod, and Smith felt about it, and they began to take measures to bring it about. As a result of their combined efforts, a charter was obtained from the legislature on September 24, 1787, establishing Washington Academy at Washington, Pennsylvania, and appropriating five thousand acres of public land, chiefly in the present Beaver County, to the uses of the school. Although there were a few representatives of other denominations on the board of trustees, it was essentially a Scotch-Irish Presbyterian institution. For some years no building was erected for the academy, classes being held in the upper rooms of the Washington County court house. Reverend Thaddeus Dod was chosen principal of the school and agreed to serve in that capacity for one year, preaching one-third of his time in Washington and the remaining two-thirds at his regular charge at Ten Mile. Not formally opened until 1789, the academy was suspended for a time owing to the burning of the courthouse in 1791. Upon the retirement of Mr. Dod from the principalship, he was succeeded by his associate, Mr. David Johnston, whose term of office lasted only till the burning of the courthouse. There now being no suitable place in which to hold classes, a feeling of depression ensued, resulting in the temporary suspension of the academy. It was soon reopened, however, but continued with only moderate success under James Dobbins and Benjamin Mills until 1805. At this juncture, Reverend Matthew Brown accepted the pastorate of the Presbyterian church at Washington and, along with it, the headship of the academy. Under his leadership,

20. D. D. Junkin, "The Life and Labors of the Rev. John McMillan, D.D.," in *Centenary Memorial of the Planting and Growth of Presbyterianism in Western Pa. and Parts Adjacent,* 30-31; James I. Brownson, "The Educational History of Presbyterianism in Western Pennsylvania and Adjacent Regions," in *ibid.,* 73-74.

21. W. W. Sweet, *Religion on the American Frontier,* II, 26.

ably assisted by David Elliott, the academy made rapid progress and on March 28, 1806, received from the legislature a charter incorporating it as a college under the name of Washington College.[22]

Meanwhile Canonsburg Academy, located at Canonsburg about seven miles from Washington, had been founded under the leadership of Dr. McMillan. When the courthouse at Washington burned and the academy there was suspended, Dr. McMillan and Reverend Matthew Henderson (of the Associate Presbyterian Church) had tried to secure a lot there for the erection of an academy building, but were unable to do so. At this juncture, Colonel John Canon offered a lot at Canonsburg for school purposes and expressed his readiness to advance funds for the erection of a building. His offer was accepted and in 1791 Canonsburg Academy opened its doors with David Johnston as principal. Like Washington Academy, it was founded and fostered under Scotch-Irish Presbyterian auspices. The new academy was fortunate in being taken under the patronage of the Synod of Virginia at its annual meeting in 1791, and under that of the Presbytery of Redstone at its meeting at Pigeon Creek in October, 1792. Contributions for its support were raised by authorized agents throughout the bounds of the Presbytery of Redstone, and also by the Associate Presbyterian Church under the leadership of Matthew Henderson.[23] In this way substantial funds were secured, which were used partly to reimburse Colonel Canon for the money he had advanced and partly to defray current expenses. In 1794 a charter was obtained from the Supreme Court of Pennsylvania. Being now strongly established, it became the most substantial educational institution in Western Pennsylvania. In 1800 it secured from the legislature a grant of one thousand dollars, and in 1802 obtained a charter transforming it into Jefferson College.[24]

22. Brownson, *op. cit.,* 75-78; Sweet, *op. cit.,* 71.
23. Typical subscriptions were as follows: James Ewing, five bushels of wheat, at two shillings; John McMillan, $1; Mrs. Vallandigham, six yards linen; James McBride, three bushels rye; and, says Moffett, "one subscription payable in whiskey, which, coming from an old-fashioned Scotch-Irishman, represents, I think, a good degree of self-denial." See James D. Moffett, "Pioneer Education in Washington County, Pa.," in Scotch-Irish Society of America *Proceedings,* VIII, 183-184.
24. Brownson, *op. cit.,* 77.

The close relationship existing between Christianity and education is nowhere better exemplified than in the combined religious and educational activities of the Scotch-Irish ministers of Pennsylvania. No other racial group in the province contributed nearly so much as they to the establishment of classical schools and academies in the colonial era. On the extreme frontier in particular they exerted "the principal cultural and educational influence in that region for at least three quarters of a century."[25] Professor Sweet, a close student of religious and educational conditions on the frontier, attributes this in part to the fact that they sent to that region the first group of college-trained men and in part to the circumstance that "in the very nature of the case the vast educational need about them, as well as the necessity of increasing their means of livelihood, would naturally lead the average college-trained minister to become also a schoolmaster. And with few exceptions that is what happened."[26]

The Scotch-Irish and Higher Education

Not content with their achievements in founding and maintaining classical schools and academies in all their principal settlements in the province, the Scotch-Irish Presbyterians were the first religious body to found institutions of higher learning in Pennsylvania. Being particularly strong in the Cumberland Valley, they established Dickinson College at Carlisle, the first denominational college in Pennsylvania and the twelfth college to be founded in the United States. While the College of Philadelphia was theoretically non-sectarian, the dominant influence in its board of trustees and faculty was Episcopalian, a circumstance which irked the Presbyterians and led them to desire a college of their own. Furthermore, though the Log College and schools of similar type had met fairly well the needs of their day, it was now felt that the Presbyterians should establish a college in Pennsylvania, where they were more numerous than anywhere else in the country. Again, it was foreseen that the interior of the state would soon be thickly settled, and hence it would be desirable to have an institution of

25. McCartney, *op. cit.,* 5-6.
26. Sweet, *op. cit.,* 69-70.

higher learning more convenient to the people of that district than was the College of Philadelphia or Princeton.[27] Though the dominant influence behind the founding of Dickinson College in 1783 was that of the Scotch-Irish Presbyterians,[28] the enlarged aims of its founders enlisted the support of public-spirited men like Dr. Benjamin Rush and John Dickinson. Dr. Rush was greatly interested in the project and was one of its most enthusiastic promoters; and Dickinson, after whom it was named, made a large donation to it. In 1786 the legislature appropriated to the College five hundred pounds and ten thousand acres of land. Its first president was Reverend Charles Nesbit of Scotland, but the other members of the faculty were of Scotch-Irish ancestry.[29] Its checkered career and later history is beyond the scope of our subject, but it may be remarked in passing that it has had a remarkably large number of distinguished alumni, among whom were President James Buchanan and Chief Justice of the Supreme Court of the United States Roger B. Taney.

The process by which Washington Academy and Canonsburg Academy emerged from the log-cabin schools of Dod, McMillan, and Smith did not stop there since these academies themselves evolved into Washington College and Jefferson College respectively. The former was chartered by the Legislature in 1806 and the latter in 1802. There had been considerable rivalry between the two academies, and this continued when they became colleges. In fact, since they were in the same county and only seven miles apart, there were two colleges where there should have been but one, each attracting students from the same general constituency and each serving to retard the growth of the other. This rivalry, which was attended by some ill feeling between the two institutions, resulted in the so-called "College War," which was finally terminated by the union of the two schools under the name of Washington and Jefferson College by an act of legislature passed March 4, 1865. This act was amended February 26, 1869, definitely

27. Wickersham, *op. cit.*, 395-398.

28. *Ibid.*, 396; H. J. Ford, *The Scotch-Irish in America*, 455; W. H. Egle, *History of Pennsylvania*, 629.

29. Ford, *op. cit.*, 455; Wickersham, *op. cit.*, 395.

fixing the location of the College at the borough of Washington, where it has since remained.[30]

Thus it is seen that in early Pennsylvania history the influence of the Scotch-Irish was large and vital in the founding and maintenance of elementary schools, of academies, and of colleges. Their record in this regard, especially in view of the crudity of the times, is impressive and serves to dissipate any idea that may have been cherished by the uninformed that the Scotch-Irish of colonial Pennsylvania were a rough, illiterate, uncouth people engaged principally in quarreling with their neighbors and in fighting the Indians.

Cultural Contribution of the Scotch-Irish

The principal cultural influence exercised on colonial Pennsylvania by the Scotch-Irish was through their churches and schools, whose history we have sketched. There was but a slight development of literature and the fine arts either in Pennsylvania or elsewhere in America during the colonial era, and this, such as it was, was due chiefly to the English element of the population. The people were too busily engaged in establishing themselves firmly on the soil and in earning a livelihood to devote much attention to the cultivation of the fine arts. Not only were they isolated from the art centers of the world, but they lacked the wealth and leisure to cultivate to any great extent the aesthetic side of life. Furthermore, it must be said of the Scotch-Irishman that his genius is practical rather than imaginative, and that he has never excelled particularly in the fine arts. Renowned for his genius for law and government, for his business sagacity and financial skill, and for his contributions to religion, education, journalism, and invention, he undoubtedly is, but he does not ordinarily write poems, paint pictures, and carve statues, nor shine as a star of the first magnitude on the horizon of architecture and music. It is not claimed for him that he is a universal genius who does all things well. His achievements in the fields of endeavor in which he does excel were tremendous and have made him an outstanding figure in Ameri-

30. Brownson, *op. cit.,* 78, 90-91.

can history. Nevertheless it is true that, in comparison with his achievements in other directions, he contributed little to the development of the fine arts.[31] In provincial Pennsylvania, while he was still finding himself, his accomplishments in this regard suffer by comparison with those of the English, who carried off the palm. However, even in this era, Charles Brockden Brown, a Philadelphia Scotch-Irishman, appeared as the first great American novelist and the first professional man of letters in the country, publishing *Wieland* in 1798, and following this in rapid succession with *Ormand, Edgar Huntley, Arthur Mervyn, Jane Talbot,* and *Clara Howard.* In journalism, a field in which the Scotch-Irish were later to excel, John Dunlap founded *The Pennsylvania Packet or General Advertiser* in 1771, a journal which appeared in 1784 as the first daily newspaper in the United States under the name of *The Pennsylvania Packet and General Advertiser.* Another eminent Scotch-Irishman of this era was David Ramsay, a native of Lancaster County, Pennsylvania, who later removed to South Carolina. Ramsay was the author of *History of South Carolina, History of the Revolution in South Carolina, History of the American Revolution,* and *Life of Washington,* winning fame as one of the most distinguished historians of his time.

In later times the Scotch-Irish, though still not as accomplished in the fine arts as in other fields of endeavor, have developed to an ever increasing degree the imaginative and sympathetic qualities required for success in this regard, with the result that they have made more important contributions to the aesthetic side of life than formerly; and they may be expected in future to contribute their full proportionate share to the promotion of the fine arts in America. As evidence of this, it need only be recalled that Stephen Collins Foster and Ethelbert Nevin, whose names loom large in the history of American music and whose songs are sung around the world, were Scotch-Irishmen from Western Pennsylvania; that Thomas Eakins holds a high place on the roll of American painters; and that Edwin Forrest, the first great American actor,

31. See Dr. Robert Ellis Thompson, in Pennsylvania Scotch-Irish Society *Proceedings,* VIII, 28-31.

whose career is one of the cherished traditions of the American stage, was, like Eakins, a Scotch-Irishman born in Philadelphia. Others might be cited, but these will suffice to show that Scotch-Irishmen are quite capable of enriching the world with imperishable works of beauty.

Bibliography

A. SOURCES

1. Manuscript Materials

Becket, Reverend William, *Notices and Letters concerning incidents at Lewes Town*. Hist. Soc. of Pa.

Dickinson-Logan Letter Book. Hist. Soc. of Pa.

Dickinson, Jonathan, *Letter Book*. Ridgway Branch, Library Company of Philadelphia.

Irvine, William, *Papers of Brigadier-General William Irvine*, Hist. Soc. of Pa.

Lamberton Scotch-Irish Collection. 2 vols., Hist. Soc. of Pa.

Logan Papers, Correspondence of James Logan. Hist. Soc. of Pa.

Logan Papers, Letter Books of James Logan, Hist. Soc. of Pa.

Logan Papers, Letters from James Logan. Hist. Soc. of Pa.

Nesbit-Addison Letters, Charles Nesbit to Alexander Addison. Darlington Collection, University of Pittsburgh.

Penn Letter Books. Hist. Soc. of Pa.

Penn MSS., Official Correspondence. Hist. Soc. of Pa.

Penn, Thomas, *Letters of Thomas Penn to Richard Peters, 1752-1772.* Hist. Soc. of Pa.

Peters MSS. Hist. Soc. of Pa.

Peters, Reverend Richard, *Letters to the Proprietaries of the Province of Pennsylvania, 1755-1757.* Hist. Soc. of Pa.

Shippen Papers, Papers of the Shippen Family. Hist. Soc. of Pa.

State Archives of Pennsylvania, *Provincial Papers*. State Library of Pennsylvania.

State Archives of Pennsylvania, *Revolutionary Papers*. State Library of Pennsylvania.

2. Published Sources

A Serious Address to such of the Inhabitants of Pennsylvania as connived at the Massacre of the Indians at Lancaster. Philadelphia, 1764.

An Address to Rev. Allison, the Rev. Mr. Ewing, and others, being a vindication of the Quakers from the aspersions in their letter published in the London Chronicle, to which is prefixed the said letter. By a Lover of Truth. n.p., 1765.

An Answer to the Pamphlet Entitled the Conduct of the Paxton-Men Impartially Represented, with some remarks on the Narrative. Philadelphia, 1764.

Anbury, Thomas, *Travels through the Interior Parts of North America.* 2 vols., London, 1887.

Ashe, Thomas, *Travels in America Performed in 1806.* London, 1808.

Bailly, Francis, *Journal of a Tour in the Unsettled Parts of North America in 1796 and 1797.* London, 1856.

Barton, Thomas, *The Conduct of the Paxton-Men impartially represented, with some remarks on the Narrative.* Philadelphia, 1764.

Beatty, Charles, *The Journal of a Two Months Tour, with a view to promoting Religion among the Frontier Inhabitants of Pennsylvania.* London, 1768.

Birkbeck, Morris, *Notes on a Journey in America from the Coast of Virginia to the Territory of Illinois.* London, 1818.

Blair, Samuel, *A Short and Faithful Account of the Remarkable Revival of Religion in the Congregation of New Londonderry, and Other Parts of Pennsylvania.* Philadelphia, 1764.

Boulter, Hugh, *Letters Written by his Excellency Hugh Boulter, D.D., Lord Primate of All Ireland, to several Ministers of State in England, and some others.* 2 vols., Dublin, 1770.

Burke, Edmund, *An Account of European Settlements in America.* 2 vols., London, 1757.

Calendar of State Papers, Ireland, 1663-1665. London, 1907.

Calendar of State Papers, Ireland, 1669-1670. London, 1910.

Cazenove Journal. Edited by R. W. Kelsey, Haverford, 1922.

Census Reports, 1790 to 1840.

Colonial Records of Pennsylvania, 1683-1790. Vols. I-X, *Minutes of the Provincial Council;* vols. XI-XVI, *Minutes of the Supreme Executive Council.* 16 vols., Harrisburg, 1851-1853.

Cuming, F., *Sketches of a Tour in the Western Country,* in Thwaites, *Early Western Travels, 1748-1846,* vol. III. Cleveland, 1904-1907.

Doddridge, Joseph, *Notes on the Settlement and Indian Wars of the Western Parts of Virginia and Pennsylvania.* Wellsburgh, Va., 1824.

Douglass, William, *A Summary, Historical and Political, of the First Planting, Progressive Improvements, and Present State of the British Settlement in North America.* 2 vols., London, 1755.

Dwight, Margaret Van Horn, *A Journey to the Ohio in 1819.* Reprint, Max Farrand, ed., New Haven, 1913.

Fearon, H. B., *Sketches of America*. London, 1818.

Fithian, Philip Vickers, *Journal, 1775-1776*. R. G. Albion and L. Dodson, eds., Princeton, 1934.

Flint, James, *Letters from America*. Edinburgh, 1822.

Fordham, Elias Pym, *Personal Narrative of Travels in Virginia, Maryland, Pennsylvania, Ohio, Indiana, Kentucky, and of a Residence in the Illinois Country, 1807-1818*. Cleveland, 1906.

Franklin, Benjamin, *A Narrative of the Late Massacres, in Lancaster County, of a Number of Indians, Friends of this Province, by Persons Unknown*. Philadelphia, 1764.

Galloway, Joseph, *Historical and Political Reflections on the Rise and Progress of the American Revolution*. London, 1780.

Gilpin, Joshua, *Journal of a Tour from Philadelphia through the Western Counties of Pennsylvania in the Months of September and October, 1809*. Pa. Mag. of Hist. and Biog., L-LII.

Harpster, John W., ed., *Pen Pictures of Early Western Pennsylvania*. Pittsburgh, 1938.

Harris, T. M., *The Journal of a Tour into the Territory Northwest of the Allegheny Mountains in the Spring of 1803*. Boston, 1805.

Historical Account of the Late Disturbance between the Inhabitants of the Back Settlements of Pennsylvania and the Philadelphians. Printed at Rome by A. S., 1764.

Jardine, L. J., *A Letter from Pennsylvania to a Friend in England Containing Information with respect to America*. Bath, 1795.

Johnson, C. B., *Letters from the British Settlement in Pennsylvania*. London, 1819.

Kalm, Peter, *Travels into North America*. Translated by J. R. Foster, Warrington, 1770.

La Rochefoucald-Liancourt, Francois Alexandre, Duc de, *Travels through the United States of North America, 1795, 1796, 1797*. 2 vols., 2d. edn., London, 1800.

Laws of the Commonwealth of Pennsylvania, 1700-1829. 10 vols., Philadelphia, 1810-1844. Usually cited as *Smith's Laws*.

Lee, Henry, *Memoirs of the War in the Southern Department*. 2 vols., Philadelphia, 1812.

McClure, David, *Diary of David McClure, 1748-1820*. Franklin B. Dexter, ed., New York, 1899.

Martin, A. E. and Shenk, H. H., *Pennsylvania History Told by Contemporaries*. New York, 1925.

Minutes of the Presbytery of Redstone, 1781-1831. Cincinnati, 1878.

Oldmixon, John, *The British Empire in America*. 2 vols., London, 1708.

Penn-Logan Correspondence. 2 vols. Historical Society of Pennsylvania *Memoirs,* IX and X.

Pennsylvania Archives. Samuel Hazard and others comps., 9 series. Philadelphia and Harrisburg, 1852-1931.

Perry, W. S., ed., *Historical Collections Relating to the American Colonial Church.* 2 vols., Hartford, Conn., 1887.

Priest, William, *Travels in the United States of America, 1793-1797.* London, 1802.

Read, Charles, *Letter to the Hon. John Ladd, Esq.* Philadelphia, 1764.

Records of the Presbyterian Church in the United States of America. Philadelphia, 1841, 1852, 1904.

St. Clair Papers. W. H. Smith, ed., 2 vols., Cincinnati, 1881.

Schoepf, Johann David, *Travels in the Confederation, 1783-1784.* Erlanger, 1788; translated and edited by Alfred J. Morrison, Philadelphia, 1911.

Smith, Matthew and Gibson, James, *A Declaration and Remonstrance of the Distracted and Bleeding Frontier Inhabitants of Pennsylvania.* Philadelphia, 1764.

Smith, William, *A Brief Review of the Conduct of Pennsylvania for the Year 1755.* London, 1756.

————, *A Brief Review of the Province of Pennsylvania.* London, 1756.

Statutes at Large of Pennsylvania from 1682 to 1801. J. T. Mitchell and Henry Flanders, compilers, Harrisburg, 1896-1908.

Stewart, Andrew, *The History of the Church in Ireland since the Scots were Naturalized.* Supplement to Rev. Patrick Adair's *True Narrative of the Rise and Progress of the Presbyterian Church in Ireland.* Belfast and Edinburgh, 1868.

The Plain Dealer; or a Few Remarks on Quaker Politics, and their attempts to change the government of Pennsylvania. Philadelphia, 1764.

The Quaker Unmasked, or Plain Truth. Philadelphia, 1764.

The Quakers Assisting to Preserve the Lives of the Indians in the Barracks Vindicated. Philadelphia, 1764.

The Susquehanna Papers. Edited by Julian P. Boyd, 4 vols., Wilkes-Barre, 1930-1933.

Thomas, David, *Travels through the Western Country in the Summer of 1816.* Auburn, N. Y., 1819.

Tome, Philip, *Pioneer Life; or Thirty Years a Hunter.* Reprint, Harrisburg, 1928.

Votes and Proceedings of the House of Representatives of the Province of Pennsylvania. 6 vols., 1752-1776.

Weld, Isaac, Jr., *Travels through the States of North America . . . . during the years 1795, 1796, 1797.* 2 vols., London, 1800.

Whitefield, George, *A Continuation of the Reverend Mr. Whitefield's Journal from his Embarking after the Embargo to his Arrival at Savannah in Georgia.* London, 1740.

Wilkeson, Samuel, *Early Recollections of the West.* The American Pioneer, II.

Young, Arthur, *A Tour in Ireland, 1776, 1777, 1778.* London, 1780.

3. Newspapers

American Weekly Mercury
Pennsylvania Gazette
Pennsylvania Journal and Weekly Advertiser
Pennsylvania Packet
Pittsburgh Gazette

B. SECONDARY WORKS

1. Books and Pamphlets

A Centennial Pamphlet Containing Addresses Delivered at Chartiers and North Buffalo, in the U.P. Presbytery of Chartiers. Pittsburgh, 1876.

Abernethy, T. K., *Three Virginia Frontiers.* Louisiana State University Press, 1940.

Abraham, Evelyn, *Over the Mountains.* Uniontown, Pa., 1936.

Adair, Rev. Patrick, *A True Narrative of the Rise and Progress of the Presbyterian Church in the North of Ireland.* Belfast and Edinburgh, 1866.

Adams, W. F., *Ireland and Irish Immigration to the New World from 1815 to the Famine.* 2 vols., New Haven, 1932.

Addresses Delivered before the Dauphin County Historical Society in the State Capitol, Harrisburg, July 4, 1876. n.p., n.d.

Africa, J. S., *History of Huntingdon and Blair Counties.* Philadelphia, 1883.

Agnew, Daniel, *History of the Region North of the Ohio and West of the Allegheny River.* Philadelphia, 1887.

Albert, G. D., *History of the County of Westmoreland, Pennsylvania.* Philadelphia, 1882.

Aldrich, L. C., *History of Clearfield County, Pennsylvania.* Syracuse, N. Y., 1887.

Alexander, A., *Biographical Sketches of the Founder and the Principal Alumni of Log College.* Princeton, N. J., 1845.

Alvord, Clarence, *The Mississippi Valley in British Politics.* 2 vols., Cleveland, 1916.

Ambler, C. H., *History of West Virginia*. New York, 1933.

Anderson, T. C., *Life of Rev. George Donnell*. Nashville, 1858.

Arthur, J. P., *Western North Carolina*. Raleigh, N. C., 1914.

Atwater, Caleb, *A History of the State of Ohio*. Cincinnati, 1838.

Babcock, Charles A., ed., *Venango County: Her Pioneers and People*. 2 vols., Chicago, 1929.

Bagenal, Philip H., *The American Irish*. London, 1882.

Bagwell, Richard, *Ireland Under the Stuarts*. 3 vols., London, 1905.

Baldwin, Leland D., *Pittsburgh: The Story of a City*. Pittsburgh, 1937.

———, *The Keelboat Age on Western Waters*. Pittsburgh, 1941.

———, *Whiskey Rebels: The Story of a Frontier Uprising*. Pittsburgh, 1939.

Bancroft, George, *History of the United States*. 6 vols., New York, 1890-1891.

Bates, S. P., *History of Greene County, Pennsylvania*. Chicago, 1888.

———, *Our County and Its People: A Historical and Memorial Record of Crawford County, Pennsylvania*. Boston, 1899.

Battle, J. H., ed., *History of Columbia and Montour Counties, Pennsylvania*. Chicago, 1887.

Bausman, J. H., *History of Beaver County, Pennsylvania*. New York, 1904.

Beebe, V. L., *History of Potter County, Pennsylvania*. Coudersport, Pa., 1934.

Belcher, E. A. and Williamson, J. A., *Migration within the Empire*. London, 1924.

Bell, H. C., *History of Cumberland County, Pennsylvania*. Chicago, 1891.

Bell, H. C., ed., *History of Venango County, Pennsylvania*. Chicago, 1890.

Bell, Herbert, *History of Northumberland County, Pennsylvania*. Chicago, 1891.

Benn, George, *History of Belfast*. Belfast, 1877.

Bining, A. C., *Pennsylvania Iron Manufactures in the Eighteenth Century*. Harrisburg, 1938.

Black, G. F., *Scotland's Mark on America*. New York, 1921.

Bolles, A. S., *Pennsylvania: Province and State*. 2 vols., Philadelphia and New York, 1899.

Bolton, C. K., *Scotch-Irish Pioneers in Ulster and America*. Boston, 1910.

Boucher, J. N., *History of Westmoreland County, Pennsylvania*. 3 vols., New York and Chicago, 1906.

Brackenridge, Hugh H., *Incidents of the Insurrection in the western Parts of Pennsylvania in the Year 1794*. Philadelphia, 1795.

Brackenridge, H. M., *History of the Western Insurrection in Western Pennsylvania*. Pittsburgh, 1859.

Bradsby, H. C., *History of Bradford County, Pennsylvania*. Chicago, 1891.

Branch, E. D., *Westward: The Romance of the American Frontier*. New York, 1930.

Breed, W. P., *Presbyterians and the Revolution*. Philadelphia, 1876.

Briggs, C. A., *American Presbyterianism: Its Origin and History*. New York, 1885.

Bromwell, W. J., *History of Immigration into the United States, 1819-1855*. New York, 1856.

Brown, I. B., *Early Footprints of Developments and Improvements in Extreme Northwestern Pennsylvania*. Harrisburg, 1905.

Brown, R. C., ed., *History of Butler County, Pennsylvania*. n.p., 1895.

Buchanan, Roberdeau, *Genealogy of the McKean Family, with a biography of Thomas McKean*. Lancaster, 1890.

Buck, Solon J. and Elizabeth H., *The Planting of Civilization in Western Pennsylvania*. Pittsburgh, 1939.

Burr, C. S., *America's Race Heritage*. New York, 1922.

Burton, J. H., *History of Scotland*. 7 vols., Edinburgh, 1870.

Butler, W. F. T., *Confiscation in Irish History*. Dublin, 1817.

Callahan, J. M., *Semi-Centennial History of West Virginia*. Charleston, W. Va., 1913.

Camp, D. I. and Kaufman, J. W., *History of the Presbyterian Churches of Path Valley*. Chambersburg, 1916.

Campbell, Douglas. *The Puritan in Holland, England, and America*. New York, 1892.

Campbell, John C., *The Southern Highlander and His Homeland*. New York, 1921.

Carey, Matthew, *Emigration from Ireland and Immigration into the United States*. Philadelphia, 1828.

Carnahan, James, *The Pennsylvania Insurrection of 1794, commonly called the "Whiskey Insurrection."* n.p., n.d.

Carroll, B. R., *Historical Collections of South Carolina*. Charleston, 1857.

Carter, W. C. and Glossbrenner, A. J., *History of York County, Pennsylvania*. York, Pa., 1834.

Centenary Celebration of the Organization of Washington County. Washington, Pa., 1881.

Centenary Memorial of the Planting and Growth of Presbyterianism in Western Pennsylvania and Parts Adjacent. Pittsburgh, 1875.

Centennial Memorial of the Presbytery of Carlisle, Pennsylvania. 2 vols., Harrisburg, 1889.

Chaddock, R. E., *Ohio before 1850: A Study of the Early Influence of Pennsylvania and Southern Populations in Ohio*. New York and London, 1908.

Chambers, George, *A Tribute to the Principles, Virtues, Habits, and Public Usefulness of the Scotch-Irish Early Settlers of Pennsylvania*. Chambersburg, 1866.

Chapman, T. J., *The Valley of the Conemaugh*. Altoona, 1865.

Cherry, T. C., *Kentucky, the Pioneer State of the West*. Boston, 1923.

Christian, Bolivar, *The Scotch-Irish in the Valley of Virginia*. Richmond, 1860.

Clare, I. S., *A Brief History of Lancaster County, Pennsylvania*. Lancaster, 1892.

Clark, Victor S., *History of Manufactures in the United States, 1607-1860*. Washington, D. C., 1916.

Clyde, John C., *Genealogies, Necrology, and Reminiscences of the Irish Settlement; or a Record of those Scotch-Irish Presbyterian Families who were the First Settlers in the "Forks of the Delaware," now Northampton County*. n.p., 1879.

——, *History of the Allen Township Presbyterian Church and the community which has sustained it in what was formerly known as the "Irish Settlement," now Northampton County, Pennsylvania*. Philadelphia, 1876.

Collins, L., *Historical Sketches of Kentucky*. Cincinnati, 1850.

Collins, R. H., *History of Kentucky*. Covington, 1882.

Commons, J. R., *Races and Immigrants in America*. 2d. edn., New York, 1920.

Craig, N. B., *History of Pittsburgh*. Pittsburgh, 1851.

Craighead, J. G., *Scotch and Irish Seeds in American Soil*. Philadelphia, 1878.

Creigh, Alfred, *History of Washington County, Pennsylvania*. Harrisburg, 1870.

Creigh, Thomas, *History of the Presbyterian Church of Upper West Conococheague* (Mercersburg). Chambersburg, 1877.

Cribbs, George A., *The Frontier Policy of Pennsylvania*. Pittsburgh, 1919.

Croskery, Thomas, *Irish Presbyterianism: Its History, Character, Influence, and Present Position*. Dublin, 1884.

Crumrine, Boyd, *History of Washington County, Pennsylvania*. Philadelphia, 1882.

Dahlinger, C. W., *Pittsburgh: A Sketch of Its Early Social Life*. New York, 1916.

D'Alton, E. A., *History of Ireland*. 3 vols., London, 1906.

Darlington, Mary Carson, *History of Colonel Henry Bouquet and the Western Frontier of Pennsylvania.* n.p., 1920.

Davis, A. J., *History of Clarion County, Pennsylvania.* Syracuse, N. Y., 1887.

Davis, T. S. and Shenk, Lucile, eds., *A History of Blair County, Pennsylvania.* 2 vols., Harrisburg, 1931.

Davis, W. W. H., *History of Bucks County, Pennsylvania.* Doylestown, Pa., 1876.

Day, Sherman, *Historical Collections of the State of Pennsylvania.* Philadelphia, 1848.

DeHaas, W., *History of the Early Settlement and Indian Wars of Western Virginia.* Wheeling, 1851.

Dexter, F. B., *A Selection from the Miscellaneous Papers of Fifty Years.* New Haven, 1918.

Dinsmore, J. W., *The Scotch-Irish in America.* Chicago, 1906.

Dobbs, Arthur, *Essay on the Trade of Ireland.* London, 1729.

Donehoo, G. P., *A History of the Cumberland Valley in Pennsylvania.* 2 vols., Harrisburg, 1930.

Downes, R. C., *Council Fires on the Upper Ohio.* Pittsburgh, 1940.

Downey, W. V., *History of Paxton Church.* Harrisburg, 1877.

Dubois, Robert P., *A Discourse on the Origin and History of the Presbyterian Church and Congregation of New London, in Chester County, Pennsylvania.* Philadelphia, 1845.

Dunaway, Wayland F., *A History of Pennsylvania.* New York, 1935.

———, *The Susquehanna Valley in the Revolution.* Wilkes-Barre, 1927.

Durant, P. A. and Richard, J. F., *History of Cumberland County, Pennsylvania.* Chicago, 1886.

Earle, Alice Morse, *Home Life in Colonial Days.* New York, 1898.

Eastman, Frank M., *Courts and Lawyers of Pennsylvania.* 3 vols., New York, 1922.

Eaton, Rebecca, *A Geography of Pennsylvania.* Philadelphia, 1835.

Eaton, S. J. M., *Centennial Discourse: A Sketch of the History of Venango County, Pennsylvania.* Franklin, Pa., 1922.

———, *History of the Presbytery of Erie.* New York, 1868.

Egle, W. H., *Notes and Queries, Historical and Genealogical.* 2 vols., Harrisburg, 1895.

———, *History of Dauphin and Lebanon Counties.* Philadelphia, 1883.

———, *History of the Commonwealth of Pennsylvania.* Harrisburg, 1876.

Elliott, D., *The Life of the Reverend Elisha McCurdy.* Allegheny, Pa., 1848.

Elliott, W. C., *History of Reynoldsville and Vicinity.* Punxsutawney, Pa., 1922.

Ellis, Agnes, *Lights and Shadows of Sewickley Life*. Philadelphia, 1893.

Ellis, F. and Evans, S., *History of Lancaster County, Pennsylvania*. Philadelphia, 1883.

Ellis, Franklin, *History of Fayette County, Pennsylvania*. Philadelphia, 1882.

Ellis, F., *History of Northampton County, Pennsylvania*. Philadelphia, 1877.

Ely, W. S., *Scotch-Irish Familes: some of the Early Settlers in Bucks County, Pennsylvania*. n.p., 1898.

Evans, P. D., *The Holland Land Company*. Buffalo, N. Y., 1934.

Falls, Cyril, *The Birth of Ulster*. London, 1936.

Fast, R. E. and Maxwell, H., *The History and Government of West Virginia*. Morgantown, 1901.

Ferguson, Russell J., *Early Western Pennsylvania Politics*. Pittsburgh, 1938.

Filson, John, *The Discovery, Settlement and Present State of Kentucky*. Wilmington, 1784.

Findley, William, *History of the Insurrection in the Four Western Counties of Pennsylvania*. Philadelphia, 1796.

Finney, W. G., *The History of Chillisquaque Church*. n.p., 1926.

Fisher, S. G., *Pennsylvania, Colony and Commonwealth*. Philadelphia, 1897.

——, *The Making of Pennsylvania*. Philadelphia, 1896.

——, *The Quaker Colonies*. New Haven, 1920.

Fiske, John, *Old Virginia and Her Neighbors*. Boston and New York, 1898.

——, *The Dutch and Quaker Colonies in America*. 2 vols., Boston and New York, 1889.

Foote, W. H., *Sketches of North Carolina*. New York, 1846.

——, *Sketches of Virginia, Historical and Biographical*. Philadelphia, 1850.

Ford, H. J., *The Scotch-Irish in America*. Princeton, 1915.

Franklin, Benjamin, *Writings of Benjamin Franklin*. Albert Henry Smyth, ed., 11 vols., New York, 1905.

Freeze, J. G., *History of Columbia County, Pennsylvania*. Bloomsburg, Pa., 1883.

Froude, James Anthony, *The English in Ireland in the Eighteenth Century*. 3 vols., New York, 1873.

Futhey, J. S., *Historical Discourse delivered on the occasion of the One Hundred and Fiftieth Anniversary of the Upper Octorara Presbyterian Church, Chester County, Pennsylvania*. Philadelphia, 1870.

Futhey, J. S., and Cope, G., *History of Chester County, Pennsylvania*. Philadelphia, 1881.

Futhey, J. S., *History of Upper Octorara Church*. Philadelphia, 1870.

Garland, Robert, *The Scotch-Irish in Western Pennsylvania*. Pittsburgh, 1923.

Garrard, L. H., *Chambersburg in the Colony and in the Revolution*. Philadelphia, 1856.

Garrett, W. R. and Goodpasture, A. V., *History of Tennessee*. Nashville, 1900.

Geiser, K. F., *Redemptioners and Indentured Servants in the Colony and Commonwealth of Pennsylvania*. New Haven, 1901.

Gibson, John, *History of York County, Pennsylvania*. Chicago, 1886.

Gillett, E. H., *History of the Presbyterian Church in the United States of America*. 2 vols., Philadelphia, 1864.

Gipson, Lawrence H., *The British Empire before the American Revolution*. 3 vols., Caldwell, Idaho, 1936.

Glasgow, Maude, *The Scotch-Irish in Northern Ireland and in the American Colonies*. New York, 1936.

Gordon, James J., *The Scotch-Irish and American Citizenship*. n.p., n.d.

Gordon, Thomas F., *A Gazeteer of the State of Pennsylvania*. Philadelphia, 1832.

Gordon, Thomas F., *The History of Pennsylvania from its Discovery by Europeans to the Declaration of Independence*. Philadelphia, 1829.

Green, Samuel Swett, *The Scotch-Irish in America*. Worcester, Mass., 1895.

Gregg, Alexander, *History of the Old Cheraws*. Columbia, S. C., 1867.

Hain, H. H., *History of Perry County, Pennsylvania*. Harrisburg, 1922.

Hall, James, *Sketches of the History, Life, and Manners in the West*. 2 vols., Philadelphia, 1835.

Hall, P. F., *Immigration and its Effects upon the United States*. New York, 1908.

Haltigan, James, *The Irish in the American Revolution*. Washington, D. C., 1908.

Hamilton, Lord Ernest, *The Irish Rebellion of 1641*. London, 1920.

Hamilton, Thomas, *History of the Irish Presbyterian Church*. Edinburgh, 1886.

Hanna, Charles A., *Historical Collections of Harrison County in the State of Ohio*. New York, 1900.

——, *The Scotch-Irish, or the Scot in North Britain, North Ireland, and North America*. 2 vols., New York and London, 1902.

——, *The Wilderness Trail*. 2 vols., New York and London, 1911.

Hanna, William, *History of Greene County, Pennsylvania*. Waynesburg, Pa., 1882.

Hansen, Marcus L., *The Atlantic Migration*. Cambridge, Mass., 1940.

Harrison, John, *The Scot in Ulster*. London, 1888.

Hart, Freeman H., *The Valley of Virginia in the American Revolution, 1763-1789*. University of N. C. Press, Chapel Hill, 1942.

Hassler, E. W., *Old Westmoreland: A History of Western Pennsylvania during the Revolution*. Cleveland, 1900.

Haywood, John, *History of Tennessee*. Louisville, 1823.

Hazard, Samuel, *The Register of Pennsylvania*. 8 vols., Philadelphia, 1828-1836.

Henderson, Archibald, *The Conquest of the Old Southwest*. New York, 1920.

Henry, M. S., *History of the Lehigh Valley*. Easton, 1860.

Hensel, W. U., *Presbyterianism in the Pequea Valley, and other Historical Addresses*. n.p., 1912.

Herrick, C. A., *White Servitude in Pennsylvania*. Philadelphia, 1926.

Hill, George, *Plantation Papers containing a Summary Sketch of the Great Ulster Plantation in the Year 1610*. Belfast, 1889.

Hinsdale, B. A., *The Old Northwest*. New York, 1888.

History of the Presbytery of Washington. Edited by a committee of the Presbytery, Philadelphia, 1889.

Hogue, W. J., *The Greatness of the Founders*. n.p., n.d.

Hollister, H., *History of the Lackawanna Valley*. 3d. edn., Scranton, 1875.

Howe, George, *The Scotch-Irish and Their First Settlements on the Tyger River . . .* Columbia, 1870.

Howe, Henry, *Historical Collections of Ohio*. Columbus, 1890.

——, *Historical Collections of Virginia*. Charleston, S. C., 1845.

Howison, R. R., *A History of Virginia*. Richmond, 1848.

Hunt, W. E., *Historical Collections of Coshocton County, Ohio*. Cincinnati, 1876.

Hunter, Margaret Adair, *Education in Pennsylvania Promoted by the Presbyterian Church, 1726-1937*. Philadelphia, 1937.

Jenkins, H. M., ed., *Pennsylvania, Colonial and Federal: A History, 1608-1903*. 3 vols., Philadelphia, 1903.

Johnson, G. G., *Ante-Bellum North Carolina: A Social History*. Univ. of N. C. Press, Chapel Hill, 1937.

Johnson, H. R., *A History of Neshannock Presbyterian Church, New Wilmington, Pennsylvania, together with some account of the settlement of that portion of North Western Pennsylvania in which the church was organized*. Washington, D. C., 1925.

Johnson, Stanley C., *A History of Emigration from the United Kingdom to North America 1763-1912*. New York and London, 1914.

Jones, U. J., *History of the Early Settlement of the Juniata Valley.* Philadelphia, 1856.

Jordan, J. W., ed., *A History of the Juniata Valley and Its People.* 3 vols., New York, 1913.

Keith, Charles P., *Chronicles of Pennsylvania, 1688-1748.* 2 vols., Philadelphia, 1917.

Kelker, L. R., *History of Dauphin County, Pennsylvania.* 3 vols., New York and Chicago, 1907.

Kephart, Horace, *Pennsylvania's Part in the Winning of the West.* St. Louis, 1902.

Kercheval, S., *A History of the Valley of Virginia.* Strasburg, Va., 1925.

Kieffer, H. M., *Some of the First Settlers of the Forks of the Delaware.* Easton, 1902.

Killikelly, Sarah H., *History of Pittsburgh.* Pittsburgh, 1906.

Klein, H. M. J., ed., *Lancaster County, A History.* 4 vols., New York and Chicago, 1924.

Klein, Philip S., *Pennsylvania Politics, 1817-1832: A Game without Rules.* Philadelphia, 1940.

Klein, T. B., *Early History and Growth of Carlisle.* Harrisburg, 1905.

Klett, Guy S., *Presbyterians in Colonial Pennsylvania.* Philadelphia, 1937.

Konkle, Burton A., *George Bryan and the Constitution of Pennsylvania, 1731-1791.* Philadelphia, 1922.

Koontz, L. K., *The Virginia Frontier, 1754-1763.* J. H. U. Studies in Hist. and Polit. Sci., Series XLIII, No. 2.

Lambing, A. A. and White, J. F., *Centennial History of Allegheny County, Pennsylvania.* Pittsburgh, 1888.

Latimer, W. T., *A History of the Irish Presbyterians.* Belfast, 1893.

Lecky, W. E. H., *A History of England in the Eighteenth Century.* 4 vols., London, 1878.

——, *A History of Ireland in the Eighteenth Century.* 5 vols., London, 1892.

Lineham, J. C., *The Irish Scots and the "Scotch-Irish."* Concord, N. H., 1902.

Linn, John Blair, *Annals of Buffalo Valley.* Harrisburg, 1877.

——, *History of Centre and Clinton Counties.* Philadelphia, 1883.

Lloyd, Thomas W., *History of Lycoming County.* 2 vols., Topeka and Indianapolis, 1929.

Lytle, M. S., *History of Huntingdon County, Pennsylvania.* Lancaster, 1876.

McAlarney, M. W., ed., *History of the Sesquicentennial of the Paxtang Church.* Harrisburg, 1840.

McCartney, C. E., *The Presbyterian Church, Western Pennsylvania, and the Making of the Nation*. n.p., 1931.

McCauley, I. H., *History of Franklin County, Pennsylvania*. Harrisburg, 1878.

McClain, Miriam G., *The Rebellion of Sir Cahir O'Dogerty, and its Influence on the Ulster Plantation*. Philadelphia, 1930.

McClune, James, *History of the Presbyterian Church in the Forks of the Brandywine, Chester County, Pennsylvania*. Philadelphia, 1885.

McCrady, E., *The History of South Carolina under the Royal Government*. New York, 1899.

McDonnell, John, *The Ulster Civil War of 1641 and Its Consequences*. Dublin, 1879.

MacDougal, D., *Scots and Scots' Descendants in America*. New York, 1917.

McGee, T. D'A., *A History of the Irish Settlers in North America from the Earliest Period to the Census of 1850*. Boston, 1855.

MacGill, Caroline E., *History of Transportation in the United States before 1860*. Washington, D. C., 1917.

Mackenzie, John, *Narrative of the Siege of Londonderry*. London, 1690.

McKnight, Charles, *Our Western Border*. Philadelphia, 1876.

McKnight, W. J., *A Pioneer Outline History of Northwestern Pennsylvania*. Philadelphia, 1905.

——, *Pioneer History of Jefferson County, Pennsylvania*. Philadelphia, 1898.

McLean, J. P., *An Historical Account of the Settlements of Scotch Highlanders in America*. Cleveland and Glasgow, 1900.

MacMinn, Edwin, *On the Frontier with Colonel Antes*. Camden, N. J., 1900.

McPherson, David, *Annals of Commerce*. 4 vols., London, 1805.

McSherry, James, *History of Maryland*. Baltimore, 1904.

Maginnis, T. H., Jr., *The Irish Contribution to American Independence*. Philadelphia, 1913.

Maguire, J. F., *The Irish in America*. London, 1868.

Marmion, Anthony, *The Ancient and Modern History of the Maritime Ports of Ireland*. 3d. edn., London, 1858.

Maxon, Charles H., *The Great Awakening in the Middle Colonies*. Chicago, 1920.

Maynard, D. S., *Historical View of Clinton County*. Lock Haven, 1875.

Meginness, John F., *Biographical Annals of the West Branch Valley*. Williamsport, 1889.

——, *History of Lycoming County, Pennsylvania*. Chicago, 1872.

——, *Otzinachson: a History of the West Branch Valley.* Philadelphia, 1857.

Meriwether, R. L., *The Expansion of South Carolina, 1729-1765.* Kingsport, Tenn., 1940.

Miller, John, *Twentieth Century History of Erie County, Pennsylvania.* Chicago, 1909.

Mombert, Jacob I., *An Authentic History of Lancaster County in the State of Pennsylvania.* Lancaster, 1869.

Monette, J. W., *History of the Discovery and Settlement of the Valley of the Mississippi.* 2 vols., New York, 1846.

Montgomery, Thomas L., ed., *Report of the Commission to Locate the Site of the Frontier Forts of Pennsylvania.* 2 vols., Harrisburg, 1916.

Morgan, G. H., *The Settlement, Formation, and Progress of Dauphin County, Pennsylvania, from 1785 to 1876.* Harrisburg, 1877.

Morgan, James H., *Dickinson College.* Carlisle, Pa., 1933.

Morrison, H. S., *Modern Ulster: Its Character, Customs, Politics, and Industries.* London, 1920.

Morrison, L. A., *Among the Scotch-Irish.* Boston, 1891.

Mulhern, James, *A History of Secondary Education in Pennsylvania.* Philadelphia, 1933.

Murphy, Thomas, *The Presbytery of the Log College; or the Cradle of the Presbyterian Church in America.* Philadelphia, 1889.

Murray, J. A., *A Contribution to the History of the Presbyterian Churches, Carlisle, Pennsylvania.* Carlisle, 1904.

Myers, Albert Cook, *Immigration of the Irish Quakers into Pennsylvania.* Swarthmore, 1907.

Nevin, Alfred, ed., *Encyclopaedia of the Presbyterian Church in the United States of America.* Philadelphia, 1884.

Nevin, Alfred, *Churches of the Valley.* Philadelphia, 1852.

——, *Men of Mark of the Cumberland Valley, 1776-1876.* Philadelphia, 1876.

Nevins, Allan, *American Social History as Recorded by British Travelers.* New York, 1923.

Newenham, Thomas, *A Historical Inquiry into the Progress and Magnitude of the Population of Ireland.* London, 1805.

Noble, W. B., *History of the Presbyterian Church at Fagg's Manor, Chester County, Pennsylvania, 1730-1776.* Parkersburg, 1876.

Norcross, George, ed., *The Centennial History of the Presbytery of Luzerne.* Harrisburg, 1889.

O'Brien, George, *The Economic History of Ireland in the Eighteenth Century.* Dublin and London, 1918.

O'Brien, Michael J., *A Hidden Phase of American Nationality.* New York, 1919.

O'Brien, R. B., *Studies in Irish History, 1630-1649*. Dublin, 1906.

O'Hanlon, J. C., *Irish-American History*. Dublin, 1903.

Osgood, Herbert L., *The American Colonies in the Eighteenth Century*. 4 vols., New York, 1924.

Osmond, J., *History of the Presbytery of Luzerne*. Wilkes-Barre, 1897.

Parkman, Francis, *History of the Conspiracy of Pontiac*. New York, 1929.

———, *Montcalm and Wolfe*. 2 vols., Boston, 1895.

Patterson, A. W., *History of the Backwoods*. Pittsburgh, 1843.

Paxson, F. L., *History of the American Frontier*. Boston and New York, 1924.

Pendleton, W. C., *History of Tazewell County and Southwest Virginia*. Richmond, 1920.

Pennsylvania Scotch-Irish Society Proceedings and Addresses.

Perrin, W. H., Battle, J. H. and Kniffin, G. C., *History of Kentucky*. Louisville, 1886.

Petty, William, *Tracts, chiefly relating to Ireland*. Dublin, 1869.

Plumb, H. B., *History of Hanover Township and the Wyoming Valley*. Wilkes-Barre, 1885.

Peyton, J. L., *History of Augusta County, Virginia*. Staunton, Virginia, 1882.

Potter, H. N., *One Hundred Years of the Shenango Presbytery*. n.p., 1908.

Pound, Arthur, *Two Centuries of Industry*. Pittsburgh, 1941.

Powell, J. W., *History of Tioga County, Pennsylvania*. Harrisburg, 1897.

Prendergast, J. P., *The Cromwellian Settlement in Ireland*. 2d. edn., Dublin, 1875.

Proper, E. M., *Colonial Immigration Laws*. New York, 1900.

Proud, Robert, *History of Pennsylvania in North America*. 2 vols., Philadelphia, 1797, 1798.

Prowell, George R., *History of York County, Pennsylvania*. 2 vols., Chicago, 1907.

Pusey, W. A., *The Wilderness Road to Kentucky*. New York, 1921.

Ramsay, David, *History of South Carolina*. Charleston, 1809.

Rattray, William J., *Scot in British North America*. 4 vols., Toronto, 1880.

Reed, William B., *Life and Correspondence of Joseph Reed*. 2 vols., Philadelphia, 1847.

Reid, J. S., *History of the Presbyterian Church in Ireland*. 3 vols., 2d edn., Belfast, 1867.

Reid, Whitelaw, *The Scot in America and the Ulster Scot*. London, 1912.

Reynolds, John E., *In French Creek Valley*. Meadville, 1938.

Richard, J. Fraise, *History of Franklin County, Pennsylvania*. Chicago, 1887.

Richard, J. Fraise, ed., *History of Mercer County, Pennsylvania*. Chicago, 1888.

Richardson, D. K., *The Presbyterian Church of Greencastle*. Chambersburg, 1876.

Riddle, D. H., *The Scotch-Irish Element of Presbyterianism*. Pittsburgh, 1856.

Roberts, E. F., *Ireland in America*. New York and London, 1931.

Roosevelt, Theodore, *The Winning of the West*. 4 vols., New York, 1904.

Root, Winifred, *The Relations of Pennsylvania with the British Government, 1696-1765*. New York, 1912.

Ross, Peter, *The Scots in America*. New York, 1896.

Rossiter, W. S., *A Century of Population Growth in the United States, 1790 to 1890*. Washington, D. C., 1890.

Rumple, Jethro, *A History of Rowan County, North Carolina*. Salisbury, N. C., 1881.

Rupp, I. D., *Early History of Western Pennsylvania and of the Western Expedition and Campaigns, 1754-1783*. Pittsburgh, 1846.

———, *The Geographical Catechism of Pennsylvania and the Western States*. Harrisburg, 1836.

———, *History of Berks and Lebanon Counties*. Lancaster, 1844.

———, *History of Lancaster and York Counties*. Lancaster, 1844.

Sanford, Laura, *History of Erie County, Pennsylvania*. Philadelphia, 1862.

Scharf, J. T., *History of Western Maryland*. Philadelphia, 1882.

Scharf, J. T. and Westcott, T., *History of Philadelphia*. 3 vols., Philadelphia, 1884.

Schell, W. P., *Annals of Bedford County, Pennsylvania*. Bedford, 1907.

Schenck, H. R., ed., *History of Falling Spring Presbyterian Church*. Chambersburg, 1894.

Scotch-Irish Society of America, Proceedings and Addresses. 10 vols., Nashville, etc., 1890-1900.

Scott, Kate M., *History of Jefferson County, Pennsylvania*. Syracuse, 1888.

Scott, O. C., *The Scotch-Irish and Charles Scott's Descendants and Related Families*. n.p., 1917.

Scouller, J. B., *History of the Big Spring Presbytery of the United Presbyterian Church and Its Territorial Predecessors, 1750-1879*. Harrisburg, 1879.

Semple, Ellen C., *American History and Its Geographic Conditions*. Boston, 1903.

Seybert, A., *Statistical Annals*. Philadelphia, 1818.

Shade, Louis, *Immigration into the United States of America*. Washington, 1856.

Sharpless, Isaac, *A Quaker Experiment in Government*. Philadelphia, 1902.

——, *Two Centuries of Pennsylvania History*. Philadelphia, 1900.

Shaw, James, *The Scotch-Irish in History*. Springfield, 1899.

Shepherd, W. R., *History of Proprietary Government in Pennsylvania*. New York, 1896.

Shimmel, L. S., *Border Warfare in Pennsylvania during the Revolution*. Harrisburg, 1901.

Shoemaker, Henry W., *Scotch-Irish and English Proverbs*. Reading, 1927.

Shoemaker, Mary Craig, *Five Typical Scotch-Irish Families of the Cumberland Valley*. n.p., n.d.

Sipe, C. Hale, *Fort Ligonier and its Times*. Harrisburg, 1932.

——, *The Indian Wars of Pennsylvania*. Harrisburg, 1929.

Smith, Horace W., *Life and Correspondence of the Reverend William Smith, D.D.*, 2 vols., Philadelphia, 1879, 1880.

Smith, Joseph, *History of Jefferson College, including an Account of the Early Log Cabin Schools*. Pittsburgh, 1857.

——, *Old Redstone; or Historical Sketches of Western Presbyterianism*. Philadelphia, 1854.

Smith, Joseph, *The "Scotch-Irish" Shibboleth Analysed and Rejected*. Washington, D. C., 1898.

Smyth, S. G., *The Scotch-Irish Pioneers of the Schuylkill Valley, Pennsylvania*. Conshohocken, 1901.

Speed, Thomas, *The Wilderness Road*. Louisville, 1886.

Sprague, William B., *Annals of the American Pulpit*. 9 vols., New York, 1858.

Stevens, Joseph, *History of the Presbytery of Northumberland*. Williamsport, 1881.

Stevenson, J. H., *Centennial History of Tyrone Presbyterian Church*. Connellsville, Pa., 1876.

Stewart, Mrs. Harriet Wylie, *History of the Cumberland Valley*. n.p., n.d.

Stewart, J. F., *Indiana County: Her Pioneers and People*. 2 vols., Chicago, 1913.

Stillé, Charles J., *Major-General Anthony Wayne and the Pennsylvania Line in the Continental Army*. Philadelphia, 1893.

Stone, R. B., *McKean, The Governor's County*. New York, 1926.

Summers, L. P., *History of Southwestern Virginia, 1746-1786*. Richmond, 1903.

Sutherland, Stella H., *Population Distribution in Colonial America*. New York, 1936.

Swank, James M., *Progressive Pennsylvania*. Philadelphia, 1908.

Swoope, R. D., Jr., *Twentieth Century History of Clearfield County, Pennsylvania*. Chicago, 1911.

Swope, Gilbert E., *History of the Big Spring Presbyterian Church, Newville Pennsylvania*. Newville, Pa., 1898.

Taylor, R. H., *Historical Sketch of the Derry Presbyterian Church*. n.p., 1929.

Taylor, Rosser H., *Ante-Bellum South Carolina*. Univ. of N. C. Press, Chapel Hill, 1942.

Temple, O. P., *The Covenanter, the Cavalier, and the Puritan*. Cincinnati, 1897.

Tiffany, N. M. and F. *Harm Jan Huidekoper*. Cambridge, 1904.

Trego, C. B., *A Geography of Pennsylvania*. Philadelphia, 1843.

Turner, D. K., *History of Neshaminy Presbyterian Church*. Philadelphia, 1876.

Turner, F. J., *The Frontier in American History*. New York, 1920.

Tuttle, J. F., *Presbyterianism on the Frontiers*. Philadelphia, 1877.

Van Voorhis, John S., *The Old and New Monongahela*. Pittsburgh, 1893.

Veech, James, *The Monongahela of Old*. Pittsburgh, 1858.

Volwiler, A. T., *George Croghan and the Westward Movement, 1741-1782*. Cleveland, 1926.

Waddell, J. A., *Annals of Augusta County, Virginia*. Richmond, 1886.

Wall, F. L., *Clearfield County, Pennsylvania, Past and Present*. 2 vols., Clearfield, Pa., 1925.

Walsh, L. G. and M. G., *History and Organization of Education in Pennsylvania*. Indiana, Pa., 1930.

Walton, J. S., *Conrad Weiser and the Indian Policy of Colonial Pennsylvania*. Philadelphia, 1900.

Watson, John F., *Annals of Philadelphia and of Pennsylvania in the Olden Time*. 2 vols., Philadelphia, 1854.

Wayland, J. W., *The German Element of the Shenandoah Valley of Virginia*. Charlottesville, 1907.

Webster, Richard, *History of the Presbyterian Church in America from its Origin until the year 1760*. Philadelphia, 1858.

Wertenbaker, T. J., *The Old South: The Founding of American Civilization*. New York, 1942.

White, W. P. and Scott, W. H., eds., *The Presbyterian Church in Philadelphia*. Philadelphia, 1895.

Wickersham, James P., *A History of Education in Pennsylvania*. Lancaster, 1885.

Wiley, Richard T., *Monongahela: The River and Its Region*. Butler, Pa., 1937.

——, *The Whiskey Insurrection: A General View*. Elizabeth, Pa., 1912.

Williamson, Hugh, *History of North Carolina*. Philadelphia, 1812.

Willis, William, *Genealogy of the McKinstry Family, with a preliminary essay on the Scotch-Irish Immigration to America*. Boston, 1858.

Wing, C. P., *A Discourse on the History of Donegal and Carlisle Presbyteries*. Carlisle, 1877.

Wing, C. P., ed., *History of Cumberland County, Pennsylvania*. Philadelphia, 1882.

Winsor, Justin, *Narrative and Critical History of America*. 8 vols., Boston, 1884-1889.

——, *The Westward Movement*. Boston and New York, 1897.

Witherow, B. J., *The Insurrection of the Paxton Boys*. n.p., 1860.

Witherow, Thomas, *Derry and Enniskillen in 1688-1689*. Belfast, 1885.

——, *Historical and Literary Memorials of Presbyterianism in Ireland*. London and Belfast, 1879.

Wittke, Carl, *We Who Built America: The Saga of the Immigrant*. New York, 1939.

Wood, S. G., *Ulster Scots and Blandford Scots*. West Medway, Mass., 1928.

Woodburn, J. B., *The Ulster Scot*. London, 1915.

Wright, J. E. and Doris, *Pioneer Life in Western Pennsylvania*. Pittsburgh, 1940.

Wylie, S. S. and Pomeroy, A. N., *Rocky Spring Presbyterian Church*. Chambersburg, 1895.

2. *Articles*

Agnew, Daniel, "The Scotch-Irish of Pennsylvania," Scotch-Irish Society of America *Proceedings and Addresses*, I.

Armor, William C., "Scotch-Irish Bibliography of Pennsylvania," Scotch-Irish Society of America *Proceedings and Addresses*, VIII.

Avery, I. W., "The Scotch-Irish Settlers in Georgia," Scotch-Irish Society of America *Proceedings and Addresses*, IV.

Bair, Robert C., "The Scotch-Irish Conquest," Scotch-Irish Society of America *Proceedings and Addresses*, X.

Baldwin, E. H., "Joseph Galloway, the Loyalist Politician," *Pa. Mag. of Hist. and Biog.*, XXVI.

Barker, Howard F., "National Stocks in the Population of the United

States as indicated by the surnames in the Census of 1790," Amer. Hist. Assoc., *Annual Report, 1931,* I.

Beam, Jacob M., "Dr. Robert Smith's Academy at Pequea," *Jour. Presb. Hist. Soc.,* VIII.

Bennett, D. M., "Concerning the Life and Works of the Rev. John McMillan, D.D.," *Jour. Presb. Hist. Soc.,* XV.

Bradley, A. G., "The Ulster Scot in the United States," *Nineteenth Century,* LXXI.

Calhoun, H., "The Acts of the Fathers," Scotch-Irish Society of America *Proceedings and Addresses,* IV.

————, "The Scotch-Irish Homespun," Scotch-Irish Society of America *Proceedings and Addresses,* IV.

Calhoun, Patrick, "The Scotch-Irish in Georgia," Scotch-Irish Society of America *Proceedings and Addresses,* IV.

Clark, Chester, "Pioneer Life in the New Purchase," Northumberland County Hist. Soc. *Proceedings and Addresses,* VII.

Condon, Edward O., "Irish Immigration to the United States since 1790," *Jour. Amer. Irish Hist. Soc.,* IV.

Cooper, John W., "The Scotch-Irish in the Cumberland Valley," Scotch-Irish Society of America *Proceedings and Addresses,* VIII.

Coyle, John G., "American Irish Governors of Pennsylvania," *Jour. Amer. Irish Hist. Soc.,* XIV.

Craven, E. R., "The Log College of Neshaminy and Princeton University," *Jour. Presb. Hist. Soc.,* I.

Dalzell, John, "The Scotch-Irish in Western Pennsylvania," Scotch-Irish Society of America *Proceedings and Addresses,* II.

Dexter, F. B., "Estimates of Population in the American Colonies," American Antiquarian Society *Proceedings,* 1887.

Diffenderfer, F. R., "The Early Population and Settlement of Lancaster County and City," Lancaster County Hist. Soc. *Papers,* IX.

Dubbs, J. H., "The Names of the Townships," Lancaster County Hist. Soc. *Papers,* I.

Dunaway, Wayland F., "The English Settlers in Colonial Pennsylvania," *Pa. Mag. of Hist. and Biog.,* LII.

————, "The French Racial Strain in Colonial Pennsylvania," *Pa. Mag. of Hist. and Biog.,* LIII.

————, "Pennsylvania as an Early Distributing Center of Population," *Pa. Mag. of Hist. and Biog.,* LV.

Eddis, Thomas A., "Irish during the Seventeenth and Eighteenth Centuries," *Jour. Irish Amer. Hist. Soc.,* II.

Eddy, F. L., "The Race and Name Scotch-Irish," *The Old Northwest Geological Quarterly,* VIII.

Egle, W. H., "Landmarks of Early Scotch-Irish Settlement in Pennsylvania," Scotch-Irish Society of America *Proceedings and Addresses,* VIII.

——, "The Scotch-Irish Pioneer Hunters and Scouts," Pennsylvania Scotch-Irish Society *Proceedings and Addresses,* VIII.

Ely, W. S., "Scotch-Irish Families," Bucks County Hist. Soc. *Papers,* II.

——, "Some of the Early Settlers in Bucks County, Pennsylvania," Scotch-Irish Society of America *Proceedings and Addresses,* VIII.

Everitt, F. B., "Early Presbyterianism along the West Branch of the Susquehanna River," *Jour. Presb. Hist. Soc.,* XII.

Fitzgerald, James, "The Causes That Led to Irish Emigration," *Jour. Amer. Irish Hist. Soc.,* X.

Flood, W. H. Grattan, "Irish Emigration to the American Colonies," *Jour. Amer. Irish Hist. Soc.,* XXVI.

Fullerton, James N., "Squatters and Titles in Early Western Pennsylvania," *West. Pa. Hist. Mag.,* VI.

Funk, Henry D., "The Influence of the Presbyterian Church in Early American History," *Jour. Presb. Hist. Soc.,* XII.

Futhey, J. Smith, "The Scotch-Irish," Lancaster County Hist. Soc. *Papers,* XI.

Gibson, John B., "General John Gibson," *West. Pa. Hist. Mag.,* V.

Hall, John, "Scotch-Irish Characteristics," Scotch-Irish Society of America *Proceedings and Addresses,* I.

Hamilton, A. Boyd, "Old Derry Church," Scotch-Irish Society of America *Proceedings and Addresses,* VIII.

——, "The Conewago Congregation of Presbyterians, Londonderry Township, Dauphin County, 1730-1796," Dauphin County Hist. Soc. *Publications,* I.

Harbaugh, Linn, "German Life and Thought in a Scotch-Irish Settlement," Scotch-Irish Society of America *Proceedings and Addresses,* X.

Henderson, Elizabeth K., "The Northwestern Lands of Pennsylvania, 1790-1812," *Pa. Mag. of Hist. and Biog.,* LX.

Henry, William Wirt, "The Scotch-Irish of the South," Scotch-Irish Society of America *Proceedings and Addresses,* I.

Hensel, W. U., "The Scotch-Irish, Their Impress on Lancaster County," Lancaster County Hist. Soc. *Papers,* IX.

Hersh, Grier, "The Scotch-Irish in York and Adams Counties," Scotch-Irish Society of America *Proceedings and Addresses,* VIII.

Houston, J. W., "Early Presbyterianism in Lancaster County," Scotch-Irish Society of America *Proceedings and Addresses,* VIII.

Houston, R. J., "A Prominent Scotch-Irishman," Scotch-Irish Society of America *Proceedings and Addresses,* I.

Huidekoper, Alfred, "Incidents in the Early History of Crawford County," Pa. Hist. Soc. *Memoirs,* IV, Pt. II.

Hunter, W. H., "Influence of the Scotch-Irish on Ohio," Pa. Scotch-Irish Soc. *Proceedings and Addresses,* VIII.

Ingham, George H., "The Story of the Log College," *Jour. Presb. Hist. Soc.,* XII.

James, Alfred P., "First English-Speaking Trans-Appalachian Frontier," *Mississippi Valley Historical Review,* XVII.

Johnson, Roy H., "Frontier Religion in Western Pennsylvania," *West. Pa. Hist. Mag.,* XVI.

Keatley, John H., "Scotch-Irish Conflicts," Scotch-Irish Society of America *Proceedings and Addresses,* VI.

Kernohan, J. W., "Irish Presbyterianism: Its Origin and Story," Pa. Scotch-Irish Soc. *Proceedings and Addresses,* XXV.

King, J. W., "Colonel John Armstrong," *West. Pa. Hist. Mag.,* X.

Learned, M. D., "The Pennsylvania German and his English and Scotch-Irish Neighbors," Lebanon County Hist. Soc. *Papers,* II.

Linn, John Blair, "Indian Land and Its Fair Play Settlers," *Pa. Mag. of Hist. and Biog.,* VII.

Lonergan, Thomas S., "The Irish Chapter in American History," *Jour. Irish Amer. Hist. Soc.,* XI.

McCall, Robert A., "The Huguenots in Ulster," Pa. Scotch-Irish Soc. *Proceedings and Addresses,* XXVI.

Macartney, Clarence E., "John McMillan, The Apostle of the Gospel and Presbyterians, in Western Pennsylvania," *Jour. Presb. Hist. Soc.,* XV.

———, "The Period of the General Synod, 1717-1788," *Jour. Presb. Hist. Soc.,* XV.

Macaulay, W. J., "The Plantation and Presbyterian Pioneers," Pa. Scotch-Irish Soc. *Proceedings and Addresses,* LV.

McCook, Henry C., "Scotch-Irish Women Pioneers," Scotch-Irish Society of America *Proceedings and Addresses,* VIII.

———, "Transplanted Scotch-Irishisms, their offshoots and Transformations," Pa. Scotch-Irish Soc. *Proceedings and Addresses,* IV.

McCracken, Henry, "What Manner of Man Was and Is the Scotch-Irish American?" Scotch-Irish Society of America *Proceedings and Addresses,* VIII.

McFarquhar, Colin, "Donegal Church, A Landmark of Presbyterian History," Lancaster County Hist. Soc. *Papers,* XVII.

McMeen, Robert, "The Scotch-Irish of the Juniata Valley," Scotch-Irish Society of America *Proceedings and Addresses,* VIII.

MacIntosh, J. S., "The Making of the Ulsterman," Scotch-Irish Society of America *Proceedings and Addresses,* II.

McKinney, William W., "Eighteenth Century Presbyterianism in Western Pennsylvania," *Jour. Presb. Hist. Soc.*, X.

McPherson, John B., "The Judiciary of the Commonwealth," Pa. Scotch-Irish Soc. *Proceedings and Addresses*, IX.

Mays, George, "The Palatine and Scotch-Irish Settlers of Lebanon County," Lebanon County Hist. Soc. *Papers*, I.

Meginness, John F., "The Scotch-Irish of the Upper Susquehanna Valley," Scotch-Irish Society of America *Proceedings and Addresses*, VIII.

Mervine, William, "The Scotch-Irish Settlers in Raphoe, County Donegal, Ireland," *Pa. Mag. of Hist. and Biog.*, XXXVI.

Moffett, James D., "Pioneer Education in Washington County, Pennsylvania," Scotch-Irish Society of America *Proceedings and Addresses*, VIII.

Myers, Albert Cook, "The Scotch-Irish Quakers," Pa. Scotch-Irish. Soc. *Proceedings and Addresses*, XIII.

Norcross, George, "The Scotch-Irish in the Cumberland Valley," Scotch-Irish Historical Society of America *Proceedings and Addresses*, VIII.

O'Brien, Michael J., "An Interesting Example of the Extent of Irish Emigration to the American Colonies," *Jour. Amer. Irish Hist. Soc.*, XXVII.

——, "Irish Immigrants from English Ports in the Eighteenth Century," *Jour. Amer. Irish Hist. Soc.*, XVIII.

——, "Irish Pioneers and Schoolmasters in Butler County, Pennsylvania," *Jour. Amer. Irish Hist. Soc.*, XVIII.

——, "Irish Pioneers in Berks County, Pennsylvania," *Jour. Amer. Irish Hist. Soc.*, XXVII.

——, "The Scotch-Irish Myth," *Jour. Amer. Irish Hist. Soc.*, XXIV.

Parke, N. G., "Personal Knowledge of the Scotch-Irish," Scotch-Irish Society of America *Proceedings and Addresses*, VIII.

Sargent, Winthrop, "The History of an Expedition against Fort Duquesne in 1755," Hist. Soc. of Pa. *Memoirs*, V.

Schlosser, Gaius J., "A Chapter from the Religious History of Western Pennsylvania," *Jour. Presb. Hist. Soc.*, XVI.

Sheppard, J. Havergal, "Irish Preachers and Educators in the Early History of the Presbyterian Church in America," *Jour. Amer. Irish Hist. Soc.*, XXIV.

Simonton, J. W., "History of Hanover Church and Congregation," Scotch-Irish Society of America *Proceedings and Addresses*, VIII.

Snowden, James H., "Our Scotch-Irish Heredity," Pa. Scotch-Irish Soc. *Proceedings and Addresses*, XXI.

Stewart, John, "Scotch-Irish Occupancy and Exodus," Kittochtinny Hist. Soc. *Papers,* II.

Stone, Frederick D., "First Congress of the Scotch-Irish in America," *Pa. Mag. of Hist. and Biog.,* XIV.

"The Scotch-Irish of Northampton County, Pennsylvania," Northampton County Historical and Genealogical Society Publications," I.

Turner, F. J., "The Place of the Ohio Valley in American History," *Ohio Archeological and Historical Quarterly,* XX.

"Ulster and Its People," *Fraser's Magazine,* August, 1876.

Ward, Townsend, "The Insurrection of the Year 1794, in the Western Counties of Pennsylvania," Hist. Soc. of Pa. *Memoirs,* VI.

Weidman, J. W., "Francis Alison, D.D. and Classical Education in Pennsylvania," Scotch-Irish Society of America *Proceedings and Addresses,* IX.

West, William A., "Scotch-Irish Presbyterianism in the Cumberland Valley; Its Origin, and Religious, Educational, and Patriotic Aspects," Scotch-Irish Society of America *Proceedings and Addresses,* X.

Wiley, Richard T., "The Scotch-Irish in Southwestern Pennsylvania," Scotch-Irish Society of America *Proceedings and Addresses,* III.

Wilkeson, Samuel, "Early Recollections of the West," *The American Pioneer,* II.

Williams, E. Melvin, "The Scotch-Irish in Pennsylvania," *Americana,* XVII.

Winner, John E., "The Depreciation and Donation Lands," *West. Pa. Hist. Mag.,* VIII.

Woodburn, J. A., "Scotch-Irish Presbyterians in Monroe County," Indiana Historical Society *Publications,* IV.

Worner, W. F., "The Old Pequea Presbyterian Graveyard," Lancaster County Hist. Soc. *Papers,* XXIV.

INDEX

Abbeville County, Scotch-Irish pioneers in, 110

Academies, of Scotch-Irish in colonial Pennsylvania, 219-228

Agnew, Daniel, 140, 142

Alabama, Scotch-Irish in, 111

Albany Purchase of 1754, 65, 146

Alamance, battle of, 111

Alison, Francis, as minister, 213, 224; as educator, 223-224

Allegheny County, settlements in, 83-84; mentioned, 138

Allen, William, 55

American-Irish, object to term "Scotch-Irish," 4

Amherst, General Jeffrey, 153

Amish, 67, 88, 156

Amusements, on frontier, 195-196

Andrews, Zedekiah, 203

Anglicans, 120

Anti-Constitutionalist Party, 135, 136

Anti-Proprietary Party, 133

Antrim, County, plantation of, 20; racial and religious composition of, 25-26; mentioned, 15, 16, 18, 33, 40, 62

Arkansas, Scotch-Irish in, 111

Armagh, County, plantation of, 20; English in, 25; mentioned, 15, 18, 33, 40

Armstrong, John, Secretary of War, 139

Armstrong, General John, leads expedition against Kittanning, 149-150; in Pontiac's War, 153-154; in Revolution, 163

Armstrong County, pioneer settlements in, 87

Aughwick (Fort Shirley), 68

Aughwick Creek, 65

Augusta County, Scotch-Irish settlements in, 104-106

Baltimore, 44, 177

Bald Eagle Valley, 89

Bannockburn, 143

Baptists, in Ireland, 12, 24, 25; in Pennsylvania, 82, 100

Barker, Howard F., conclusions questioned, 49n

Barter, in colonial Pennsylvania, 178

Barton, Samuel, defends Scotch-Irish, 125-126

Beatty, Charles, 212, 221

Beatty, Patrick, 68

Beaver County, settlements in, 86

Becket, William, 8

Bedford (Raystown), founded, 66

Bedford County, settlers in, 66; mentioned, 132, 161

Belfast, linen manufacture of, 30; port of embarkation, 39, 43, 44

Bench of Bishops, oppresses Dissenters, 32

Berks County, raises German regiment, 161

Bethel Presbyterian Church, founded, 87

"Beverly Grant," 104

Beverly, William, 104

Big Spring Presbyterian Church, founded, 63

"Big Runaway," 90, 91

Bingham, Samuel, 67

Black, Jeremiah S., 142

Blaine, Ephraim, 162, 164